More Reflections on
The Day I Lost the President

Captain Jones shares a wealth of humorous anecdotes from his many and varied life experiences, especially stories of living during WWII in Wilmington, where I grew up.
- Ken Howard,
Director of the North Carolina Museum of History

Jones paints a vivid picture of his lifetime of independence and determination, and of his ethics and values shared with the Greatest Generation. This book is a gift to future generations.
- Bill Vassar, Executive Vice President, EUE/Screen Gems Studio, Wilmington, NC

Captain Jones' memoir is an historical walk through some very important times, events and places. He shadowed, tended to, and advanced for some people at the pinnacle of American politics and military power, and has captured his observations magnificently.
- Dick McGraw, former Principal Deputy Assistant Secretary of Defense, Public Affairs and Legislative Affairs

Jones brings history to life through his Southern way of storytelling and was invaluable in documenting Wilmington.
- Honorable Bill Saffo, Mayor, City of Wilmington, NC

It has been my pleasure to work with Jones on various WWII projects through the years. He is very passionate about the role that Wilmington has played.
- Honorable Ted Davis, Member, North Carolina House of Representatives

Jones is revered on the home front, at the office, and by principle and institution. Wilmington is better for having him in our lives.
- Jon Evans, Anchor/Assistant News Director, WECT TV-6 and Fox, Wilmington, NC

Other Books By the Author Include:

"She Shot Her Way to Success": How China's Empress Dowager Ci Xi Launched a
Photographer's Trail-Blazing Career, with Carroll Robbins Jones

"Football! Navy! War!": How Military "Lend-Lease" Players Saved the College Game
and Helped Win World War II

The Journey Continues: The World War II Home Front

A Sentimental Journey: Memoirs of a Wartime Boomtown

Forget That You Have Been Hitler Soldiers: A Youth's Service to the Reich, with
Hermann O. Pfrengle

Hawaii Goes to War: The Aftermath of Pearl Harbor, with Carroll Robbins Jones

Condemned to Live: A Panzer Artilleryman's Five-Front War, with Franz A. P. Frisch

Arming the Eagle: A History of U.S. Weapons Acquisition Since 1775

Gyrene: The World War II United States Marine

Giants in the Cornfield: The 27th Indiana Infantry

The Day I Lost
President
FORD

By Wilbur D. Jones Jr.

The Day I Lost President Ford
Memoir of a Born-and-Bred Carolina Tar Heel
First edition

Published by
Dram Tree Books
P.O. Box 7183
Wilmington, NC 28406

www.dramtreebooks.weebly.com

ISBN 978-0-9844900-2-8

DEDICATION

My memoir is dedicated to my parents, Wilbur David and Viola Murrell Jones, who placed me on the right track with their love, discipline, a work ethic, love and respect of God and country, and the desire to achieve.

TABLE OF CONTENTS

PROLOGUE

Remembering how I began, and the time in which I grew up, I was born to be a military historian and career armed forces officer in service to my country . . .

. . . and as a writer.

Therefore, this memoir intends to show how this grounding and core factors, interests, and devotions guided every stage of my working career and family life.

March 2018. On a balmy backyard afternoon in Holly Springs, North Carolina, an octogenarian gently pushed the swing of a precious little girl of two. Happily holding tight, she snickered short laughter bursts lighting his face. Murmuring between laughs, she honed a beginner's speech and practiced her budding charm. "Pop pop, I wuv you. Tee hee. Pop Pop, I wuv you."

"Carrie," the octogenarian exclaimed to her nearby mother, "this child is the exact age you were when your grandmother and I took legal custody of you thirty-two years ago. Same size. She reminds me so much of you then."

Of the myriad paths I've chosen, bringing all their hundreds of successes, none have surpassed how my late wife Carroll and I accepted God's challenge to raise our granddaughter Carrie. We produced a crown jewel of a wife, mother of Charlie and son Brooks, seven, and a dedicated third-grade school teacher. Carrie's life is mine's proudest achievement.

Now, let's go.

Wᴇʟᴄᴏᴍᴇ ᴛᴏ Tʜɪs Exᴘᴇʀɪᴇɴᴄᴇ ᴏꜰ ᴀ Lɪꜰᴇ Wᴇʟʟ Lɪᴠᴇᴅ

Readers might learn something about which they probably knew little or nothing. Like inside White House politics, work-life in the Pentagon, and umpiring in Little League

This screed is neither autobiography nor meant to be life's complete story. Ergo, it's called a memoir, a.k.a. the story of my adventures, experiences, and influences, and their impact on me today. Hah. It's only about things I want the reader to know. I don't include everything that happened. Otherwise, I'd still be writing and you wouldn't be reading.

Why divulge deep, dark secrets and a thousand indiscretions, if there were any? That trail is left to a biographer fifty years from now attempting to dig it out. Then again, that's purely illusory. The mark I leave here may be non-discernible, and this work relegated to a library basement.

Also, nobody wants to read about someone commiserating over a hundred bad times. This isn't a relationships training manual. I handle the only bad times with my lifelong principal credo: Never Give Up.

Meanwhile, I proceed. Memoir pressure on me has been increasing. My children, particularly David and Andrew, have been after me to write my story. Dad, they said, you've written eighteen books about everybody else. It's time we read one about you. Okay, okay, even if I have to do it myself. I turned 85 years old on July 9, 2019. So, what more inspiration must one have? My life remains a work-in-progress; always a vision, always a goal; someone to help; something to accomplish.

Wʜᴀᴛ's ɪɴ ᴀ Mᴇᴍᴏɪʀ?

In sum, this book is about a strait-laced, multi-directional working life which redefines the term "diverse." Varied, checkered working years as "Tinker, Tailor, Soldier, Spy," as spy novelist John Le Carre might have it. Meaning: a lifetime traveling many divergent roads through success and failure, but with the strength to learn and bounce back, and envision the future. Ultimately, it results in satisfaction for a job well done for family, community, and country.

Sounds a bit like Creative Writing 101 maybe. But, is this boastful? Not necessarily, and here's why. It doesn't shy from identifying early- and mid-life ups and downs where a ticket-punching pattern en route to the top occurred in only one of my career adventures, the Navy. I want the reader to see how my early life's exposure to character-building strengths appear openly or sublimely at subsequent stages through the years, congealing into the man I became. And, with adequate revealing details.

The experience of writing one's own memoir heavily re-immerses the writer. Getting lost in or subsumed may be better stated. For me it became a concentrated task heretofore never foreseen, done only once. Do guidelines exist? Not to my knowledge. Everything passes by in one form or another, flashing or deliberate, detailed or hazy, absolutes or uncertainties. Facts from memory are checkable only in my private papers or the family collection at the University of North Carolina Wilmington's Randall Library, or the Google search bar.

Generalities are easier to remember, which I discovered right away. Necessary details not always. Subsequently, as I reflected, typed, and reflected more, certain scenes, instances, conditions, and people edged into view more clearly. Oh yes, I remember that! Starting with a blank sheet of paper does not mean starting with a blank mind.

All right, what do I say and how? Who's the audience? Well, the wise old sage advises, go back as far as you can. So many moments come to mind: situations, opportunities, paths, actors, conditions, decisions, tragedies, victories, roadblocks, defeats, disappointments, rallies, standoffs, congestions, rewards.

So, it covers my life beginning to present. Some memoirs recount period experiences in war, in government service, or while shipwrecked on a Pacific atoll. With mine, you get much more.

But I will say this. If you want to write yours, start it NOW.

It's called resisting putting off things to another day.

Very old age is not conducive with procrastination. Something has to give.

Do I remember only the good and shun the not-so? Returning to this Prologue's opening, the memoir likely produces only what the writer wants the world to know. That's okay, assuming it's factual and interesting. A historian such as I must write accurately, but this is not a diary, and no framework dictates writing an exhausting chronicle. But, this work is factually correct and meant to educate, enlighten, and entertain.

WHY THE MEMOIR'S TITLE?

Of course, the title uncovers an untold one-of-a-kind story, certainly destined for Big History. You'll see in Chapter 8. No, no, don't go there yet. Patience. All in due course. The reader must work his way through.

The title might also be "Mountaintops," because I've climbed many, mostly small ones, not the Rockies or Alps, with some in-between or ascensions close to the summits. No matter how they are measured, they represent achievements. My life continues generating countless. The subtitle reflects various extra-strong positive influences on my decision-making. More exist, just not enough space to list them.

What are these mountaintops? Thinking hard, because I've never done this before. Many come to mind and consequently find themselves in Appendix A. Except for the government positions, they're primarily as an unpaid volunteer.

Most of my positions involved leadership and management roles, where I excel. Chairman of one, commanding officer or executive director of another.

Those important, visible positions generated unlimited opportunities to serve and succeed for community, state, and country. Someone in command recognized I could do the job, and granted appropriate responsibility, reins, and authority. Other leadership positions I created myself to fill voids and needs. All positions built upward on each other, uncovering additional service opportunities. *This really is the first time* they've been written down.

A note. Historians will find my personal papers in Randall Library. Among a vast amount of material, much from my political career, the collection is a treasure trove of "inside" information on the 1972 and 1976 presidential campaigns, loaded with information on Presidents Nixon and Ford and their acolytes, White House photographs, illustrations, official documents, artifacts, campaign mementoes, and media clips documenting my experiences.

Besides being referenced, some illustrate this memoir.

Fortunately Randall Library and I established a close working relationship making them my papers' permanent home. For their highly professional assistance I thank current special collections librarian Rebecca Baugnon and her retired predecessor, Jerry Parnell.

FORMULATING FIVE CAREER CHANNELS

I've had five different career channels, let's call them. For the first time I am formulating and matching them with the mountaintops climbed. From childhood, I've been blessed with a
character backbone consisting of perseverance and a willingness and desire to work hard, lead, organize, manage, be decisive, and get along with people—teamwork. I never stopped to be simply satisfied, or wonder what would have happened "if." What's next? I ask. I'm in.

Those five career channels, plus the obligatory everyman's Formative Years, are:

• The Formative Years: Growing Up During World War II, Education , and Carolina Tar Heel Jock

• Service in the Navy, Pentagon, and Armed Forces Academia

• Seventeen Years in California and Washington Staff Politics, and Service to Presidents Richard Nixon and Gerald Ford

• Military Historian Preserving North Carolina WWII History

• Writer, Photographer, Speaker

• Professional Baseball Umpire and Basketball Official, and WWII Battlefield Tour Leader

My writing career began in Forest Hills elementary school in the eighth grade in 1946. Perfected over the past thirty-five years—now nineteen books, hundreds of newspaper and magazine articles, and more—my conversational style should translate into easy, comfortable reading. It's packed with of lighthearted, fresh, sprightly views employing both serious and carefree vignettes and anecdotes, fascinating experiences, and Oh-My-Gosh moments. For instance, readers will fantasize about the Mediterranean storybook romance with my future wife (boss's daughter) and our Naples marriage. Much time is spent poking fun at myself and my mistakes, which ought to encourage the reader's chuckles.

Adequately described is how political conservatism of the 1960's and the Republican Party corresponded with my principles and incubated a future successful path in political staff work. But otherwise, readers will not be diverted to retrospective policy-wonk blathering, esoteric world views, scandalous exposes, second guessing, palace politics, or overreaching judgments. Nothing necessarily weighty. No turn-offs.

A note: In sticking to history, having participated in much of it, I avoid connections to, or comments concerning, current national issues or politics.

Once readers finish, I care only that my life's journey has enriched them, whether or not they remember the author's name. The story's information and pleasure are what matters.

THE THRILL OF NO JOB

Have you ever lost a job, been laid off, been fired, quit in dissatisfaction? No? Then let me tell you about the thrill of being out of work four times with a wife and three children, when every non-employed day must be met as if it were an otherwise normal work day. And the searching begins, then continues. To stay stable and sane, accept individual responsibility, cope with the stresses, maintain confidence, and keep fighting. It continues until a better place is found. Thus evolved my lifelong credo of Never-Giving-Up! Never.

My take on failure is this. Some are self-generated; others appear from sources one can't control. Unless one mistakenly launches a nuclear missile toward Rome, failing, or making wrong decisions, generates character building. Strengthens resoluteness. That is, *if one is strong* and takes advantage of lessons learned, and wishes to recover. The earlier in life for failures, the more one determines to succeed. Are today's young people shielded from responsibility, decision making, and fear of failure? A question. I wasn't, thank goodness.

I hold with diminished respect those individuals who grow up in the family business, working there during summers, sliding right into it after graduation, never having to apply for a job anywhere else, or face a pressure interview, or compete against others. Or be fired. I've often felt they are missing a rich experience by inheriting what daddy built. A road not hard enough, perhaps? Their problem, not mine.

When I resigned from active Navy duty in 1964 (see Chapter 5), my father, who was chief executive of Wilmington's Carolina Savings & Loan, offered me an attractive opportunity. Join the firm. Having been "around the world" a few times, I respectfully declined. No way would I be comfortable taking over from

Daddy, and Wilmington then had zero appeal after seeing "Pah-ree" and Tokyo.

Therefore, Before Diving in, for the Record Allow Me to State

I've never been arrested or sued . . . Never used illegal substances and haven't smoked since 1967 . . . Remained sober since taking my first drink at age twenty-six on New Year's Eve . . . Vote in every election, occasionally for Democrats locally if we share mutual opinions and are friends. . . .

I'm in perfect health because: I eat right, rest right, handle stress right, exercise frequently, can unwind, find work stimulating, enjoy a challenge, stay upbeat, use common sense and rationale, keep my wits, read and continue learning, wake up daily with a project in hand, keep my feet moving and brain cells percolating, love my family, drink lots of French and Italian red wine . . . and . . . since late 2013 as a widower after fifty-four years, have the shared love of the dearest woman on earth, my steady lady friend, the widow and lovely fellow Rotarian Ann LaReau. God knows I'm blessed beyond belief, health and otherwise.

NOW, WHAT SHALL THIS MEMOIR DIVULGE?

Here are some of the subjects which characterize the five career channels. First, presidential politics.

• Forty-nine advances for President Ford and the White House—All successes, but some close calls, such the undersized Oklahoma University football helmet that splashed national news; and the trepidation relating to the book's title.

• Running President Nixon's re-election campaign in New Hampshire, my association with the Nixon White House and CREEP; and what mighta-coulda-but-didn't involvement with the Watergate fiasco.

• My Hatch Act violation and Senator Barry Goldwater pioneering a patchwork but upward career climb in Republican staff politics through Los Angeles and Washington.

This general medley:

• Being molded, matured, and directed by participating in Carolina varsity lacrosse and soccer and campus activities.

• A Navy officer's challenging career assignments, responsibilities, decisions, travels, relocations, and saving a sailor's life.

• Marrying the boss's daughter in Italy during a whirlwind storybook Mediterranean romance.

• Enjoying seven-and-a-half years of duty in "Purgatory," a.k.a., The Pentagon.

• Professionally umpiring baseball and officiating basketball at the college, high school, and recreational levels.

These passions and devotions:

• Growing up and contributing to the war effort on the home front in the

"First American WWII Heritage City" of Wilmington.
  • Returning to that Old Home Town after forty-one years to start a new-culture lifestyle.
  • Organizing and leading tour groups to WWII battlefields and sites in the Pacific Ocean islands, Europe, and Mediterranean Sea: Normandy to Iwo Jima, French Riviera to Less-Than-Third-World nations, and ship voyages.
  • Assuming, almost by default, the lead 22-year role in identifying, preserving, and interpreting Southeastern North Carolina's rich WWII history, and its enduring accomplishments.
  • Entering and adjusting to (sorta) military and university academia life at the Defense Acquisition University and UNCW.
  • Writing all those books and articles, and giving all those lectures, presentations, media interviews, book signings, and taking all those photos—and what they're about.

THE OPENING PROTOCOL

So, I begin by replicating the standard memoir-author's opening protocol. On July 9, 1934, in the Marion Sprunt Annex of James Walker Memorial Hospital in Wilmington, North Carolina, I was born.

Dr. J. E. Evans delivered me, charging my Father $50. Hospital expenses for ten days were $81. I weighed eight pounds, 12 ounces. My family lived at 2004 Pender Avenue in the older Carolina Place neighborhood until moving in 1936 to 102 Colonial Drive, a home they built in the new, upscale Forest Hills development outside and east of the city limits.

Stay with me, folks. The exciting stuff begins just a page turn away.

Wilbur D. Jones, Jr.
Wilmington, North Carolina
February 2020

CHAPTER 1

INTRODUCING MY PARENTS, THE ESSENTIAL COMPONENTS OF MY LIFE: AND WILMINGTON, OF COURSE, WAS THE SOUTH

Before this life story begins, my parents want to meet you. They created the path for attaining much of what I am today. Either purposely or by association, my character collection of moral and ethical fibers, Christian baseline, respect for others, service to country and community, and common sense which sustained me, are traceable to my childhood and formative years.

Their memory lives. I thank God for their loving direction and influence. For the twenty-two years I've lived back in Wilmington, on Sundays after church, and on birthdays and death dates, I visit their gravesites. I am forever grateful to *Wrightsville Beach Magazine*, a superior regional slick cultural publication, for publishing in Februry 2019 the article I wrote saluting my parents' amazing World War I love story.

Their beginning relationship corresponds with what I perceive as early Twentieth Century generational norms originating in the lower class, into which they were born and raised originally. Ultimately, they reached an almost upper-middle class level without necessarily aspiring for such. That evolution came naturally, a sort of economic and cultural "upward mobility" because of my Father's business acumen, successes, and earned reputation.

Without any pedigree, they climbed no society ladders, which they eschewed, partly because they weren't invited, and partly because they just "didn't fit" into Wilmington's privileged country club domain. In Mother's case, she held such with both disdain and envy. Born on "the wrong side of the railroad tracks" in Wilmington, she had underlying reasons. Neither drank alcohol, a sure unwelcome social greeting.

ONLY EIGHTH GRADE EDUCATIONS

My Mother was Viola Elizabeth Murrell, born March 25, 1903, in Wilmington. My Father was Wilbur David Jones, born February 25, 1892, in Onslow County, North Carolina. My sister and only sibling Viola Elizabeth (Lib), born in Wilmington in 1922, was twelve years older. Their other child, daughter Helen Blanche, died in 1932 at age two.

For years I wondered what to do with the large amount of information about my parents' unusual storybook World War I courtship, and considered sharing it with the public. They left diaries, scrapbooks, letters, photos, poems, a wedding book, and keepsakes, amassed in a love affair the emotion and impact of which I finally understood upon returning to Wilmington in 1997 and closely examining what they left me.

Mother: Viola Elizabeth Murrell Jones, photographed during World War I.

My Father grew up in a large family of tenant dirt-farmers near the White Oak River in North Carolina's Onslow County. He was twenty-five when the two met here in 1917 during World War I. He joined the Navy as a hospital corpsman (Hospital Apprentice 1st Class), and was stationed at the Naval Hospital in Charleston, SC He had worked here briefly while learning the bookkeeping trade before enlisting. She was fourteen, lived on the down side of North Fifth Street, and was attending Hemenway grammar school, which fire destroyed many years ago.

Her divorced mother Hattie Murrell supported three children by keeping the Front Street public rest room. Mother helped raise the younger brother, William. The older one, David, became a journalist for the *Wilmington Morning Star* and as a freelance writer for publications such as *Police Gazette*. He drowned in the harbor of Hamburg, Germany, in 1937, so ordered by the Nazis, Mother told me.

My recollections of my maternal grandfather, Joseph Murrell, a lifetime Western Union employee, who left my grandmother and moved to Virginia long before I was born, are faint. He is buried on my family plot. I have none of either maternal grandmother or paternal Onslow County grandparents. Shamefully, I regret failing to track my parents' genealogy. My late wife Carroll, exceptionally interested in the subject through her own ancestors, compiled some Jones records, including men who served in the Revolutionary and Civil Wars, my qualifications for Sons of the American Revolution and Sons of the Confederacy. Strangely, unfortunately I never pursued these. Again regrettably, I have been more concerned with the history of others in World War II and neglected my own lineage. My default choice, but now it might be too late to reconstruct.

Neither parent advanced past the eighth grade in school—no high school. From their handwriting ability, creativeness, passion for life, command of the 1918 discourse, particularly my father, plus my memories of them, nevertheless they created classics in their own right.

WORLD WAR I SERVICE, THEN WILMINGTON ROOTS

Daddy later deployed for six months to the Dominican Republic with the 4th Marine Regiment and treated Marines in the Santiago, Dominican Republic field hospital. He was discharged in 1919. The photo of him in his Marine tunic in my office is the one I treasure most of his service. He took a business course, worked in Alexandria, VA, and relocated to Wilmington about 1920 to work for the Carolina Building and Loan Association. I'm uncertain what mother did after graduating from eighth grade, besides caring for her mother and William. Regular meetings replaced letters, and their love continued.

In June 1921 they married in Wilmington's St. Andrews Presbyterian Church and honeymooned "up north in the big cities" (love her accounts of that trip) before settling here. They transferred their church membership to the new Church of the Covenant in the early 1920's. St. Andrews and Covenant merged in June 1944 to form a new church, St. Andrews-Covenant, my church today.

Father: Hospital Apprentice 1st Class Wilbur D. Jones, Sr. during World War I.

Daddy worked his way to become the Association's chief executive officer during a forty-four year career. He was also associated with a companion company, Moore-Fonvielle Realty, whose principals also owned the Association. His office desk sign, "Smile and Hustle," reflected his approach to business and serving customers. The original office building at Second and Princess Streets remains, although its changed occupants numerous times after Daddy built the new building at Third and Chestnut in the early 1960's. That property is now city offices. The side door he always entered remains. So often I snuck through there. I make out the very faded B&L painted sign on the brick wall on Second Street, if no one else does.

FOR THE WORLD WAR II WAR EFFORT

During WWII, both parents were exceptionally active volunteering on the Wilmington home front. Daddy served the community in numerous civic areas, including commander of American Legion Post 10 in 1930 where was one of the early members, and headed the committee that dedicated the vehicle bridge over the Northeast Cape Fear River north of town (now Isabel Holmes Bridge). He was a long-time church elder, and a member of the Exchange Club, state leader of the International Order of the Odd Fellows. In WWII he served on the New Hanover County Defense Committee that worked with the federal and city governments to build and open in December 1941 the Second & Orange Streets USO (United Service Organizations) building, now the Hannah Block Historic USO/Community Arts Center.

With my father during World War II.

One simply could not determine his lack of education from his activities, energy, composure, involvement, and genteelness. He really was a well-read, self-made man, who could discuss almost any subject, but was never active politically. He was the quintessential Southern gentleman and courteously treated everyone, customers, all races, and strangers on the street. He smoked heavily and smiled a lot, was about 5'-6", slight, balding, and enjoyed greeting and serving people. He loved North Carolina and his roots.

Mother never went to high school and never had a paid job outside the home, but excelled in volunteer and civic work during the war. She was an attractive, clean-cut young woman who made the most out of what she had. She always wanted to be a nurse, and when war came, she became a volunteer-certified Red Cross Nurses Aide, somewhat tantamount to being a CNA (certified nurses assistant) today. Her primary duty station was James Walker Memorial Hospital at Tenth & Red Cross Streets, the county's white hospital, where she recorded the most volunteer hours of anyone. She spent time at the German prisoner of war camp dispensary at Bluethenthal Army Airfield (now Wilmington International Airport, ILM), and administered on the day he died to the only POW of some 550 who were interned here during the war.

She also served the Legion Post 10 women's auxiliary as both president and historian, maintaining four exceptionally valuable wartime scrapbooks of the area scene and records of our men in the armed forces, including those who died. I helped her "sell" the Legion's paper poppies around Memorial Day at the Front Street post office for donations used to help veterans. Both parents frequently were away from home, leaving me as a "latchkey" kid trusted to do my homework, go play war, and then be home for dinner. She was active with the North Carolina Sorosis and the Rebecca organization of the Odd Fellows.

Until WWII, Mother took care of her mother as well as my sister and me. Later she lost a knee cap falling from the Belk-Williams department store escalator, contracted breast cancer and had one breast removed without reconstructive surgery, and battled diabetes. He exercise was neighborhood walks. She garnered

My sister Elizabeth, Mother and me at home during World War II.

news from headlines and talking to friends, and enjoyed life's simple things, romanticizing and daydreaming of a lifetime of things she could only visualize. She reminisced in her girlhood and what might have been. Her handwriting, poetry, and use of the language amazes considering her education. Her hobbies included peppering our large backyard with concrete flamingos, bird baths, deer and other wildlife, and feeders to keep the critters coming back. Mowing

the lawn was like navigating an obstacle course.

Mother doted on me, her "Junie Boy Jones," which attracted the attention of everybody in town and proved to be a mantle I needed to lift gently. See that day in Chapter 3. She never had to prove her love.

He died here in 1967, and she here in 1973. They are buried in our family plot in Section S of the Oakdale Cemetery.

Their material is split between what I possess—including his military service record and photo album, and two of her WWII Legion scrapbooks—and what I donated to the University of North Carolina Wilmington's Randall Library special collections years ago.

EXITING THE GREAT DEPRESSION

Wilmington, of course, was the South. Among its culture, begin with total segregation. This wasn't the driving force in town but played prominently. Whites had little idea of what went on in the black communities. Blacks knew more about the whites, because their housekeepers and janitors went home nightly with news. My parents hired occasional black "help," but Mother's main job was maintaining the household: cooking, cleaning, and raising.

By 1941, Wilmington, like the rest of America, had mired in the Great Depression almost a decade. The city of about 34,000, and New Hanover County of about 43,000, isolated at the end of nowhere it seemed, overnight welcomed an economic transfusion. The Newport News Shipbuilding & Drydock Company opened the North Carolina Shipbuilding Company (the Wilmington Shipyard) on the Cape Fear River south of the city limits to construct cargo ships. The Army constructed a new anti-aircraft artillery training base out of wilderness swamp north of here called Camp Davis at Holly Ridge on Highway 17. Hiring opened. The Marine Corps built Camp Lejeune near Jacksonville. Hope abounded. Still, recovery required the upcoming war.

My Forest Hills neighborhood environment and roots typified the times. I graduated from Forest Hills Grammar School in 1947 after skipping the first grade because I had

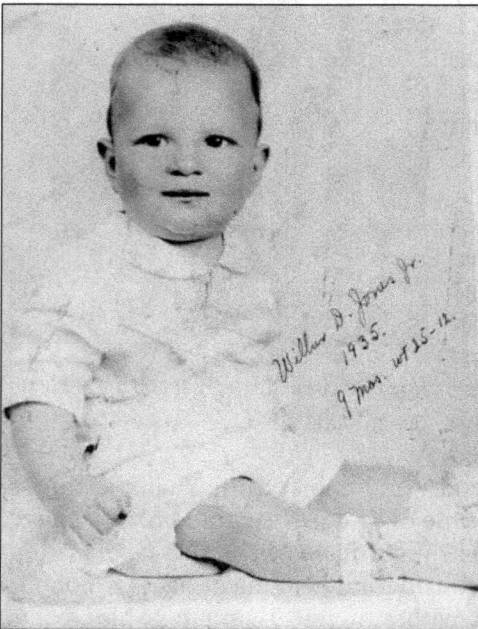

Nine months old in 1935, I weighed in at 25 pounds.

two solid years in Mrs. Hinnant's kindergarten. You could do it then. Therefore, forever, I was the youngest by a year in all my classes. New Hanover High School in 1951 (sixteen), and the University of North Carolina in 1955 (twenty).

The year I finished Carolina, mother gave me my baby book which she'd been keeping since 1934. Under "People Who Inspired Me," I wrote "My Mother, My Father, all my life"; and Carroll Robbins: "I became engaged to her on 27 April 1959 in Naples, Italy." My bachelors history degree served me little purpose in The Real World and would lie dormant for many years until I joined the faculty of the Defense Acquisition University in 1984, when finally I could "use my degree." About time. See Chapter 10.

MY SISTER FOUND LOVE IN THE ARMY

Hey, that baby book contained lots of exciting historical information. I mean, you never knew, I might grow up to be president. One major event: I pooped and peed in the nursery chair for the first time on January 23, 1935. "Was I proud!" she wrote. First word was "Da-Da" at six months, then "Ma-Ma" at nine. Making steady progress, eh? First formal photo taken on March 29, 1935. Oh come on, you need to know this. Off we go: great start to a rich life.

Oh yes, my sister Elizabeth, my only sibling, wants to meet you. Born in 1922, she graduated from New Hanover High School in 1939, Peace College in Raleigh, NC, in 1941, and Agnes Scott College in Decatur, GA, in 1943. During the early war years while she was away, my parents rented her bedroom to Army officers stationed at the Camp Davis anti-aircraft artillery training base. Ah, but that story belongs in Chapter 2.

Nevertheless, after earning her degree she returned home, took a typing class, and found employment at the Wilmington Shipyard as a clerk typing forms at a speedy "36 words per minute," she remembered. In 1943 she met her future husband of almost sixty years, Army Lt. George H. "Bud" Garniss, of New Jersey, a Virginia Tech graduate, through the

My sister Elizabeth with her Army sweetheart, Lt. George Garniss, whom she met via Wilmingtor's Second Street USO in 1943. They were married in 1946; their marriage lasted sixty years.

Second & Orange USO. Stationed at Camp Davis, Bud got his commission and soon deployed overseas. On weekends, the USO staff sent visiting armed forces personnel to local homes for dinner from a list of hosts they maintained. Ours was one. He and a buddy arrived, and, she always said, it was love at first sight. Furthermore, he secured his future position as the man of her dreams that evening by donning an apron and volunteering to wash dishes.

Wouldn't you know it? There was a war on. Quickly, they became engaged. Following his service in India, in 1946 they were married in our church. There you had it, a classic typical wartime love affair, and this one ended well. He pursued a lifelong career with the YMCA in Wisconsin, New Jersey, Hawaii, and finally thirty years in the Seattle, Wash., area. She was a career social worker and bank clerk. They raised two children, Robert ("Bud") and David.

My last visit was in their nursing home just weeks before they both died in 2006. They are buried in Tacoma, Wash. I'm real proud of my nephew Bud, a retired US Navy SEAL chief petty officer, and retired motorcycle and SWAT team officer with the Seattle Police Department. We keep in constant touch. He and wife Geri visited me in 2015.

CHAPTER 2

FIGHTING WORLD WAR II ON THE WILMINGTON
HOME FRONT, AND A TAR HEEL BORN AND BRED

Calculating the magnitude of the impact and fascination of World War II on my life would take forever. It seemed like the war dominated everything I did growing up, and to a large degree still does. WWII has been a principal factor in steering my life since 1941, and I am devoted to preserving its history and meaning. For the last nineteen years my Lexus license plates shout: "WW2HSTRN." Carroll used to kid that WWII was all I was known by, that people didn't realize I could talk about anything else. If that's still the case, then maybe the dynamics of this book will invigorate opposing opinions.

During the war, I thought military thoughts and acted them out, learned to love history, and even began writing my mindsets. That I was born and inspired to have a naval officer career, followed by a career as an author and military historian is easily predicted in those definitive years.

Like other kids, patriotic indoctrination influenced me. Watching theater newsreels and war movies every Saturday in movie houses downtown, listening to the radio news, scouring the *Wilmington Morning Star* and *Wilmington Evening News* papers and *Life* and *Saturday Evening Post* magazines. I learned the reporters and commentators, popular songs, singers, bands, actors, and celebrities. Engrossed in the armed forces, I energetically collected uniform

My childhood home, 102 Colonial Drive in the Forest Hills neighborhood of Wilmington, North Carolina.

pieces and insignia, war toys, scoured maps, sketched battle scenes, clipped pictures and articles, all the while acting out in neighborhood war games with my buddies.

Mother and I saved a unique collection of boyhood memorabilia, the kind of things a WWII boy would collect. I toted them around over the years in many moves, show them occasionally, and promised them to Randall Library among my military history collection. Newspapers she saved for me include the three December 7, 1941 *Sunday StarNews* editions, and others which are part of the home front mini-museum at our restored WWII USO.

I felt a juvenile compassion for the conditions affecting our fighting boys, recoiling thinking about their suffering and dying. Gruesome interludes plagued my reverie and sleep, especially when the news showed concentration camp horrors in 1945. Haunting, lying awake at night. Almost within two stones' throws from my house, five neighbors did not come home. How they died and when and where and how many at first frightened then revolted us neighborhood boys, but it toughened an element of youthful maturity. Retrospectively, we were probably a lot more mature then corresponding children in today's pampered childhood under helicopter parenting.

AH, TO REMINISCE: 1941 TO 1945.

I've done it so often I honestly believe the Third Dimension shuttles me in and out of that universe without needing a cue, leaving me there alone with clarity of purpose. I look backward to project its history forward, for preservation of that period in Wilmington, say even North Carolina, by default fell upon my shoulders twenty-two years ago. As life's clock hastens, accordingly my motivation and drive to finish it, and preserve it, accelerates before it's too late to record it forever, and for me.

A status report on the 11-year-plus project to have Wilmington designated nationally as the first "American WWII Heritage City" by congressional legislation appeared in the *Wilmington StarNews*, July 29, 2018. It lists what the city and Southeastern North Carolina did for the war effort, and preservation accomplishments since. It can be found, with updates on the twelve-year-plus project (see Chapter 11) on www.wilburjones.com.

A note. This memoir touches on but does not replicate the volume of my previous books on wartime Wilmington, *A Sentimental Journey: Memoirs of a Wartime Boomtown* (2003), and its sequel, *The Journey Continues: The World War II Home Front* (2005). No need to. That foundation is already laid. So, why not buy both and completely immerse yourself.

On the cool Sunday afternoon of December 7, 1941, I stayed inside to play alone in the sun parlor. Here on the largest radio set in the house we could get only a few stations. I tuned into our local WMFD station and half-heartedly listened to the Redskins professional football game from Washington. I heard something that sounded important about the Japanese bombing the US military base at Pearl Harbor in Hawaii. The news statement cut into the broadcast, and later the game announcer remarked hearing for high-ranking government persons were being paged on the public address system to go this place or that. At age seven-and-a-half, and a third grader, I realized much of the world was fighting, but of course failed to grasp the significance. I continued to play until my parents summoned me for serious talks. My sister was away at college, and they would try reaching her by phone.

"Where and what is Pearl Harbor?" people everywhere seemed to ask. Children went further than that as details unfolded over ensuing days. Passively perhaps, we sought answers to questions about war and dying and how it might impact our families. I'm unsure just how my parents explained it to me. My mother's tendency was to protect me from bad things and much of what I absorbed was from sources outside the home, or from the newspaper, magazines and radio. My father was too old for service, and he had already dived into the defense effort. What they exposed me to reflected their immense patriotism, sound judgments, and news awareness, more so my father in the latter. I believe the war forced kids to grow up real fast, a fierce test of concentration, adjustment, and adapting. Yes, it certainly did, which proved a positive character trait molding successful lives.

HOW WE BOYS WON THE WAR

A speedy bike ride would get you to the Solomon Islands or Central Pacific within three minutes from anywhere in my Forest Hills neighborhood. Such dispatch was important when warriors were gathering to execute the day's plan of attack against the hated Japanese enemy. Plans formulated by quick, short phone calls (in allegiance to wartime phone usage restrictions), or agreements ending the previous day, were necessary for picking sides to play war. In my wartime Wilmington childhood, the boundaries of one's world were most likely the neighborhood, expanding on weekends to downtown for shopping and movies, church, or beaches if gasoline was available for the family Pontiac.

About the time of WWII, I aspired to be a Royal Canadian Mounted Policeman and liked wearing that uniform. Don't know why. During the war, the lives of my friends and I revolved around playing war games, following the war news, and informal sports activities. We had no Little League structure or parents dictating the rules. We just chose sides and played pickup football and basketball and beat each other butts without rules. My backyard driveway had a basketball goal which encouraged healthy exercise. I was a decent student, mostly A's, according to my periodic report cards, except for shortcomings in "Conduct " (eee-uuhh, not always good).

We boys wore a lot of knickers. The 1943 photo which became the cover of my book *A Sentimental Journey* shows me in a one-piece shorts and shirt outfit with belt, popular in those days, holding a box of popcorn. I devour popcorn to this day. My terrier's name was Jip. I was a Cub Scout for at least a year, but dropped out after wounding myself carelessly on the right lower leg with a hatchet in the field.

Aspiring to be a Canadian 'Mountie,' I posed in my RCMP uniform in 1942.

The city hosted displays and demonstrations of our army's equipment, vehicles, weapons and the like, particularly around the Front Street post office, which was the unofficial "gathering place" for local war news and gossip. I remember seeing, touching, and crawling over and through all sorts of rolling stock from jeeps to tanks, and machine guns and howitzers, and tents to sandbag emplacements. The very idea of standing next to and talking to a real live American soldier in battle uniform! It added true realism to our next day's war games in Forest Hills. I can still smell the oil-steel of trucks, feel the rough canvas cots, and sense the smooth wood Garand rifles they actually let us hold. Upon visiting these exhibits, the rest of the world stopped.

On my ninth birthday, Daddy gave me a Smith & Wesson 1914 model revolver captured from bandits in the Dominican Republic during WWI as recognition of his service. In 1999 I donated the pistol, which had been placed safely away unused, to the Cape Fear Museum of History & Science.

MY PARENTS, OUR CHURCH, AND THE WAR EFFORT, AGAIN

My parents were very active in St. Andrews-Covenant Presbyterian Church, Daddy as a lay-leader deacon, then a ruling elder for forty years all told, and mother in women's activities. During the war, I was immersed in Sunday school and learning the Catechism, and was confirmed as a full member at age nine in June 1944 when the churches merged. Thus, I will always be the youngest SACPC Charter Member. Post-war activities with the church youth groups stemmed from both religious and social reasons.

My Mother's two old maid aunts, Kate and Lillian (Bill) George, lived on Fifth Street at Red Cross Street across from the black St. Stephen AME Church, a small two-story wood house which still stands. Her aunt Jean and husband Mervin Archer lived there also. Kate spent her career at the Atlantic Coast Line as did hundreds of locals—the largest employer in a one-horse-town before and after the war. Bill, a retired nurse, with one telephone ran the city's nurses register, assigning them all over. Jean and Mervin helped run Farrar Transfer Company on South Front Street. The building still stands. My maternal grandmother Hattie Murrell, my aunts, and uncle David lie in the George plot in Oakdale's Section O.

Boyhood knickers, 1942.

During the war I spent many an hour in their house. Mother dropped me off and did her volunteer work. I'd play in the backyard shed with the chickens and sit on the front porch watching people go by eating Bill's favorite snack, white bread smeared with thick yellow wartime margarine and sugar. On Sundays I watched the ladies and gentlemen of St. Stephen in their finery with services and resonating music that seemed to last all afternoon.

Why this memory sticks out is beyond me. Mother frequented Brownie's

Sharing a box of popcorn with my future brother-in-law, Lt. George Garniss, and my dog Jip, 1943.

Beauty Shop in Gladys Brown's home on Grace Street downtown. I'd go with her and hang out with neighborhood kids, particularly Perry Whitman who was related to Brownie. Perry and I were NHHS classmates. He glued the reunion group together all these years, but died suddenly in 2017. Not long after returning to Wilmington in 1997, I visited Brownie's for old times' sake (I admit to being extremely nostalgic). She lived, but the salon hadn't been used in years, yet everything was still in place, hair dryer chairs, shampoos, utensils, etc. One smelled the pungent hair coloring scents of an old-fashioned beauty shop. Almost toxic. A bit creepy, like an amateur home museum left untouched for years.

While writing my two wartime Wilmington books, I was continually reminded of my parents and their generation, what they made of themselves, and what they raised me to become. These reflections caused consideration of what tremendous strains and stresses community leaders and parents were under during the war. Somehow, Daddy earned a living and they maintained their volunteer, personal, and family lives in rational balance. How, I will never know, because I was a natural boy getting into natural mischief.

WAR DOMINATED, BUT DID NOT TOTALLY PREOCCUPY

How well I remember daydreaming in class looking out the windows at towering pines sketching war scenes of burning Japanese airplanes and German tanks, when I ought to be doing my school work. I loved drawing and included numerous sports, mostly football, scenes. My favorites were a portrait of Navy halfback Clyde "Smackover" Scott whom I saw play against Duke in Durham in 1945, and action from the historic Great Lakes Navy 19, Notre Dame (No. 1 in the AP poll) 14 in 1943. Sixty years later I interviewed him twice while writing my wartime football book, *Football! Navy! War!*

War dominated but did not totally preoccupy my life or my friends' lives, including playtime. Proper growing up came first. And we played pickup games of football and basketball without really know either rules or what we should be doing. Our parents saw to it that we learned, thought, and did the right things as necessary groundwork for a full, productive and virtuous life. My generation, born in the Great Depression or otherwise between 1932 and 1940, are sometimes called the "forgotten generation." Our childhood blurred radically during the most fearsome conflict the world has seen. Now long retired and very "elderly," by default we are the bridge generation between those who won WWII and their offspring. It's easy to disrespectfully view some Baby Boomers, whose indelible traits often include protests against traditions and authority their parents fought for and built during and after the war.

Our gang's successful efforts to win the war left no distinguishing neighborhood scars, even though our war games continued a year or so until petering out. Yard foxholes eventually filled in, and temporary structures and fortifications headed for the woodpiles or dumps. We watched the boys come home, heard their stories, but also saw them shift gears at their own speed. Some time after the war was over, we boys realized we needed new important occupations. In no particular

A moment in my backyard war games, complete with a toy machine gun.

order, they became girls, organized sports teams, and jumping into New Hanover High. From adolescence to young adult almost overnight. Breathtaking, and without TV, social media, and electronic devices.

During this 1946 transformation period, at twelve I created my very first job: mowing lawns, raking, and weeding in the neighborhood. I've worked steadily ever since. To this day, I am extremely proud of this burning work ethic. Among my strongest qualities, fortunately it passed to my children.

Now, interpreting for and mediating the two generations might be my generation's unwelcome task, surely not an easy one. The task also includes passing history along to those who follow, a devoted challenge which I meet daily. Some of the proven tenets and values that got us through the war crises now might be considered outmoded, if one hears certain media and political spokespersons. But they are the cornerstone of my generation's upbringing, the strength and fabric gained from the denials and deprivations to which we adjusted.

May time and history record, and appreciate, my efforts to explain and archive it.

GOOD SCHOOLS, MEMORABLE TEACHERS

In 1947 I graduated from Forest Hills School at nearly age thirteen and entered New Hanover High in the ninth grade. The school system had no middle schools and grammar schools ran through the eighth. At Forest Hills I sang (oh, really?) in the glee club, and was editor of the school newspaper, *The Forest Hills Echo*—my introduction to lifelong writing. Gonna like this gig, I must have said.

Played on the school football (lineman), basketball (substitute), and baseball (a bad third base) teams. Year-around jock. Schools played football games at the 13th and Ann Streets field, basketball and baseball around the county. Forest Hills had no gym; so we practiced on an asphalt outdoor court. I remember letting a ground ball go through my legs for an error to let in the home team's winning run at Wrightsboro School. Lifted my head and glove. Humiliated.

An end-of-the year group photograph with my eighth-grade graduating class at Forest Hills School, 1947. I'm in the striped shirt, third from the right, in the second row from the top.

During the summers of 1949 and 1950, I visited my sister Elizabeth and husband George in New Jersey. Went to numerous baseball games over in New York's Polo Grounds and Yankee Stadium, and Brooklyn's Ebbets Field either with a YMCA boys group or took buses or subways on my own. This was a load for a boy of fifteen: buses, subways, and walking through Harlem to the Polo Grounds without incident was a risky adventure absolutely not attempted today.

Can you believe this, baseball historians? I saw Jackie Robinson, Monte Irvin, Henry Thompson, Larry Doby, Roy Campanella, Don Newcombe—so many of the early black players. And the rise of the Dodgers' "Boys of Summer." The 1955 team, World Series champs over

With Mother at my sister's wedding, 1946. I was 12.

With the Forest Hills basketball team, 1947. I'm second from the right, back row.

the Yankees, is still my all-time favorite. Holy cow, what thrills. And, oh yes, jumping ahead to 1956, I watched the Dodgers play the Tokyo Yomiuri Giants in Korakuen Stadium in Tokyo before 35,000. Newcombe and Joe Black pitched. Man alive! "Did You See Jackie Robinson Hit That Ball?!"

Back to 1950 and the junior class play. I played Ted Hartley, a young businessman, the stage production "Here Comes Charlie," my only attempt at acting. The serious theater world rejoiced! I was a decent basketball player and from 1949-51 playing in the YMCA church league for my church and Trinity Methodist as a 6'-1" center, often leading the team in scoring and rebounding. Osgood-Schlatter's disease, a growth problem of excessive bone matter below the knees, ended my plans to play varsity sports after playing on the freshman football team. Growing too fast, as I recall the doctor said. The knee growths never went away and bothered me forever.

How I Launched Sonny Jurgensen's Hall of Fame Career—and Teachers Who Saw the Future

I also played sandlot baseball on the still-famous Eighteenth Street Commodores, a ragtag outfit of boys from Forest Hills, Carolina Heights, and mid-town. Sonny Jurgensen beat me out for third base and I became a utility player—nice way of saying I wasn't very good. We played most of our games on Saturdays at the baseball field at the south end of the 13th and Ann field. The metal backstop stood until 2016. Years later I told Jurgy that my inability to stop him from winning the third base position launched his National Football League Hall of Fame career. He later made millions, and I made chump change umpiring college baseball games.

The *StarNews* constantly filled its pages with high school chatter and social news, and my name frequently appeared in a group activity or party. A newspaper column called "Teenage Tattler" was a gossip column without going overboard. If you didn't make the high school news or that one reporting local college students, you were a nobody. My first "real" girl friend, my senior year, was Gloria Smith, a fourteen-year old sophomore. We broke up after my June graduation, and she died in 2002. My biggest senior year achievement was a perfect attendance record. I threw a 1949 New Years Eve party at my house: "They ate too much, played records, and did just about everything else to welcome the new year," so said The Tattler. My father always drove Pontiacs. I learned

New Hanover High School, 1950.

to drive our Chieftain in 1950 and used the car a lot on dates my senior year.

A junior year highlight was attending an interscholastic journalism conference at Washington & Lee College in Lexington, VA, a boon to my inevitable writing career as I was next year's editor-in-chief for the school newspaper, *The Wildcat*. When asked to name those who most influenced my life, I often cite two high school teachers who taught me to write—the way one should write—and who believed in my future. They made me diagram sentences, use gerunds and participles properly, not split infinitives, or end sentences with prepositions. In the classroom. Mrs. Lassiter. On *The Wildcat*, Mrs. Symmes,

New Hanover High School graduate, class of 1951, showing my diploma to my father, who completed only eighth grade.

who guided, critiqued, and encouraged my work. Memorable teachers. Thank you. This memoir should also be dedicated to you. The principles they taught last till this day. In a time when people have lost the ability or desire to write properly, or succumb to laziness, these ladies remain paramount bulwarks for my profession. Can you believe people now print and don't write in cursive? What?

In 1951 I graduated from NHHS at age sixteen, the youngest in my class of about 225, and would forever be the Class Baby. I believe NHHS was the state's largest high school then by student enrollment.

Mother spoiled me on one hand and was a disciplinarian on the other. My butt still stings from hairbrush whacks after misbehaving in church as a kid. Yet, I was the apple of her eye, the child who replaced daughter Helen Blanche who died two years before I was born. To my eternal regret, Mother never lived long enough to see me really make it.

CAROLINA TAR HEEL BORN AND BRED

Funny that I went to Carolina. For years I'd been a Duke fan and by default believed Duke it was. OMG, how I hate the thought even though it was 1,000 years ago. My neighbor Dr. James Lounsbury coaxed me to enroll in his Hotchkiss New England prep school for my senior year which all but guaranteed Princeton acceptance. Well, Mother wanted me to be (a) a Presbyterian minister (Princeton would fit nicely), or later (b) a doctor—physician (Duke would fit nicely). What steered my college choice was my passion for writing. At sixteen, I really wanted to be a sportswriter/journalist, and Carolina had one of the country's finest journalism schools. So, off to Chapel Hill. Thank goodness I did.

I'd spent a little time away from home, but nothing like freshman-college life. First, the school assigned me to room with two small-town buddy-buddies whose goal was not earning a degree, but to torment their roommate and others in the dormitory. After months of pleading, my room changed. Meanwhile, the other most memorable event was hearing on my radio "the shot heard round the world"—the New York Giants' Bobby Thomson's homer to beat the Brooklyn Dodgers and get to the 1951 World Series. "The Ji-Unts Win the Pennant! The Ji-Unts Win the Pennant!" forevermore resounded. Crazy. I knew all the players and all the statistics.

I spent weekends of my first two years on campus studying and learning my way around, occasionally getting over to Raleigh or Durham to see basketball games, like Duke's Dick Groat score forty-four points against the Tar Heels in 1952. I wrote for the *Daily Tar Heel* newspaper for a while with Charles Kuralt and Ed Yoder, both of whom achieved national distinction, and decorated my dorm room with pictures of baseball players. Then I went out for the lacrosse

Carolina's lacrosse team, senior year, 1955. I'm number 82, at the far right in the back row.

team which pretty much kept me there all spring. Otherwise I hitchhiked rides to and from campus to home on weekends, safe to do in those days, or grabbed rides with classmates.

1950S CAROLINA LACROSSE: LACKING SKILLS, WE JUST BEAT UP ON THE OTHER TEAMS

Ah, lacrosse, the most important activity of my Carolina four years. It literally made a man out of me. Because I hadn't played high school varsity sports (the knee growth problems), I was bound and determined to play one in college, for one reason just to show those back home what I could do (was made of). Participating in Carolina varsity lacrosse, and later varsity soccer, instilled in me the lifetime principles of teamwork, leadership initiative, physical fitness, motivation, and desire to succeed. Those institutions still run my life.

Our lacrosse teams "underachieved," to say the least, losing more than winning for my four seasons. Having never picked up a stick until the first day of practice in 1952, I had no idea what I was doing. The first game I ever saw was the one I played in—third midfield, a few minutes. But, I laced up the cleats versus Dook/Dewk/Duque in two varsity contact sports. Ever since, I hate . . . no, let's gentlemanly say that I want to Beat Their Butts in every sport. Honey, it's Much More Than Just a Rivalry between Carolina and Dook.

A passable mid-fielder in my second season, 1953.

Most teammates came from Baltimore, New York, or New England schools. They patiently showed the rest of us how to play. Yesterday's game was much less skilled and technical than today's, but more physical. We beat up on each other to compensate for experience of ability. My favorite punching-and-counter punching bag was Virginia's Tom Scott, a football All-America who played lacrosse in the spring of 1953, and made All-America

In action on the University of North Carolina's Navy Field. I am wearing #80, just to the right of the goal.

there, too. Our sticks and bodies became well acquainted. He prevailed, and went on to a twelve-year National Football League career. Those NFL guys got the best of me, didn't they? Never received a "thanks."

I'd always been a physical fitness nut, earning varsity letters (monograms) my last three seasons after progressing from third to second midfield, and then starting at attack my junior-senior seasons. We played on the World War II-era Navy Field which today has been converted into football practice fields before very small crowds. Almost sandlot-style. Our uniforms consisted of hand-off football jerseys and shoes, gloves, arm pads and non-football-like helmets with masks. Otherwise, the sport was a social sport—mostly fraternity boys—and you were considered cool if a girl you were dating dropped by to watch a game. My parents came up for a couple. No bleachers or concessions though. Sort of a seat-of-the-pants varsity game. Today, the way Carolina sports have expanded, you wouldn't recognize Navy Field.

Fearless, dauntless, lacking skills, nevertheless I fought hard in every game. My senior year I led the Atlantic Coast Conference in penalty box minutes, for which I received a trophy: an unhinged decorated toilet seat. No kidding. Hmm, where did it go?

Actually, I became a decent player, scoring three goals in a victory over Trinity College of Hartford, CT, there in 1954. The team played a New England early-spring break tour to beat Williams College and Trinity, and lose to Massachusetts and Harvard. After Trinity I came down with the measles, and ended up in the UMass infirmary for three days to recover, missing that game. At Harvard, it was so cold we wore sweat clothes attempting to keep from freezing, but the ground was frozen so solid our cleats just wouldn't dig in. And, we also got mauled in lacrosse.

The coach I remember most favorably was Alan Moore, a WWII Navy veteran who taught me the game and eventually was a professor emeritus at

Florida. He stayed in touch with us for years. Our final reunion was in 2010. Also favorable: good old legendary Sarge Keller, the Woollen Gym equipment manager, who for four years kept me in clean, dry practice uniforms (jocks & socks) and towels. Reminds me that I still have a pair of shorts with a faded "North Carolina" striped on a leg, and identical sweatshirt. Ooops, they never came after me.

How (Not) to Shut Down Maryland's All-America Soccer Player

My junior and senior years I also played varsity soccer under Coach Marvin Allen on Fetzer Field. Nothing else to do, making good grades, dating a little, relishing in campus life. Feeling my oats as a jock. Once again, never played it before. Knew nothing. Soon discovered my teammates who played in prep school teammates saw me as no threat to their starting positions. But my developing trademark was learning and innovation. Still is. My position was fullback, or sweeper, a defensive player in the last line of defense in front the goal. Meant I didn't have to run down field a lot. Also, my large feet and shoes allowed me to boot the heck out of the ball. Never learned sideways soccer style. Was I suppose to body block the other team, sacrifice my family jewels? (More on that later.) Poor goalie. Good luck to the team with me back there.

And, after graduation, I played soccer only a couple of times in the Navy while deployed to the Far East in 1961, once on my ship's team versus a British ship's team in Subic Bay, Philippines. Of course we lost badly.

Most memorable experience? Senior year, fall 1954, a starter (what was coach thinking?), versus national power Maryland in College Park the morning of the UNC football game. The day before Hurricane Hazel clobbered the North Carolina coast, causing transportation problems. My team took the train to Washington and then to College Park where we stayed in a dormitory for two nights. The football team took buses and were delayed by hurricane damage. My team got a decent night's sleep that Friday. The football team slept in the buses.

Sleep didn't help us. We lost something like 9-0, and Maryland's All-America left wing scored four goals on me in the first half. Coach took me out and I'm not certain I re-entered. Whew! The football team lost 33-0. UNC shutout twice in same day. But, we finished second to Maryland in Atlantic Coast Conference soccer at 3-2-1, with two wins over Deuwque (Go To Hell Dook!) and one over State, and were 6-3-2 for the 1954 season. Of course, it was all my doing. LOL.

Man, can you imagine the pride I feel in telling people I laced up the cleats against the

Durham school, a.k.a. the University of New Jersey, South, in two varsity contact sports?! Only guy in town who can claim it.

Leadership in the Monogram Club

Through active membership in the Monogram Club for letter winners, I practiced leadership and management skills. Was elected president for my senior year spring semester, had been vice president for fall semester, junior year served as secretary. The *Wilmington Star-News* sports editor's column read: "[Jones] has been afflicted with lacrosse, a sport he lettered in. It is his misfortune, for he has to explain what he is doing for extra-curricular activity at Chapel Hill."

Each spring the club sponsored the annual Blue-White varsity football scrimmage game which raised money for student scholarships, and allowed high school students and orphans as guests. I chaired the 1955 Blue-White game. My committee include cross-country-track runner Jim Beatty who later would break the indoor four-minute mile, and four-sport letter winner Albert Long, the last of that breed in major colleges as I recall. Football, basketball, baseball, track. Great guy, always in shape. Club members journeyed to Myrtle Beach during spring break. My senior year, when our lacrosse team was idle, my weekend date was coed Amy Morse, daughter of Oregon Senator Wayne Morse. Too bad, it went nowhere. Most memorable was having two roommates, football backs Eddie Sutton and Kenny Keller, who went on to NFL careers. No, they didn't need my help.

My varsity letter qualified me for UNC's Mongram Club.

My senior year I was kicked in the groin during a soccer game, missing the future family stones by a hair, and bore a huge black and blue groin mark for weeks. That year, a senior sorority coed I'd been dating came to see our game. Afterwards I introduced her to teammate Calvin Lane, a junior who later broke his leg mid-season. They began dating and eventually married for sixty-two years. Betsy and Cal lived in Wilmington where he taught school and coached soccer and golf, and she taught high school. Sadly, she died in March 2018.

Monogram Club committee plans the Blue-White football game. I'm in the middle flanked by Albert Long (standing) and Jim Beatty (right).

A big man on the Carolina campus, Chapel Hill, 1954. I'm second from right, n fashionable white bucks.

BLACKBALLED FROM KAPPA ALPHA

In 1954-55 I was a non-fraternity "Big Man On Campus (BMOC)," a rare breed. Cutting short summer vacation, I reported early for fall soccer practice and to serve as a freshman orientation counselor. I also served as a dormitory officer in Old East, the first building on the country's first state university—1789. I never joined a fraternity but went through rush my junior year at Kappa Alpha. I'm told a member blackballed me because I didn't shake his hand firmly enough. Oh, well, I didn't drink and really wasn't the frat-boy type anyway. Looking back, I couldn't give a crap less.

My early years personal letterhead featured a UNC ram resting on the Old Well: "Wilbur Jones—A Wilmington Tar Heel." Until my junior year I never dated campus coeds. Carolina's student population then was about 7,000, overwhelmingly men, and all white. Women were admitted only for

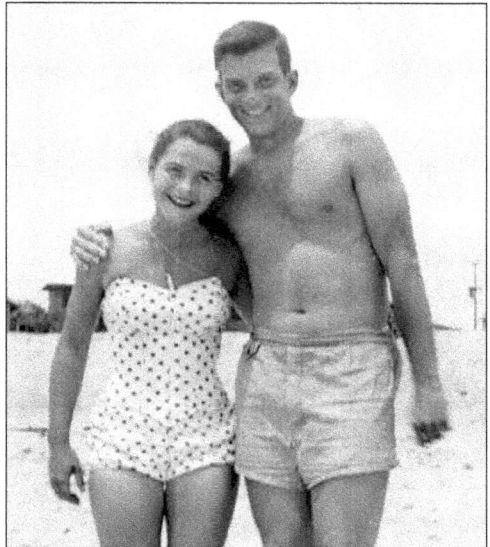

At Myrtle Beach with Amy Morse, whose father was the powerful US senator Wayne Morse of Oregon.

their final two years as transfers, unless they were "townies" from Chapel Hill or nursing students. Many transfers came from our sister school "WC," or the Women's College, now UNC Greensboro. Occasionally I'd thumb a ride to Durham or Raleigh to date a coed at Duke or a Raleigh college. Thumbing a ride was doable then, strange as it seems today, but getting home very late was brutal on the 8:00 a.m. classes.

Mostly my first two years I'd date younger Wilmington high school girls, including Jane Gardner, Louisa Otersen, and Karen Kurka. This was easier in the summer or winter when I wasn't playing weekend varsity soccer and lacrosse. Wearing the navy blue monogram-letter-winner wool sweater with the white block "NC" helped get attention, or at least I thought so. Donning it in August heat at Wrightsville Beach was pushing it for female attention. Sometimes it scored, but most thought I was nuts for wearing wool. The Kappa Delta sorority took pity on me. My first formal, black-tie social was the "Germans Club" dance in 1955. Dragging a sorority girl, I thought that was big stuff. But, taking a date to a Louis Armstrong concert in Memorial Hall was the gold medal. My closet securely houses the "block NC" sweater. Wish I could show it off.

A HISTORY DEGREE—OKAY, NOW WHAT TO DO WITH IT?

On June 6, 1955, I graduated with a bachelor of arts degree in history at age twenty. History? Now what? A card at graduation from my parents read: "Son, we love you more and more all the time. Yep, and I have many good things to talk over with you. Love, Daddy"; and, "With love and best wishes to a very fine young man. May God bless & keep you always. Mother & Daddy." I wrote my parents: "Mom and Dad, I'd like to thank you again for being so wonderful to me and giving me this chance to go to school and learn, play and meet people. You are certainly wonderful and I will always thank you. May the Good Lord bless and keep you always. Love, Junie."

With my parents at Carolina graduation in Chapel Hill, 1955.

Still her "Junie." For another year anyway. "Many good things to talk over with you." For unknown reasons, Daddy and I never really got around to discussing much about whatever he had in mind. Maybe it was what he raised again nine years later when I resigned my Regular

Navy commission. Meanwhile, God has blessed and kept me at least until age eighty-five. Because of my inside connection through son Andrew, the sports journalist who publishes TarHeelIllustrated.com, nowhere in New Hanover County is there a better informed, or rabid, Tar Heel and ACC basketball fan than I.

I'm a Tar Heel Born, I'm a Tar Heel Bred, and When I Die,

I'm a Tar Heel Dead.

So, It's Rah-Rah Carolina-lina, Rah-Rah Carolina-lina,

Rah-Rah Carolina-lina, Go to Hell Dook!

CHAPTER 3

A NAVY CAREER: THE BEST DECISION I EVER MADE:
THE LAST OF THE WOODEN SHIPS AND IRON MEN

After graduating from Carolina, until settling my next move, I went back to work as a summer-fall laborer for Moore-Fonvielle Realty Company in Wilmington. We built houses in Beaumont, a new subdivision in Forest Hills; Whitey's El-Berta Lodge; motels, and other facilities. Lacking construction experience nevertheless I worked long hard hours and made some money, and got even tougher physically sweeping floors, digging holes, and hauling kegs of nails. A holding pattern for whatever came next. Hey, I had nights off. But the best was on its way.

Meanwhile, desiring to become an officer, I investigated joining both the Army and Navy. The Navy interested me more and I pursued it diligently during the summer and fall of 1955. Because my eyesight was not 20-20 uncorrected, initially they balked at taking me as a line (command at sea) officer, which I desired. In order to "train" my eyesight, I drove with my Mother to Raleigh twice a week for several months for treatment by an eye specialist. Our congressman, neighbor Alton Lennon, and US Representative F. Ertel Carlyle wrote letters endorsing me. The eye treatment enabled me to pass another test in the Raleigh recruiting office, where I enlisted as an officer candidate seaman apprentice. I then awaited orders to report for duty at the Officer Candidate

School in Newport, Rhode Island.

In late January 1956 I headed by Pullman train overnight for Providence, RI, and from there bused to Newport. Although I'd pretend-played military roles during WWII, I just wasn't prepared psychologically for the entry into Navy life. However, didn't take long for an adjustment for obvious reasons. No choice, either that or wash out with immediate transfer to enlisted boot camp and the fleet. A few did. But, man, welcome to frigid New England.

OFFICER CANDIDATE, E-2

Officer candidates—all white males—without previous naval service entered as pay grade E-2 enlisted men. We wore peacoats and white teacup hats, boxer white draw-string skivvies (undershorts, which I hated because it didn't pack them in tightly), and thirteen-button pants without pockets. We froze our butts off during the 1956 winter as a snowstorm of unprecedented proportions hit Narragansett Bay where the OCS was located, stopping everything for two days and causing a destroyer to run aground. We lived in drafty wood WWII barracks. My "D" Company took on C Company in a massive snowball fight that drove the officers nuts. Silly, but we let out some steam while being frost-bitten.

Officer Candidate School barracks, Newport, RI, 1956. I wrote, 'Our barracks (top deck, Sec. 3) Lousy looking guy. Beautiful architecture.'

Regular Navy officers and petty officers supervised the OC's. They subjected us to tough discipline, traditions, protocol, shipboard life, and naval traditions; and rigorous academic studies in navigation, seamanship, gunnery, communications, and more. And, watch them bounce a quarter on the cot's top bed sheet. If it flails, a demerit and re-do the bed. Bounces up like on a trampoline, you pass.

Each day a different OC led the section march to its next evolution, class, drill, or meals. My turn at leading the section was disastrous and rather amusing. We were marching on the main street past OCS headquarters where the commander and other officers watched us from the second floor balcony to my right. In order to avoid hitting an incoming marching section, I gave the command "right oblique," and we veered at a 45-degree angle to the right. At the same time I snapped a salute up topside but forgot to command the section to "forward march," or get-going-straight-ahead. Consequently, my section kept marching and stumbled up on the lawn, flower beds, and shrubs before I bailed us out by shouting "HALT!" That finally stopped 'em. We reassembled and proceeded, but I didn't want to look up again. Careless. Extremely embarrassing. I reckoned that military life was still a steep learning curve.

Probably this snafu caused me to fail for selection to admiral in 1984 before I retired in the Pentagon. Had to be valid reason, I surmised. Someone wrote it down and remembered. LOL.

After a few weeks we got liberty and most of us wandered into beautiful Newport. Once I took the train and bus to New Jersey to see my sister and George and catch a Yankees game, a long haul considering I was required to be back on the base by a certain time. Usually I stayed on base, went to the gym, shined shoes and wrote letters. After the halfway point, we ordered officer uniforms—tan for summer with blouse, and blues for winter—hat, ensign rank insignia, shoes, gloves and other accessories from a New York naval officer clothing company. Putting on and replacing the white and khaki hat covers was not as simple as first thought.

SALUTING A BRAND NEW OFFICER, OR NOT

On June 1, 1956, at age twenty-one, I graduated with an ensign's commission and orders. We wore tans with blouse and shoulder boards. By Navy tradition, a newly commissioned officer receiving his first salute from an enlisted person would give that person one dollar. Hah. After the ceremony I walked back to the barracks to collect my gear, call a taxi, and check in at the bachelor officers quarters in the schools area nearby. A young sailor passed me smirking, failing to salute, obviously sensing I was rather fresh caught. (He could tell?) I stopped and chewed him out, my introduction into rendering discipline rather than receiving it. Strengthened by my actions, I proceeded into an entirely new way of life as an officer. Of course, he got no dollar bill.

A newly fledged ensign, OCS Newport, 1956.

My duty assignments began with a six-weeks communications officer school in Newport where I learned everything except how to send and receive Morse code. My first orders assigned me to the ammunition ship USS *Paricutin*,

Aboard USS 'Paricutin' in Hong Kong harbor with my commanding officer, Captain Thienes. The ship was built in the Wilmington Shipyard during World War II.

constructed in the World War II Wilmington shipyard, and homeported in Port Chicago, CA, north of San Francisco. Meanwhile, hey, what better way for a brand-new ensign to spend the 1956 summer than in this glamorous grand resort town. The Black Pearl restaurant, where young officers hung out, still rules the waterfront. Elvis Presley was taking off, and *My Fair Lady* dominated theater with its classic songs.

Once settled into my quarters on commissioning day, I checked in with my parents using the hall telephone. I needed a mild showdown with them, especially Mother, who enjoyed overseeing my life, for my benefit she always noted. Her adult friends commented on it decades afterwards. I told her I was cutting the umbilical cord. I was now a naval officer and no longer her "Junie Boy." This didn't mean I loved her less. She made a huge positive impact on my young life and I respected her opinions and wishes. But, now I had new, enormous responsibilities and must make it by myself with totally different rules. Regardless, she remained quite proud of me and pined to show-me-off to her friends when I spent time at home in uniform.

Daddy told me later this upset her but together they rationalized the meaning and she accepted it. Never had anywhere near this situation with him. Dear reader: Have you tried doing this in your case with mom? It sure ain't easy.

A WILMINGTON BOY
OFF TO SEE THE WORLD

Gulp, look at me, soon off to see the world. What excitement. What anticipation. Thousands of unknowns. The following years generated crisp memories, some of which are shared now. Most were oddball incidents that any young naval officer could have incurred in the maturing and toughening process. In the end, daily growth and increased confidence.

Two weeks of home leave, where Mother toured me (always in hot uniform) among her klatches like the

Proud parents with their naval officer son on home leave.

Hope Diamond Exhibit. Ooohs and ahhhs, all while she bubbled. And Daddy bestowed me to his Exchange Club and Legion Post 10 cohorts. When they allotted me free time, I hit Wrightsville Beach for old-times-sake and thrilled a few star-struck younger girls on "platonic" dates. My parents deserved prideful satisfaction. From their hardscrabble up-bringings, lacking a high school education, they put their two children through college, and one was now a naval officer.

In late August 1956 I headed west under official orders on an unforgettable tour-lite odyssey to report to my ship, the USS *Paricutin*, somewhere in the Far East. Commercial aircraft to Dallas-Fort Worth. Greyhound bus to San Diego, CA, riding through West Texas, New Mexico, and Arizona, fabled cowboy and Indian country. Just thrilling, never knew what critter would pop up around the bend. These were in days before interstates and uber-development devoured Route 66, when a driver really must attach a canvas bag of water to the radiator because there was "no gas or water for next fifty miles." Yes, and Howard Johnson's and Harvey's restaurants if we were lucky. Then Greyhound to the San Francisco area and Moffett Field Naval Air Station.

At Moffett I caught a Navy aircraft hop to the air station at Barbers Point, Oahu, Hawaii, remaining for several days awaiting the next military flight westward. Couldn't resist Waikiki for the swim-trunks photos on the beach with "hula girls," Diamond Head behind me and "swaying palms" overhead. Man! Hard to believe. This Navy life sure was swell. Sent photos home. Look,

The 'boot ensign' ready to hand out condoms to sailors at a Far East port liberty call, 1956.

mom, your only son. Next, military flights via Midway, Wake Island, Kwajalein, Guam, and into Atsugi Air Force Base near Yokohama, Japan. Honestly, flying military air in those days in uniform, carrying only two pieces of luggage, no uniform changes, was rough riding. Bare comfort minimum including seating, meals, reading material, and toilets. Rear-end numbness and no circulation. If the boys of 1941-45 could handle it, then I could.

From Atsugi, a bus to Yokosuka, the US Navy's large naval base south on Tokyo Bay, and the wartime home to much of Japan's fleet. Good facilities, welcoming officers club, and my introduction to famous Kobe beef. Oh, almost forgot, I finally reported to the *Paricutin*. How long to reach my ship? At least two and a half weeks. Now it's mid-September, 1956.

But, few things in my life were more intimidating. Here I am, twenty-two, a brand new ensign in my fresh khaki uniform, with bags, waiting that morning on the fleet landing for the ship's boat to pick me up, after a sailor makes the morning mail run. What lay ahead? Sure, nervous. Like scared sh . . . less, maybe?

Paricutin carried ammunition to replenish ships underway at sea. No glamour cruiser or swashbuckling destroyer, its function, nevertheless, was absolutely essential to the fleet. Overseas, it usually didn't tie up along a pier and anchored or moored off in the harbor. Meant a long boat ride regardless of the weather, a fact of life soon accepted. So, if we blew up in the harbor, only those on board would be hurtled to the high heavens. The late 1950's witnessed the pre-dawn of a totally generational transformation of American sea power as guided missiles, single-sideband communications, and computer controlled warfighting lay way-around the corner. Newer ships were on the drawing boards, but for now, be patient with the Old Navy.

Welcome, young man, to the bridge era from The Last of the Wooden Ships and Iron Men.

A TRAUMATIC FIRST DAY ABOARD AND IT WOULDN'T BE THE LAST

Officer Candidate School could not prepare me for a traumatic first day upon reporting aboard. My job as communications officer meant a quick intro to my operations department head (a lieutenant j.g.) and the executive officer (No. 2, a lieutenant commander) and my senior petty officer, then shown my stateroom I

Overlooking harbor at Hong Kong, one of my many exotic western Pacific ports of call in 1956 and 1957.

shared with another ensign. On to dinner served in the wardroom by Filipino stewards. I made two Massive Rookie Mistakes. Seated as the junior among about twelve officers, I got served last, and when being passed a communal platter of food, skimmed some off the top rather than taking it from the offering officer. So, he politely dropped it within inches of my plate. I got his point, as all hands watched, and sheepishly found vacant space for it elsewhere while shaking inside.

Second, I planned to go ashore for another night in Yokosuka. I liked the town and at dinner wore the allowed civvies, a coat and tie. But by not checking protocol, I neglected requesting permission to go ashore from my department head and the exec. Emphatically reminded, I realized another message sent and received. They let me go This Time. I took the first liberty boat. What a day! So here I was in Japan, our nation's defeated enemy just eleven years before, and a country I would love .

During the ship's 1956 and 1957 Western Pacific deployments, we participated in numerous underway replenishment operations of carriers, cruisers, destroyers and other ships, rigging lines between ships alongside to transfer ammunition and receive supplies. We called on Hong Kong; Sasebo and Kobe, Japan; Subic Bay, Philippines; and Pearl Harbor, Hawaii.

Having never been at sea on any platform, my initiation to rolls, pitches, poundings, tall whitecaps,

Water buffalo ride on route of the infamous Bataan Death March, Luzon Island, Philippines, 1957.

and gusty winds came the day we left Yokosuka, several days after reporting. Never heard of Dramamine. During a gunnery exercise, firing first at towed targets from the stern's 5-inch deck gun, my roommate Rock Stoner and I were assigned to train on this monster, prodded by gunners mates. What's this? The ship is moving up and down back here? Well, yes, I threw up; was pretty awful. Someone took me to sick bay for treatment, which just meant trying to lie down in a bunk that also was moving. At first I thought I was going to die. Soon I just wanted to die. Couple of days to recover, learn to eat again, and return to duty.

Embarrassing as hell. Bad enough just to be brand new. Enlisted men saw me suffering. Will I gain their respect? But, I don't recall getting this seasick again in my many days afloat, including years later riding through the eyes and bad quadrants of Pacific typhoons as my ship's navigator, when the only ones on the swaying bridge were the quartermaster on the helm and myself.

My thirty-man operations division included seven black sailors, my first time associating with blacks to this extent. This sounds goofy, but inner forces moved me immediately to try to disguise a slight southern accent, being tempted to introduce myself as being from Brooklyn, New York, by its slightly gnarled accent. That lasted less than a day. No one probably noticed. The division consisted of radarmen, radiomen, quartermasters, signalmen, electronics technicians, and the like—vital, skilled people, a huge responsibility. Textbook leadership case studies no longer relevant. Get going, learn quickly, try, then correct mistakes.

Fitting the likely pattern of young shipboard division officers universally in the 1950's, I transfigured into a combination bad cop-good cop, disciplinarian and godfather. Held jurisdiction and power over their liberty and special requests, advancement, aches and pains, and problems at home. And, man, did they have problems at home. Relied enormously on my chief and first-class petty officers because they ran the Navy. What an incubator for leadership, organization, and management. Learning, seeking guidance, fits and starts, and moving ahead, a firm foundation for the rest of my life. Thank God I began my professional life this way.

DRIVING A STICK-SHIFT CAR BEHIND
A SAN FRANCISCO CABLE CAR, BUT NOT IN JAPAN

When we hit Pearl in 1956, the war between Israel and Egypt raged, and momentarily we awaited orders to re-deploy to the Western Pacific. We gained a few extra days of in Honolulu (tough luck), and continued eastward to Port Chicago, CA, our home port.

Ah. Port Chicago, the Navy's West Coast ammunition depot in Concord, was Boondocks City, an hour from Berkeley, longer to Oakland, and much longer to San Francisco. What a haul into bright lights.

Yet, one enjoyed the dramatic and colorful (cold and windy, too) ship's

Aboard USS 'Paricutin,' sailing through the Golden Gate into San Francisco Bay, 1956.

passage under the Golden Gate Bridge, into San Pablo Bay with Alcatraz to starboard, north past Vallejo, and into Suisun Bay.

In 1957 I bought a used 1954 Chevy and burned lots of miles. Learning to drive this stick-shift transmission car on San Francisco's steep hills, and over cable tracks, was one huge harrowing challenge. Whew. Immediately master left-foot-on-clutch-pedal or you're doomed. Each visit I envisioned stalling and getting demolished by the Fisherman's Market-Nob Hill-Angels Flight cars with all bells clanging, or crashing out of control on wicked Lombard Street. Good fortune, luck, skill—and a horn to alert others behind their wheels. It all worked, and my Chevy escaped accident-free, if not nervous.

My '54 Chevy, dubbed 'The Green Hornet,' on the wharf at Alameda. I learned to drive the thing, stick shift, clutch and all, on San Francisco's hilly streets.

Didn't date much. Couple of times with a cute cheerleader I'd known at Carolina. I guess every young guy has a young gal he always remembers as the "first." Mine was a knockout Cal Berkeley junior named Diane Arnaud. Yes, but it just wasn't what I dreamed. Another of the "firsts" Diane and I shared was my introduction to Italian pizza. Pizza? Would love to know what ever became of her. Diane . . . ?

This super-adventuresome North Carolina boy just had to go sightseeing, and away I went, sometimes with another officer, often alone in a totally foreign world. Japan fascinated the inquisitive. Entirely new customs, smells, food, clothing, sanitation, music, structures, and the language. One picked up please, thank you, toilet, wait-a-minute, good evening, the extreme basics, yes-no, and many signs and menus doubled in very broken English. But, don't eat ubiquitous street food. Frequently I swapped on-board duty days with married officers. They took mine so I could travel, and in the States, I took theirs for family time.

As I visited Honshu and Kyushu islands, the courteous people and their industriousness impressed me the most. Signs of the war's destruction had disappeared, Tokyo in particular, where lightweight Datsuns and Toyotas, horns blaring, careened like disoriented wild animals. I saw some

With youthful Japanese baseball enthusiasts, 1957.

I was privileged to see Jackie Robinson and the Brooklyn Dodgers play the Yomiuri Giants in Tokyo, 1956.

disabled ex-soldiers in old uniforms soliciting money in parks. Street walking, taxi riding—you held your luck. What seat belts and head rests? No, I did not and would not rent or drive a car in Japan, ever. Not yet, but eventually I would own innumerable Lexuses and Toyotas, plus a Honda, for quality and performance. Didn't take me long to get over any dislike of the ex-enemy. Needed their products.

Japanese cameras already achieved world prominence by 1956. I carried my first one, a Nikon F 35-mm, throughout the Pacific and the USA for years, again eventually ramping up to more sophisticated Nikons and Canon film cameras and their extra lenses and accessories. Consequently, overseas I began a side career with a passion and degree of excellence in shooting photographs, not snapshots, with a keen eye for subjects, backgrounds, and perspectives.

This interest culminated in my well-staged 2015 exhibit of some 200 images titled "Nagasaki to Normandy: Seven Global Decades of Images: War and Peace, Peoples and Cultures." Some sold. For the past fourteen years frequenting Western Europe on business, my several pocket Canons have provided some exceptionally neat photographs, as my dear lady friend Ann LaReau would attest. Lots of café scenes, people watching, WWII memorials, and art masterpieces, descriptively organized into history albums.

How About This: I'm Actually Going to Europe!

After two Western Pacific deployments, my inquisitive horizons yearned for expansion. I should have advertised: Will Work For Navy Travel Experiences. In 1958 my transfer request for sea duty in the Mediterranean or Europe produced orders to the USS *Alameda County*, a former WWII LST (landing ship, tank) amphibious ship homeported in Naples, Italy. Now the ship served as an aviation advanced base supporting North Atlantic Treaty Organization (NATO) operations. Man, what a treat. I have advised young people since: Do it while you're young.

Mother flew to San Francisco to join me for the drive across country via Southern California and the Cowboy and Indian Southwest: Disneyland, Grand Canyon, Billy the Kid's grave, OK Corral, et al. A grand time together. Destination: West Palm Beach, FL, where my sister and husband were living and Daddy awaited. Mishap: one day he followed me too closely and rear-ended my Chevy—driveable, but needing repairs once we got to Wilmington. After I left for Europe, he sold the car and deposited the check into my savings account, which a couple of months later in Naples I used to help buy a brand new German Opel Rekord two-door red and white sedan. This car transported me, and subsequently wife Carroll, all over Southern Europe and America for several years.

Three weeks of leave and authorized travel time passed quickly at home, and after a few blah dates and again being exhibited to friends by a gleaming

Mother, I left by military air from Charleston, SC, ultimately for the naval air station at Port Lyautey, Morocco. There I waited on transportation to the *Alameda County*. However, one famous last word from mother. Before boarding the Charleston flight, she admonished me: "Don't you go bringing home one of those girls from over there, you hear me!" Seriously. Still rings in the ears. God Bless Her. Mother's limits saw "Italian," and "Catholic," interchangeable, I guess. More on this later after Carroll entered my life, and how Mother flipped.

Considering my extensive lifetime international travel, that was my only visit to Africa. At the officers club I caught the movie "Three Coins in the Fountain," about Rome's Trevi Fountain, increasing the anticipation. Oh, not to forget. More unknowns. New responsibilities ahead lay ahead for a twenty-four year old naval officer, but this time feeling exceedingly more confident than eighteen months prior.

SUMMER VACATION WITH CRETAN GOATS AND DONKEYS

Alameda County was in Cagliari, Sardinia, when I reported aboard in February 1958 as operations officer. The ship had seven officers and a crew of about 150. Our mission was to provide support for any NATO ad-hoc, temporary airfield needed in an emergency. When we deployed to the eastern Mediterranean, we pitched camp at Souda Bay, Crete (Greece), a dry, barren outpost with a lovely swimming lagoon but about five miles from the port of Khania, the only nearby city. Germans fought the British on Crete in WWII, and traces existed, namely blonde, blue-eyed Greek children, and refurbished, serviceable German army vehicles. Goats and donkeys comprised most of our Souda Bay neighbors. We took Navy jeeps sightseeing to the Minoan Palace of Knossos and other ancient Mycenaean ruins, symbolizing an archeology passion I've enjoyed all over the world. If not archaeologists to Knossos, in 1958 no one else on earth was visiting Crete. Several times I sent postcards or notes back to my ancient Carolina archaeology professor thanking him for culturally prepping me.

Three things I'll always remember about Souda Bay. When once the ship sailed, the commanding officer left me in charge of the NATO airfield with a handful of sailors, working with French, British, and Greek forces.

At the height of the 1958 first Lebanon Crisis, when internal turmoil threatened the pro-Western government, the US stood ready to provide stability. Before Marines landed there, they trained on Crete. I took a few days off and bivouacked with them in the rocky hills proving my manhood. No way could I think that one day the Assistant Commandant of the Marine Corps, General Ray Davis, Medal of Honor at Korea's Chosin Reservoir, would write the foreword to my book *Gyrene: The World War II United States Marine*, and speak at one of my history events. He made me an Honorary Marine, a distinction still pridefully felt. The experience readied me to command a real neat Naval Beach

Group Reserve unit in 1976, which supported, landed, and lived with Marine amphibious operations.

The Navy pulled me away from the Crete Marines for a trip out to the carrier USS *Essex* off the Lebanon coast. So, I hopped a carrier-on-board-delivery aircraft with my overnight gear and tail-hooked with the movies and mail. Tried sleeping in the junior officers bunkroom forward right under the launch catapult during all-night air operations. Tried, I write. After breakfast, departed *Essex* the way I came in. Such was my only carrier landing. Just wasn't cut out to be a carrier jet jockey, but admire those who are.

Adventuresome young men like me did crazy—perhaps unorthodox—things like those. How about this one? With a couple other officers, in civvies I drove a jeep into Khania for dinner and, for them, a night of drinking. I didn't drink, postponing it until 1960 New Year's Eve champagne. Anyway, my companions grew noisier and more obnoxious enhanced by Greek bouzouki music and too much ouzo. Got real late. I couldn't get them to leave but had to return to the ship. So, I walked the five miles. Mostly roughly paved rural roads, no sidewalks or street lights, an occasional farmhouse light, their animal bleats noting my passage. The jeep returned shortly after and everyone bedded down. Next day, some smirks and whispers and that was that, but I showed what could be done. They had the hangovers, not me, but my feet ached.

UGH, SIX MONTHS ON ALAMEDA COUNTY WAS ENOUGH TICKET PRICE TO ITALY PAID IN FULL

Six months on *Alameda County* was punishment enough for any sane junior officer desiring to get ahead. I felt under-worked and off the path. The ship really was The Backwater. You talk about reincarnation of the hit movie, *Mr. Roberts*. That was our commanding officer, the idiot Cmdr. Smokey Gordon, a passed-over WWII aviator, and his ship. We broke down at least twice, once in the Strait of Messina with Mt. Etna belching fire, requiring towing. Gordon was so bad that duty under him caused me to be constipated for seven days, seven days, a record I've never attempted to match. The only good thing about the ship, aside from seeing places, was that we docked downtown at the main Naples commercial harbor. Could easily walk to a taxi or to our parking spot.

The Navy quickly blessed my request with orders to the staff of Commander Service Squadron Six, a.k.a. Commander Service Force Sixth Fleet, headquartered on the fleet oiler USS *Mississinewa*, also—thank goodness—homeported in Naples. What a relief! Gordon and I parted on adequate terms, but now I was back in the Real Navy. Now the Navy could cash-in and utilize my ability and desire and continue grooming me.

Our squadron commodore commanded the oilers, supply, ammunition, repair, and other service ships that rotated deployment from the US Atlantic coast for six months Sixth Fleet duty in the Med. As his communications officer and chief cryptologist, I had immediate access with my value recognized. From September 1958 to early 1960 when I departed, the ship visited many of the Med's great ports—Barcelona, Mallorca, Toulon, Cannes, Genoa, Piraeus (Athens), Beirut, and Istanbul—while also refueling underway hundreds of ships alongside. Each stop expanded my inquisitive cultural appetite for sightseeing and shooting pictures.

Because duty on this sea-going staff essentially is the story which follows, one in the same, continuing to describe my Navy service simply merges into the next best decision of my life: Carroll Robbins. Had the inside track on her, which follows.

CHAPTER 4

A STORYBOOK EUROPEAN ROMANCE
AND STARTING A CALIFORNIA FAMILY

I met Carroll Eloise Robbins and her parents in Naples, Italy, in September 1958 when her father, Captain Berton A. (Bob) Robbins, Jr., arrived to take command of the Service Force Sixth Fleet. Since I had been there a few weeks, he inherited me as his communications officer and added the title of flag aide, whose protocol responsibilities included accompanying the commodore throughout the Mediterranean as he called on port captains and Allied naval commanders, and attended social events. You already know where this going, right?

The first time I saw her was the day he assumed command. She wore a gray tweed-ish suit and heels, which made it difficult for her to walk across the ship's steel-grated deck. We chatted briefly at the evening reception. She struck me solidly, but, why was she in Naples? Soon thereafter, on outright dares from the ship's junior officers, taunts more like it, I asked her for a date. This just accelerated the business of "going out with the boss's daughter" from those jealous fellows. They ain't seen nothing yet. Carroll and I began dating and developed a friendship which grew into love.

CARROLL STAYED BECAUSE OF PAT'S HEALTH

But back to the origin. Patricia O'Meara (Pat) Robbins, Carroll's mother, a world-class trailblazing, award-winning photographer, unwittingly instigated this liaison. At Pat's request, Carroll took leave from an assistant buyer position at Garfinkels fashionable department store in Washington, DC, to accompany her and Bob to Italy for their new assignment. With declining health, Pat believed she needed Carroll's help in adjusting in Europe. Being at her beckon call was more apt. Carroll planned to return to Washington to her job after a couple of months, but two life-changing factors kept extending her stay. Pat made her feel guilty for "abandoning" her mother (she was a demanding person and expected continuous doting and "servitude"), and we began dating.

With Carroll on the Spanish island of Mallorca, 1959.

I guess I was nuts—it just wasn't done in the Navy of that era—but I liked her, and she reciprocated. Also, Naples was absolutely devoid of other eligibles for each of us. Slim pickins. For years we occasionally wondered aloud what if we had met in the States rather than romantic Europe. But that never really mattered. Our first date was to Pompeii in my Opel Rekord. I picked her up at the Hotel Vesuvio on Santa Lucia harbor where they were temporarily staying, and returned her there announcing I had another date for the evening. Not good, I would learn. Over the months we enjoyed weekend drives to Rome, Cassino, Paestum, Amalfi, all over the region. We loved Italy, she especially, and made ourselves at home there becoming comfortable with each other as we grew closer. The glamour of Italy facilitated our transition into married life.

As my ship sailed the Mediterranean, Pat and Carroll often joined us in port—Athens, Barcelona, Mallorca, Cannes, and more. Those were the late 1950s, the omnipresent Cold War under control, Americans welcomed, and no terrorist threats. We became friends, then good friends, then realized we were in love. Ours was the classical Storybook Novel Romance that people would die for. The Med became our private lake, and Riviera films with Cary Grant and Grace Kelly could as easily

The Parthenon on Athens' Acropolis was one of many Mediterranean destinations Carroll and I visited.

been shot with Wilbur and Carroll.

On April 27, 1959, the day before her twenty-fifth birthday, and after a trip to Capri where I proposed, we announced our engagement to her parents over dinner at their apartment. That night, "Wilbur got all pink in the face when he started talking," Carroll wrote in her diary, "and the way he was leading up to it I felt sure they knew what was to come. Daddy got up from the table and was about to leave the dining room when Wilbur said, 'come back and sit down, commodore!!!' He did. Mother turned to me and said, 'you're kidding, really?' They both seemed more surprised than we expected, but at the same time pleased . . . . Later, after the dishes were done, we went out for ice cream and a drive."

SORRY, MOTHER, BUT NO SURPRISE: I'M BRINGING ONE OF THOSE GIRLS HOME

Goodness, this was not like eloping to the Maryland Eastern Shore to a justice of the peace like back in the olden days. To get married overseas, I had to go through the chain of command to the Commander Sixth Fleet, Vice Admiral Charles "Cat" Brown, for permission. This simultaneously with navigating through the Department of State and our embassy in Rome. I must have really wanted that girl.

So, Lt. (j.g.) Jones, a.k.a mama's "Junie Boy" of Wilmington, married the boss's daughter on August 11, 1959, in the Anglican Christ Church in Naples.

Everybody in the Sixth Fleet—admirals and captains and Italian and US dignitaries and their decked-out ladies, including the Gallantins—came from everywhere for the year's grandest Mediterranean social event. Cat Brown, too, if you wondered. Hottest day of the year, the Neapolitans informed us, as sweat filled her sloshing wedding shoes. "Mike the driver," a seaman on our staff, drove us in a Navy car through teeming city streets to the NATO officers club reception as onlookers, seeing who we were, shouted "auguri! auguri!"

Two days earlier, the mayor of Naples married us in a required civil ceremony (Italian law, I believe) at city hall. This was cool. There authorities posed to Carroll: what nationality are you? You see, she was born in Shanghai, China, of American parents, baptized in Vladivostok, Soviet Union, turned eighteen while living in West Germany, and now lived in Italy. Guess which. They didn't have to ask me that question. For the church wedding rehearsal two days before, Joy Gallantin, daughter of Sixth Fleet Rear Admiral Pete Gallantin, stood in (tradition...) for the bride at the rehearsal. Boy, was she dynamite. She later married a Wilmington friend, Ed Veazey. After my Naples duty, Carroll and I saw them only once many years ago.

The newlyweds exiting Anglican Christ Church in Naples under ceremonial arch of swords held by my fellow naval officers.

With two weeks of leave, we drove our honeymoon through northern Italy, Switzerland, Bavaria, and Austria. We were so lucky. Our favorite collectible was a lovely hand-carved creche set acquired in Oberammergau, which still decorates my house each Christmas.

Sorry, Mother, but surprise. I'm bringing one of those girls home with me, and you and Daddy will love her! Phone calls homeward had eased the shock, and once we alighted in Wilmington to visit en route to San Diego in early

1960, as was well.

We rented a marble-floor apartment at 94 Via Orazio, bought used furniture chairs and a table and slept on a mattress on the floor. While I was working Carroll made her way through Neapolitan culture and got to know the American ex-pat Lucky Luciano of Mafia fame, banished after the war to Italy. She fit right in.

Damascus, Syria, is frequently in today's news. Here's what I remember about being there in 1960. Never have I been so frightened. While my ship docked in Beirut, Lebanon, two other officers and I hired a private car to drive us to Damascus. Toufik Asley was the driver. At the Syrian border we waited an hour for the large entourage of the emir of Kuwait to pass. In those days, US armed forces personnel could travel with an identification card only, no passport necessary. Security hassled us a bit but we proceeded.

Our sightseeing destinations were the world famous Great Mosque of Umayyad, and the adjacent Grand Bazaar. Asley

The happy couple, Wilbur and Carroll, August 11, 1959.

instructed us on protocol and we left shoes at the door, knelt inside, and were awestruck by the fact it looked nothing like Europe's cathedrals. Err, did I expect otherwise? Heading into the long, winding network of narrow streets, I noticed three indigenous men obviously following us. I just knew they were up to something bad. Our walking pace quickened, then we jogged, finally sprinted through shops, stalls, donkey carts, and other vendors. They stayed with us until outside, when we lost them and re-connected with Asley. No cell phones then to contact the driver. By pure luck we located each other and got heck outta there.

ARRIVEDERCI, ITALIA

Time for my reassignment stateside. Carroll and I spent our last two nights in the Hotel Paradiso where, forty-seven years later, I stayed in my first return trip to Naples since then. We sailed to New York on the fancy liner SS *Independence,* ate dinner with the captain, brought the Opel, and shipped our meager belongings into a "hold" in California until we finally landed. Stopping in Wilmington, we received the royal welcome from family and friends. Mother staged a Southern tea for Carroll, inviting her Little Old Lady buddies in their feathery-lacy hats, gloves, purses over arms, and spotlighted us at the St. Andrews-Covenant Presbyterian service. As expected, Mother glowed with pleasure. It might have been the nicest things that ever happened to her. Daddy, while less expressive, proudly approved and smiled.

On a stop in Wilmington, Carroll meets my parents.

The Opel took us westward to San Diego in June 1960, but not before Carroll began a series of daily morning sicknesses signaling but one thing. In Arkansas honestly the pavement was so torridly hot the tires almost melted. The car lacked air conditioning. Yee gads.

We were blessed with three children, Patricia, David, and Andrew, and eventually raised our only grandchild at the time, Carrie, born in 1994. Carroll, born and raised a Catholic, never had a problem joining me at church anywhere. As the years passed, especially in Wilmington, she went to her St. Mary's Catholic Church and I returned to my root church. Occasionally I joined her. Our children were baptized in the Catholic church.

Before continuing with the Navy story, let's conclude with my lasting tribute to Bob, Pat, and the Robbins family, whom I loved very much. The book I wrote titled, *'She Shot Her Way to Success': How China's Empress Dowager Ci Xi Launched a Photographer's Trailblazing Career.* Published in October 2016, it was my promise to Carroll before she died in 2013. This was my second book on the Robbins-O'Meara families, following *Hawaii Goes to War: The Aftermath of Pearl Harbor,* in 2001.

Bob died in 1983, Pat in 1988. Both are buried in Arlington National Cemetery.

Concluding this Robbins vein, I mention here that Carroll died in Wilmington on September 22, 2013, following a long illness. She is buried with my parents and maternal grandfather in the Oakdale Cemetery family plot. On the day I write this, we would celebrate our sixtieth wedding anniversary. I will always remember how lovely she was that day as we began our fifty-four years together. But wait. As you will see throughout this memoir, she continued to be a large part of my life.

MEANWHILE, BACK TO CALIFORNIA AND MORE SEA DUTY

My new ship duty was the amphibious attack transport USS *Lenawee* out of San Diego. We rented in Coronado across the San Diego Bay, familiar territory from the Korean War days when her father commanded a similar ship, and they lived there. Our ship carried Marines and their vehicles, equipment, and supplies as a key force in amphibious assaults on hostile beaches. This was the "Gator Navy."

With my Deck Department Master Chief Boatswain's Mate West on 'USS Lenawee.'

This cool assignment began as navigator on the first Far East deployment, ploughing through typhoons and dodging fishing boats at night among the myriad Philippine Islands. Later, after being promoted to full lieutenant, I became ship's first lieutenant heading the deck department of 150 men responsible for deck, cargo, and assault boat operations, and embarked Marines. Into this duty I poured everything I knew about leadership, management, and working together, and passed the test. Never after that would I doubt my abilities.

A perfect "literary" match arose. The ship needed new and revised internal regulations and procedures manuals, and I accepted the offer to write them. This extra responsibility was right in my wheelhouse, and I relished the assignments to start, little did I foresee, what became a writing career. A long jump from high school editor of *The Wildcat*, but the commanding officer needed help and I saw opportunity.

A favorite souvenir of those days, a super-sized ceramic coffee mug made to order in Yokosuka from our 1961-62 cruise, lists ports visited. They included: In Hawaii: Maui, Pearl Harbor, Kiahlua; Okinawa: Naha, Buckner Bay; Japan: Yokosuka, Numazu, Kobe, Sasebo, Iwakuni; Hong Kong; Philippines: Mindoro, Subic Bay; and Korea: Pohang, Chumunjin. Also, four amphibious exercises in Hawaii, Japan, and Korea; and six different Marine units carried.

One afternoon in Hong Kong, I took the Star Ferry from Kowloon to the island. By chance, I landed a seat next to Christine Jorgensen, one of the first persons to receive sex reassignment surgery, ergo a surgically transformed transgender person, then famous worldwide. A delightful conversation ensued. She was nice.

Three episodes stood out.

The only person's life I've ever saved was a young black sailor from my ship who fell overboard from a boat off of Maui, Hawaii, during an exercise. He was stunned and had trouble swimming. I dived in, held him for the lifesaving strokes, and negotiated our way to the beach. I got to him before anyone else could, or maybe he went under for good. The sailor returned to duty.

Deploying landing craft for the Marines from the amphibious attack transport USS 'Lenawee,' 1962.

Another was a joint landing exercise with the Republic of (South) Korea marines just a couple miles south of the demilitarized zone from North Korea on the east coast, in the middle of January with sub-freezing, gnawing temperatures and strong winds. On deck supervising for at least seventy-two hours, I nearly froze to death, got just a few hours' sleep, then topside again, and fell exhausted as we departed. Never have I been so frigid. An earlier goodwill visit to a Pohang family for dinner, loaded with the volcanic cabbage kimchi, with its fiery attack on one's innards, must have been my refuge from literally freezing. I could only imagine our 1950 Marines at "Frozen Chosin" Reservoir farther up in North Korea during the Korean War.

And the best, an occasion I rank among my life's most memorable and productive.

CHRISTMAS WITH ORPHANS FROM HIROSHIMA, SIXTEEN YEARS AFTER ATOMIC BOMB NO. 1

We spent the Christmas 1961 period in Iwakuni, on the Inland Sea about twenty miles south of Hiroshima, devastated by the August 6, 1945, first atomic bomb. The *Wilmington StarNews* of February 25, 1962, reported on my role staging a Christmas party the ship gave for thirty-five Japanese school children between the ages of nine and twelve, from a deaf and blind orphanage in Hiroshima. "As the ship's public information officer, I originated the idea for the party for our People to Peoples program, and made all the plans for the party and saw to their execution. Luckily, the party was a tremendous success." It included a tour of the ship, lowering the assault boats, operating anti-aircraft batteries, a signaling exhibition, a Western movie, and "all the ice cream, cookies and candy they could hold." There's more: gifts, sailor hats, and the ship's "welcome aboard" pamphlet printed in Japanese. Two Japanese TV stations and two newspapers covered the event.

The *StarNews* noted that "I felt quite warmed by it, and had to choke back tears at the end when those little kids—some partially blind, others completely deaf—left the ship happy. We have many opportunities out here to engage in public relations for the good of our country."

In planning the event, I worked with Reverend Kiyoshi Tanimoto, whose Methodist church succumbed to the bomb about a half mile from ground zero. He rebuilt it there, but became known globally for organizing the famous Hiroshima Maidens, a group of fifty girls badly scarred by the bomb whose treatment and return to normal life he sponsored. He took many to the United States, where he delivered more than 1,600 speeches. What a privilege for me.

SPRINGBOARD IN CORONADO

The springboard to my future life came in with late 1962 orders ashore to the staff of commander Amphibious Force, US Pacific Fleet (COMPHIBPAC), in Coronado, CA. No residence change. By then Carroll and I had Patricia (1961) and David (1962), and the "Ming Steed," a lovely Ford station wagon. My job heading the Pacific Fleet attack transport type desk required extensive West Coast traveling, but was a welcome respite from arduous sea duty.

As the captain/coach, I played on the staff's Amphibious Base championship basketball team in 1963-64. Prior to a November 22 game, we heard the news that President John F. Kennedy had been assassinated. Carroll and the kids were in the bleachers. We postponed the game, but that night, for some reason, we kept dinner reservations at the fashionable old Hotel Del Coronado. Surprisingly it served to a nearly empty dining room. So many other activities had shut down in shock and mourning.

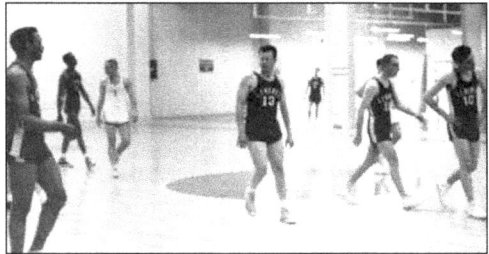

No. 13 on USS 'Lenawee team during Far East competition.

In 1964 I pined for destroyer duty, considered in "career circles" mandatory for long term ticket-punching promotions: the verve combatant ship duty one required. I applied through the Bureau of Naval Personnel, but struck out. Nothing available, and my background in the service and amphibious forces didn't translate into destroyers. So, after nearly nine years I resigned from the Regular Navy active duty, and reverted back to the Reserve.

But, not before the politics of 1964 grabbed me lock, stock, and barrel. A smart life transformation opened up named Arizona United States Senator

Barry Goldwater. Hang on, I thought, 'cause their ain't no road map for this business and what might come. Will have to make my own way.

CHAPTER 5

SENATOR BARRY GOLDWATER
AND THE POLITICS OF LIFETIME TRANSFORMATION

Purists could say I violated the Hatch Act in 1964 by working as a volunteer for Republican presidential nominee Senator Barry Goldwater in his San Diego, CA, headquarters while still on active Navy duty at Coronado. I guess so, but hush. Statute of limitations expired. Anyway, if someone in authority cared, the subject never arose.

Apparently even my three-star boss, Vice Admiral Ephraim Holmes, Commander Amphibious Force, Pacific Fleet (COMPHIBPAC), surely knew. From what I gathered, staff political sentiment leaned toward the conservative Goldwater vs the liberal President Lyndon Johnson. The admiral and I played tennis often (he usually won: smart of me, eh?) during and after business hours at the Coronado Amphibious Base courts. I kept my gear in the office standing by my day job awaiting his aide's call to play.

By then I had integrated into the Regular Navy as a full lieutenant whose resignation request was known. Having been denied immediate career-enhancing destroyer sea duty after eight years on active duty, the choice was to remain in non-career enhancing billets, or get out. The blow stung; I mean stung. The Bureau of Personnel kept me on a tether and I remember well cycling home in the afternoons hopefully singing the musical "Gypsy's" big hit, "Everything's

Carroll and me with US Senator Barry Goldwater, R-Arizona, and US Representative Barry Goldwater, Jr., R-California. I worked on the senator's 1964 presidential campaign, and later for his son.

Coming Up Roses." Untransferable aspirations need not apply.

BARRY GOLDWATER

Why Goldwater? Three books raged over the 1963-64 political landscape.

Goldwater's *Conscience of a Conservative* grabbed both heart and brain. Raised in the conservative South, but hardly political, I nevertheless eschewed the Democrats' and Roosevelt-Truman New Deal and Johnson's liberalism which placed government control over individual responsibility. Just never took to national liberalism. Suddenly a savior, Arizona United States Senator Goldwater, appeared, urging a common sense message easily understood.

From growing up during World War II and through college and into the Navy, basic conservatism grounded my ideological instincts. Whether I recognized them as such then was immaterial. I studied political science but life was not classroom. Those instincts came naturally based on my parents' influence as much as anything, reenforced by the determination to succeed within the rules and values of our great country. Self reliance, self starting, responsibility for my actions, strong national defense, serving the less fortunate through non-governmental means—seeing reality as things are, not as we wished they were. And, the less government running my life the better.

Nothing about my instincts has changed except I'm much more "open and practical" in assessing our country's needs. That includes the human need to take care of others through some expanded government assistance, rights of all citizens, a hatred of all racism, protection of our environment, and equal opportunity—but not guaranteed equal results—for all. The conservatism of those earlier year remains principled, but its identification is factored by political and world events moving far faster than that of my youth. I'm flexible; I see reality clearly. Life isn't fair, but I do not blame others. I consider myself a lifelong patriot, devoted to my country's security and those who have served it.

As such, my debt to fellow veterans living and dead is to preserve and memorialize their service, rather than to join organizations, act on behalf of their rights, and march in parades. They made the history. I devote my life to recording and recognizing it for present and future Americans, as reflected in my books and articles and many hundreds of presentations. Please see Chapter 10.

Since becoming a Wilmington Rotarian in 1998, the Rotary International motto of "Service Above Self" has doubly focused my life. I am a proud Rotarian.

Now, return to 1964. Besides Goldwater's book, we had *A Choice, Not An Echo* by the iconic Phyllis Schlafly, instrumental in founding the modern conservative movement; and *None Dare Call It Treason* by John Stormer, which alleged all kinds of shenanigans in Johnson's elective career. Together gave cause to doubt the country's existing progressive path.

At age twenty-six (the legal voting age then was twenty-one) I first registered as a Republican after returning with Carroll to the States in the summer of 1960 from duty in Naples, Italy. Quite a drawn-out experience. We visited my parents in Wilmington en-route San Diego for my next ship. Our trip to the city hall registrar's office humorously could be considered an outlier of the Old South. She expected us to register as Democrats because that party had dominated Southern politics since the post-Civil War period—a one-party region. To her shock, we said "Republican." Voter registration books were recorded manually, and were large ledger/log-type used for decades. She had to reach to the upper shelf to find the Republican registration book, dusted it off, and opened it. Few registrations appeared. Spider activity jumped out. We added ours using my parents' address as "permanent."

Note: My father, a typical Southern gentleman, raised on an Onslow County tenant dirt-farm, World War I Navy veteran, therefore by default was a Democrat. After Roosevelt assumed power, he always voted Republican for president. I suspect he never voted Democrat for president again. A true ideological conservative, who advanced from poverty by his own boots only through the eighth grade, he worked his way up in finance to become chief executive officer of a local building and loan association. Not active in Democrat politics, nevertheless he personified conservatism. But his views on segregation and race relations were far more liberal than the Joe-On-the-Street Democrat, an enlightened compassionate trait he passed to me. I remember how he saved black families from losing the mortgage on their homes. With his roots, he understood, and I have ever since.

NIXON FOR PRESIDENT IN 1960

By absentee ballot, I voted for the first time in 1960 for Richard Nixon for president. The bug had bit, and as best I could, I followed national politics while deployed twice to the Pacific and Far East on my ship, the USS *Lenawee*.

At the 1964 San Diego Republican Republican headquarters, I launched my political career as a peon to no fanfare. Stuffed envelopes, licked stamps, assembled posters, and was a grassroots gofer—the best way to start a political infatuation. When Goldwater flew into San Diego for a fall airport campaign rally, I joined thousands who cheered.

We lived in Coronado, a solid Navy town across the bay from San Diego while I served on the *Lenawee* and the COMPHIBPAC headquarters staff. Patricia was born in 1961 in San Diego's Balboa Naval Hospital, stricken with the cerebral palsy birth defect, later also stricken with grand mal epilepsy. David was born in 1962 in Coronado Hospital. My children, to be joined in 1966 by son Andrew who was born in Los Angeles' St. Vincent's Hospital, are fifth-generation Southern Californians by birth (and direct descendants of the Mayflower pilgrims).

Well, although Johnson creamed Goldwater as history records, I found the entire experience and process challenging and stimulating. Certainly I was on to something big. After resigning from the Regular Navy, Carroll (we were both 30), Patricia, David and I moved to Los Angeles in late 1964 after driving across country roundtrip to see my folks. Ever tried it with three small kids? My ears still vibrate from the "he hit me"—"no I didn't" and "I've got to pee" shrieks from the rear of our Ford station wagon. Whack! Be Quiet! What today would be held "child abuse" was then normal "parenting."

Anticipating leaving the Navy, not only did I transfer into the Ready Reserve to retain my commission and rank, I investigated professional careers as a stock broker and in the US Foreign Service. Took aptitude examinations for both, interviewed, decided stocks were not my tea, and did well on the Foreign Service application. But, together the FS and I decided on "no," and I was left looking.

LOS ANGELES, OUR FIRST CIVILIAN HOME:
HELLO, CORPORATE WORLD

Carroll spent much of her childhood in Los Angeles, her nominal home, close to her mother's large Irish family. Their "Old Los Angeles Blue Book" heritage stemmed from ancestors who trekked over on covered wagons in the 1800's. Her parents finally settled there five years after Admiral Robbins retired, living in their Indian Wells desert residence in between. In 1964 Los Angeles thus became our home for five years. We bought a house for $24,000 at 454 Mansfield Avenue in Central LA in the Wilshire District near Wilshire Boulevard and Hollywood. When we moved to Alexandria, VA, in 1969, it sold for the same price. Today it's got to be at least half a million.

Carroll's uncle Bill O'Meara's statewide bank, Union Bank, hired me as a marketing trainee to learn the ropes. Wham! Within six months the bank let me go in a company staff cutback, last in-first out. Now I felt isolated in this monstrous city where I knew no one. Get going. Carroll would not work for compensation until 1976 when she began a successful real estate career in Northern Virginia. So, just me.

This was my first of four times out of work with a family to support. In those tests, one learns and adapts quickly or survival crashes. Must bounce back. Soon I landed an executive trainee position with Wilshire Oil Company, a subsidiary of Gulf Oil, starting at the bottom. That meant donning Wilshire coveralls (name tag: "Wilbur") pumping gas, changing oil, lube-ing, and cleaning up the station and rest rooms. Well, they paid me. My station was near the Watts area of South LA, from where I watched the fire and smoke rising from buildings less than a mile away: the great Watts Riots of 1965.

BAPTISM BY OVERWHELMING FIRE:
A REPUBLICAN IN THE LIBERAL LOS ANGELES PRECINCTS

The 1964 election debacle traumatized the Republican Party in Los Angeles and California. However, the daze provided an opening into local party operations, and as the shockwave diminished, immediately I became an important volunteer as congressional district precinct chairman. Hah. The district was so Democrat that filling a room with a dozen Republicans was like finding a Sahara Desert McDonald's.

Forever, liberals represented the district and still do. Nevertheless, I gave it a go and compiled lists and held canned training sessions. I worked hard and established a positive name, even ran for the county

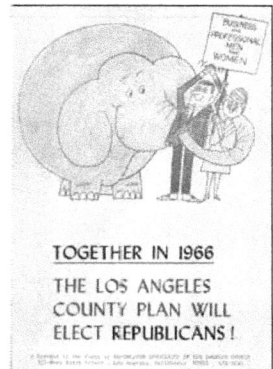

TOGETHER IN 1966

THE LOS ANGELES COUNTY PLAN WILL ELECT REPUBLICANS!

A 1966 GOP poster from L.A.

central committee and barely lost, my only "attempt at public office." Thus saving the Republic.

Bob Finch, California's lieutenant governor under Ronald Reagan, later served in the Nixon administration. He was one of my political mentors.

Somehow, only God knows how, I put my best foot forward and met the right people, including Robert (Bob) Finch, who gave me a shot at full-time employment with the party. Finch was elected lieutenant governor in the 1966 Ronald Reagan-for-governor sweep, and later became President Richard Nixon's secretary of Health, Education and Welfare, then White House counselor. Bob gave me the ultimate break. His relationship facilitated my meeting Nixon intimates H. R. (Bob) Haldeman and John Ehrlichman, among others, in California and subsequently Washington politics. Eyes and ears open, mouth shut, be alert to openings seemed to work.

But that's down the road a bit.

Finch recommended me to the board of Republican Associates of Los Angeles County, an independent education, public relations, and grass-roots organizing team of ten professionals who worked closely with the party organization and office nominees. My principal job was to recruit and train volunteers in companies and other groups for the 1966 campaign and thereafter, called The Los Angeles County Plan. As such, I worked closely with many of the county's leading business and professional persons, valuable contacts that paid off for promotion to my next position. The 1966 election saw Reagan demolishing incumbent Governor Pat Brown. Republican Associates played a role. We all campaigned for Reagan and Finch.

REAGAN AND ME, THEN FORD

California Governor Ronald Reagan and me, 1968.

Following his election, Governor Reagan and I met again at a Century City hotel event. I was starting my business at a restroom urinal when in he walks and settles into the adjoining urinal. "Hello, Wilbur," he said, "how's it going?" "Just great, Governor, thank you. Hope you are." I recovered quickly, and away we went back to the reasons we were there. In 1976 I would stymie his attempt to upstage First Lady Betty Ford at the Iowa Republican state convention in Des Moines during the presidential primary, a bodacious move. Really, I loved him personally and as governor, and fondly remembered how he inspired voters for Goldwater, but never forgave him for challenging President Ford in 1976. His premature desire for the presidency helped cost Republicans the White House, and who knows how the nation would have turned minus the four years of Jimmy Carter.

The keynote speaker at one of Republican Associates' 1967 downtown hotel events was Michigan Congressman Gerald Ford, the House minority leader. My assignment included escorting him from his hotel room to the conference floor. In the elevator I noticed he still had shaving cream around an ear. What to do? Well, his handkerchief took care of that and he thanked me. I don't believe I ever lightly brought that up in the numerous times I was around him in 1975-77 while serving the White House. Not that it mattered. If I had, he would have laughed it off. He was human, so easy relate to.

I first met Gerald Ford in 1967, when the Michigan congressman, then minority leader in the House, spoke at a Republican event in Los Angeles.

You probably can't tell, but I'm sometimes an introvert. Jump way ahead momentarily. The Meyers-Briggs tests I took in the late 1980's at the Defense Acquisition University showed me smack on the border between introvert-extrovert. I could go either way. Ideal. The situation dictated which, whether to shut up, or start talking. That's what I had figured, and as such usually kept my mouth shut to size up an opportunity before committing—or rushing in and losing it. I'm still the same, can be hail fellow one minute, and then quiet to stake out my surroundings the next. A positive characteristic I always thought: you can't pull back something already spoken or done. The alternative: saying "sorry" or facing immediate embarrassment.

Anyway, aspiring in politics meant invoking the introverted side, breaking out if necessary to raise a point. This was probably my approach to landing a plum position, moving up the ladder in GOP staff politics: ergo, the right place at the opportune time. As a member of the LA Junior Chamber of Commerce, my 1966 accomplishments earned me runner-up for the outstanding member of the year award.

ANOTHER BIG BREAK—WORKING FOR THE US CONGRESS

The field representative, a.k.a., district chief of staff, to Republican 27th District Congressman Ed Reinecke of Burbank, decided to move on. My networking contacts influenced Ed to hire me to run his Van Nuys office in the San Fernando Valley. Man, I grabbed it. The 27th was a widespread, fairy-tale district, beginning with the film studios of North Hollywood and Burbank in the south. Then up the Valley through Canoga Park and Northridge to Sylmar in the foothills, then a straight shot into the Antelope Valley and the edge of the Mojave Desert and its ghost towns and abandoned mines, and Edwards Air Force Base. High temperatures, dry heat, no rest stops. Traveling the district, especially if I had to battle traffic from the middle of LA to get to work, was an exhausting chore of many miles. At least I was going against those commuting into downtown.

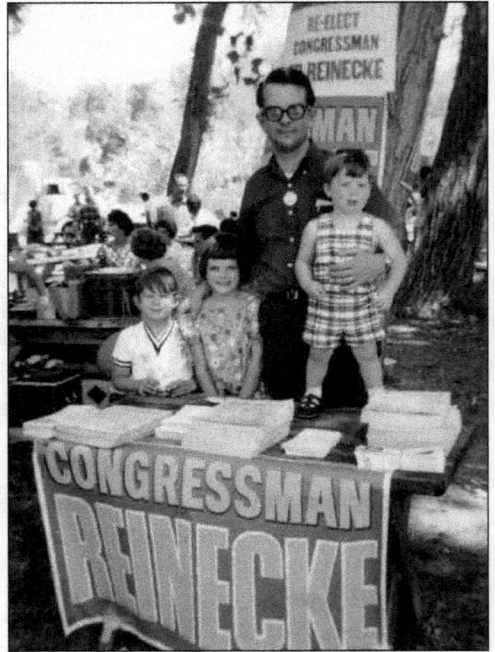

Campaigning for Ed Reinecke in Antelope Valley, California, 1968, I took the kids along. From left: David, Patricia and Andrew.

Honestly, I enjoyed navigating the northern parts of the district representing the congressman at Chamber of Commerce, church, social and other events, usually called on to make brief remarks or present something on his behalf. Spreading the Reinecke gospel. Lots of good Republicans there around Lancaster and Palmdale, which were considered very rural and out-of-the-way. The big business was at Edwards Air Force Base. People were friendly and receptive, which would pay off in my next job. One leads to another to another, without road maps. Keep track of this unorthodox "climb."

ABANDONED GOLD-MINING TOWNS, DESERT, AND BOB HOPE'S HOUSE

My favorites were the old abandoned gold mining "towns," left as if they were a movie set, and the 20-Mule Team Borax mine. On the way home one afternoon I stopped at a lonely desert bar/grocery store/one-pump gas station for a beer. Outside the entrance hitched to a post was a burro with saddle bags. Inside, the only customer was just what you would expect: a real old timer miner with long beard, soiled, dusty clothes and hat, and willing to chat. For a beer, naturally. We did. Last of a dead breed. Too real to be Hollywood. He promised to vote for Reinecke.

With Ed Reinecke in Hollywood, 1968.

Our competent Van Nuys staff of four took care of constituents' business and helped get Ed reelected to his third term in 1968, and his reputation swelled. Ed already was a successful businessman. Wife Jean was a low-profile movie actress and therefore they linked to the entertainment crowd, and enjoyed a fine lifestyle. Both were pleasant and businesslike to me. Bob Hope's Toluca Lake home hosted one of his fundraisers. Neither Dolores nor Bob were present, but what a place. We held another in the Sherman Oaks home of one of the Warner Brothers Studio owners. Believe it was Jack's. Or, I might be confusing this one with a fundraiser for my next boss. Oh well. You see so many of them around town it's hard to keep accurate track. Heck, it was that type of environment. Lots of shoulders to rub even if mine were dwarfed.

Ed's star rose quickly, and when Bob Finch in 1969 departed for Nixon's Washington cabinet, Reagan named him lieutenant governor. Bam, the seat was vacant, calling for a special election. Next move.

GOLDWATER RE-VISITED:
NOW, WHAT CAN I DO FOR YOUR SON?

The Goldwater name which launched my journey in 1964 intercepted it squarely five years later. The senator's son, Barry, Jr., a Burbank resident and stock broker, filed for Reinecke's seat. Because of my knowledge of the district, its movers, shakers, issues, and bars, he hired me to be his campaign eyes and ears, body man, and personal advisor. That valuable role paid off immensely for each of us.

We immediately hit it off. He was likeable, personable, but hardly one of deep intellect. Had to keep him on the basics. A private pilot and well-to-do bachelor, he ran with the trendy,

With newly elected Barry Goldwater, Jr., 1969.

upscale set, who descended on his home for leisure and to be with-it after he announced. Fine. The national media locked on to him—name association. My children appeared with him in a national magazine spread during the campaign. No doubt, his name drew people and got votes in this fairly conservative suburban district. We milked it.

I drove him all over the 27th District introducing the right people and getting him before groups and the media, a dawn-to-midnight operation of several months that ended with his election to Congress on April 29, 1969, defeating Democrat John Van De Kamp, 57-43%. My own star shot up not quite as fast, but it would land me on Capitol Hill. Barry asked me what I wanted for my service for getting him elected, and I said I wanted to go to Washington to help him get settled, and then move into the Nixon administration. He agreed, and off we went.

DEFEATING REAGAN'S DAUGHTER, AND SEVENTY-TWO HOURS TO WASHINGTON

But, before that, he had to defeat six opponents in the Republican primary, including one sponsored by Governor Reagan's daughter, Maureen. Thus, two big names battled, and sometimes it got publicly nasty. I liked her before and after, but not during. Her man's campaign manager was veteran journalist Lyn Nofziger who served both President Richard Nixon and Governor and President Reagan. The Goldwater team worked overtime to beat this machine. I respected Lyn. Association with him was added exposure to Nixon's Haldeman and Erlichman crowd. Having spent minimum time for the last two years with my family, nevertheless I was on to something and had mouths to feed. Survive and advance.

I bought a used Plymouth from Reinecke's Burbank dealer friend. Excited, packed it and drove across country adorned with a "Goldwater for Congress" sticker to be present when Barry was sworn in. Seventy-two hours to get to Arlington, VA. True, seventy-two hours, long before Red Bull and 5-Hour Energy. No sane person would try that again. There I rented an apartment in Arlington and opened and ran his confined junior-congressman office in the Longworth House Office Building. My salary was about $24,000 with medical insurance and extremely long hours and a US House of Representatives ID card as a keepsake. That's what they gave me. Carroll remained in LA to sell our house and would reunite later.

Two memorable experiences with Barry. The first took place in the cockpit of his Cessna single engine aircraft en route from Burbank to Bakersfield for a speech. Flying over, nearly into, the Tehachipi Mountains, we caught a huge downdraft that pushed our plane toward the peaks. Nowhere to go, I clutched the passenger dashboard so tightly while praying that it left indented hand-marks forever. Skillfully, keeping cool, he maneuvered the plane just high

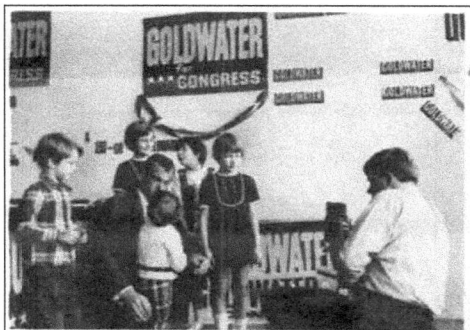

Barry Goldwater Jr. proved an energetic and canny campaigner. He posed with neighbors' kids prior to election.

My three children appeared with Barry Goldwater, Jr. in New York 'Daily News' photo-story about the 1969 special election that put him in Congress.

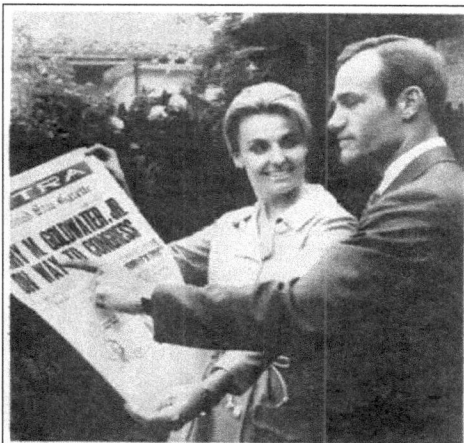

He surveys mock newspaper heralding his election to Congress. Secretary, Jeanne Swallow, gives him a smile.

enough to make it over and into Kern County. I was drained for hours, but we got back over without problems. Months later I read that Barry safely landed his fuel-exhausted aircraft on a Burbank street at night returning from the Antelope Valley. Man. I haven't ridden in this type of aircraft since, and won't.

For the second, I became a date broker for Barry with President Nixon's younger daughter Tricia. He'd dated her before, but asked me to arrange their date at the July 23, 1969, Major League Baseball All-Star game in Robert F. Kennedy Stadium. Hey, nice extra duty. I worked with the White House and Secret Service and the game host Washington Senators team. They gave us box seats behind home plate. A few days prior, I met with Senators officials and team manager Ted Williams—Ted Williams!—in the dugout prior to a game. Went out on the field, swung a bat. Could hardly contain myself. Yes, Ted Williams, the game's greatest hitter. National League won, 9-3. The president had expected to attend but because of the Apollo 11 landing sent Vice President Agnew instead. To we three it mattered none, and we left together long before the final out.

THE FAMILY MOVES TO ALEXANDRIA:
STRANGE NEW LIFE FOR ALL

Carroll had been exceptionally understanding and tolerant of my work ethic and desire to make a living in staff politics. She grumbled, but who wouldn't? Being divided by 3,000 miles meant separate bank accounts, and she alone tolerated the three rambunctious children. She had our 1961 Ford station wagon. In a down Los Angeles market, she sold the house in December 1969, gave away the Ford, and flew with the kids to Washington, arriving right before Christmas. Meanwhile, we purchased a newly constructed house in a

In the early 1970s I worked with Washington Mayor Walter Washington promoting President Nixon's Minority Business Enterprise Program.

As a Navy Reserve lieutenant commander in Washington, DC, 1970.

south Alexandria-Mount Vernon area development called Fort Hunt where we would raise our children. Our belongings were delayed for days. We started a completely different new life.

By then I had left Barry's office and through the senator's assistance, landed a prestigious Schedule C confidential assistant political appointee position "down town" in the General Services Administration. Two of Barry's closest friends from Los Angeles whom he brought to Washington created an uncomfortable working environment. My departure was mutually acceptable, and Barry and I stayed in touch for several years. My professionalism got him elected, set up his shop, and was rewarded. Hey, this stuff happens in Washington, with who knows what's to come.

I developed an amiable relationship with the senator and wife Peggy and staff and helped in his Senate office occasionally. Carroll and I enjoyed dinner in their apartment. The Goldwater connection had come full circle: the father inspired me into politics, and I repaid him by leading his son into the US Congress. Forever am I grateful to the senator for what he did for conservatism and the Republican Party, and how he opened my eyes into the potential minefield of earning a living at it while serving my country. And, what he did to influence my life.

Two years later, the senator wrote me.

Occasionally I get a letter from a young man like you who credits me with getting him started in public life, and I can't think of anything that brings me a warmer, better feeling. I've always looked upon 1964 as one of the great years of my life even though I got my tail beat off. I say that because thousands, many thousands if young people who probably would never have gotten interested in politics got a start, and thank God they never quit. I appreciate everything you've done for me more than I can tell you.

—*With best wishes, Barry.*

CHAPTER 6

IN SERVICE TO PRESIDENT NIXON
WHILE AVOIDING THE WATERGATE MESS

By "keeping my nose clean" and never burning bridges—lifetime credos so applicable in Washington—I maintained both contacts, jobs, and equilibrium. Forever I engendered a display of common sense and tolerance, and keeping my wits, in an otherwise non-sensical and intolerant town. A wise little fish senses the pond size and schemes accordingly.

From late 1969 until 1973, I held confidential assistant (Schedule C) positions in the General Services Administration's (GSA) Public Buildings Service in the District of Columbia, and the Federal Supply Service in Crystal City, Arlington. These were considered political appointments outside the career Civil Service patterns. As such I advised the services' commissioners who directed the agencies, engineered projects, was a defacto public affairs face, and was the political contact and go-fer. Now I was under the Hatch Act again, and had better watch out.

More important, the Nixon White House staff knew where I was situated and kept in touch.

In 1971 presidential assistant Fred Malek, whom I knew in California, began assembling a team of guys like me in government agencies who could be trained and utilized as advance men, looking ahead to the 1972 presidential election. I became part of their team of about twenty-five reporting to Bart Porter. We attended training sessions in the White House, received a procedures manual, and somehow got "certified." In Chapter 7 I thoroughly explain the definition of advancing for a president and all that entails. For the moment, we concentrate on the Nixon staff approach. A procedures manual copy is in my collection in the University of North Carolina Wilmington's Randall Library, along with more details about this Nixon White House connection. Some of those men went down with Watergate.

HALDEMAN, ERLICHMAN, COLSON AND AVOIDING WATERGATE

At first we would advance just government officials on government business—no politics. Yes, we brushed with Bob Haldeman, John Erlichman, Chuck Colson, and other Nixon heavies whose names splashed across the *Washington Post* front pages as the scandal exploded. For someone at my level, forging close alliances with the inner sanctum was impossible and relegated us mostly to the side. Those men were hardened and a bit intimidating, dead loyal to the president. Oh well. Read their rules. Washington was a far cry from Los Angeles or Sacramento in every manner. As it turned out, my good fortune was being excluded from any inner loop, thank God. Besides, why would I imagine otherwise?

The GSA administrator, political appointee Bob Kunzig of Pennsylvania, was a decent, ambitious man with good management skills. We blended. But when asked by the White House to free me for some advance assignments on company time, unsure, he tightened. Not about me, but the prospect of something going wrong and impacting GSA and his standing.

This played out in perhaps what to me became the closest call I ever had in politics, or elsewhere I guess, aside from being chased down for blocks by Syrian hoodlums through the Damascus bazaar in 1960 (Chapter 4).

The unusual request to advance was a doozy. Even I could see that and hesitated, skittish, but stayed in there not wishing to alienate my White House handlers by teetering. How could I decline if I wanted to stay on The Team for '72? I'd watch it play out from the second row.

The task actually appeared simple, but I was skittish. Take Martha Mitchell, the wife of Attorney

'I'm a Political Prisoner' Post 6/26/72

Martha Is 'Leaving' Mitchell

The 1972 Martha Mitchell story was a sideshow to the main Watergate circus. I dodged a bullet after being asked to help keep her out of the limelight.

General John Mitchell, to Florida for a few days in winter to stay out of town and bake in the sun. Martha, so told, was embarrassing Official Washington with loose lips and too much alcohol. Florida might dry her out a bit. She was not a government official, so no matter how much I said Team Player, while the White House awaited a reply, Kunzig said no. Whew, thank you. Bob, I knew we both were right. I'll advance the attorney general if offered, thank you. How things might have been if strong pressure had been applied, and I'd been directed to go.

WHAT WAS MY CLOSEST CALL IN POLITICS?

Plain. Somewhat hypothetical, but never leave anything to chance. The Mitchell episode turned out to be an indirect link to the Watergate scandal, and, had I accepted the assignment, might have swept me up. Might have..., but trust me, my head was on straight. The guy who accepted was Alfred Baldwin, a former FBI official. To someone, he must have succeeded with Martha and got "promoted." Baldwin, you may remember, was the rooftop lookout across the street from the Watergate Hotel the night of the break-in. In no way would I have accepted any role in that Watergate caper, absolutely no way. But, the hypothetical link will forever ring in my ear, and to political history junkies, makes quick table talk. Might it have been me as the lookout? However, Baldwin skated: questioning, interviews, but no charges. That makes no difference.

Watching re-runs of *All the President's Men*, about the *Washington Post*'s Carl Bernstein and Bob Woodward, who stayed on the Watergate coverup story, and the recent release of *The Post*, about its publisher Katherine Graham, punches all kinds of memory buttons. Watergate was huge in its time and still rings today in Washington's whirligig of scandal, deceit, and mistrust, drawing similarities.

Meanwhile, I thoroughly appreciated my role at GSA as a torch bearer for the president's Minority Business Enterprise Program. This role included much nationwide travel speaking to groups and holding live media interviews hyping and describing the MBE opportunities for black, women, and other minority entrepreneurs. I know very well I contributed to this program's success. The valuable experience paid off later in my Wilmington preservation efforts.

Point of View

Post 3/27/72

To Martha:

Thanks for

The Memories

Post 2-27-72
By Mary Russell

Martha Mitchell, we'll miss you. While it's true you're not entirely "gone with the wind," nevertheless, your days as an official Cabinet wife are over, and the wife of President Nixon's campaign director just won't have the impact the wife of the Attorney General did.

So in these times of instant nostalgia, we're already remembering fondly your early morning telephone calls, your blasts at Sen. Fulbright, your castigating of peace protesters, your three-inch stiletto heels and your Scarlett O'Hara dresses.

And we salute you.

You infused a shot of adrenaline into a good gray Republic administration. Before Henry Kissinger you were. And while you startled us, stunned us, outraged us sometimes, you also gave us a glimmer of lightheartedness in those days which followed the upheaval of the '60s, which seemed so grim, so full of anger, frustration and hopelessness.

But there was more than that. While you scorned women's lib, you made it pretty plain that you believed in being anything but submissive. "Outspoken" was used so often before your name it became a cliche.

And while you scorned the hippies and the peace freaks, you were pretty anti-Establishment yourself. You refused to curtsy to the queen of England, you protested when the Supreme Court put a woman on the Supreme Court and you said flatly you didn't want your husband to leave the campaign. You also wore a style of clothing that was distinctly nonconformist, and if anybody didn't like it that was too bad.

But in each case, it was not what you said or what you did, but the sheer bravado of your doing it that lent you that special something that turns a public figure into a very human, and more often than not, likeable being.

And it is in this sense that we hope you've started a trend, perhaps even something so exalted as a tradition.

Because the wives of Cabinet members, congressmen, diplomats and sometimes even First Ladies have tended to treat their roles very delicately. Easily on in their husband's careers they were told that everything they did reflected on their spouse's image. And so public officials' wives have tended to rein in, to go out of their way to appear "normal, proper

So, I did no advances while at GSA but stayed on the White House list and attended some of their socials. In mid-1972, after Watergate broke, the Committee for the Re-Election of the President (CREEP),* mainly Rick Fore, sent me to New Hampshire to take over a foundering Nixon campaign. I had to resign from GSA, but was assured I would come back on the rolls after the election. This evolved into one of my most successful-ever ventures. What I was able to accomplish in a little over three months was "one for the books."

* The media have tortured the name. Historically, it is not The Committee to Re-Elect the President, as Dustin Hoffman and Robert Redford keep saying.

RESCUING NEW HAMPSHIRE

I'd never visited New Hampshire and knew little about New England "culture." Uncharted waters for certain, but the Nixon Campaign team dispatched me, ready or not. Former New Hampshire Governor Lane Dwinell, our campaign chairman, and the state party bigwigs, recognizing my "political creds," greatly eased the transition from "Washington" and welcomed me with open arms in August.

Lethargy permeated the state's Nixon Campaign organization following his overwhelming, first-in-the-nation February primary victory, requiring a serious boot-in-the-butt. My job, they informed me. I opened the state campaign headquarters in Concord across from the capitol building and began recruiting district chairmen, courting the media, raising money, and organizing volunteers. Helen Martin, an old timer who knew everyone in the state, came forward

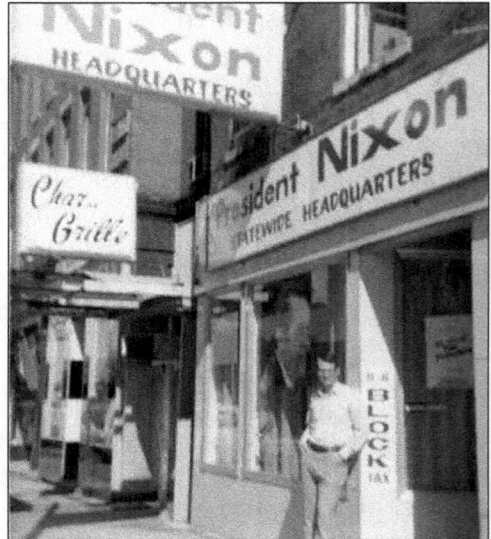

At the Nixon campaign's New Hampshire state headquarters in Concord, summer of 1972.

as my chief assistant. With Margaret LeMay, a hard-charging veteran campaigner as field operations director, the stars blessed me with two valuable, irreplaceable wings. My ten-year old son David got a Northern Virginia school leave of absence to accompany me for weeks and assisted me everywhere. I even enrolled him temporarily in a Concord school. We always remember those bonding times together.

I lived in a rent-free house and tirelessly traveled the entire state numerous times in a dealer loaner-car from the Massachusetts line to Berlin on the Canadian border and Dixville Notch, the first town reporting national elections. Fell in love with the state and her people immediately. Somehow I broke through the Granite State-stoic, "oh yeah," facade of its natives, and persuaded them to work for the president, essentially rebuilding our operation in weeks. New Hampshire was where Democrat presidential candidate Senator Edmund Muskie of Maine had "cried" in the primary's snow, leaving their party in shambles and a ripe target.

To campaign for Nixon, we attracted Vice President Spiro Agnew and Republican notables such as David Eisenhower, President Eisenhower's grandson, and his wife Julie Nixon, the president's daughter; Nixon's brother Ed; campaign director Congressman Clark McGregor; and Ed Cox, daughter Tricia Nixon's husband. Whew—the folks loved the VIP's, but I had work to do! In retrospect, viewing my personal papers of the 1972 campaign, I am amazed how organized, proficient, and productive was the Nixon Campaign emanating from its Washington headquarters in a day of only fax machines, telegrams, the Postal Service, and phone calls. The demands—and assistance—they levied on us state directors: surveys, advice, forms, get-out-the-vote and finance reports required, campaign materials to distribute, media guidance, and much more, came daily. All of this descended upon me, but somehow we handled them.

On election eve the president telegraphed me (and I suppose my

Vice President Spiro Agnew came to New Hampshire to campaign for Richard Nixon in 1972.

Nixon's son-in-law Ed Cox. Note campaign operative in the background keeping a close eye on things.

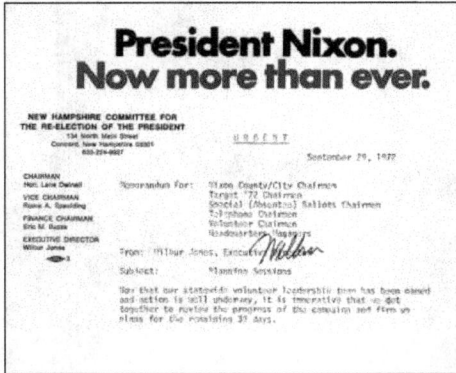

I sent this memo to members of the campaign staff in the home stretch before the election.

Among those who came to New Hampshire to help in the campaign was the First Brother, Ed Nixon.

state counterparts) touting the election's importance and extolling my "major impact on the outcome of the decision. We will be counting on your leadership— and the dedication of your fellow campaigners—to help us achieve the largest voter turnout in American history. I have never worked with a finer team. Your contributions have been invaluable, and I am deeply grateful.—Richard Nixon"

All our resources clicked and everything came together. We walloped Democrat nominee Senator George McGovern 63-37%, the highest Nixon margin east of the Mississippi River in his totally landslide re-election. No Watergate effect there. How we did it in four months I'll never figure especially in that non-digital, low-tech age (as we know it).

The state's elective spirit excelled, and thus my productive reputation also. I consider New Hampshire 1972 as perhaps my single most successful professional achievement—pending the outcome of my now twelve-year-plus project to have Wilmington designated as the first "American World War II Heritage City (see Chapter 11).

Governor Dwinell, one of the finest and most genuine persons I have known, wrote me:

> No one could have come into our state as a stranger and made more friends while accomplishing a difficult assignment. All the time you have been here, you have demonstrated the highest organizational and administrative capacity. In my many years if experience in business, in government and political activities, I have never worked with a more competent person than yourself. We will miss you.
> —Lane Dwinell

Carroll left the kids with someone and came up for a joyous election night. Afterwards we said so long to those wonderful people and drove to Montreal

This cover story in influential 'Saturday Review' magazine focused on New Hampshire.

Carroll came to New Hampshire to join me at Nixon campaign headquarters on election night 1972.

and Quebec City for a very cold holiday. Very cold. Enjoyed pub crawling in Montreal's underground passages. But I was absolutely beat.

A PRESTIGIOUS NIXON WIN, THEN INAUGURATION

Back in Washington, I re-entered the GSA workforce and the Admninistraror and White House immediately assigned me to direct the logistics support functions for the 1973 Nixon inauguration. In about six weeks I assembled an agency-wide team which provided the necessary administrative, space, transportation, medical, supply, food. and other items for inauguration participants. On that day, I coordinated support and watched the parade from a ground level office in the Department of Justice building on Pennsylvania Avenue. That night, Carroll and I performed among as inaugural ball docents, for us the Smithsonian Museum. Very long day, very long.

With former Gov. Lane Dwinell, Nixon's New Hampshire campaign chairman, on election night 1972.

Julie Nixon Eisenhower in Concord, NH, 1972.

For an inauguration season highlight, Carroll and I hosted in our Mount Vernon home a cocktail party for the New Hampshire delegation, primarily to thank them for treating me so warmly and cooperating so steadfastly. Governor Dwinell led the group. "Live Free or Die" is their state motto. Forever I see why.

Inauguration Committee Chairman J. Willard Marriott, founder of the now massive Marriott Corporation, wrote the head of GSA:

The 1973 Inaugural Committee could not possibly have become operational so quickly and efficiently had you and your personnel not made the maximum effort. We are most grateful. Two individuals deserving of special recognition are Wilbur Jones and Woodrow Swanson whose dedication and invaluable assistance not only established the Committee but have kept us in operation. My thanks again.

—*J. Willard Marriott*

In early 1973 President Nixon rewarded staff such as me with a nice artifact and invitation to meet British Prime Minister Edward Heath in the White House. Got to shake their hands. I think that's the only time I actually met Nixon. My last trip to New Hampshire was in 1975 advancing President Ford's speech to their legislature (Chapter 8). Soft spot in my heart forever, but never have returned.

The Watergate investigation continued. Thank God I never got close to the shenanigans or was called on account. Forever after, the acronym CREEP would ring detrimentally in political history as Nixon remains vilified, and those who were close who didn't go to jail had to hide, then attempt to restart their careers and lives. My connection? Because I was employed by CREEP as New Hampshire campaign executive director, my name is on the employee roster. That's it only, thank God.

POLITICAL REWARDS FOLLOWED: GREAT JOB AT HUD

The overwhelming re-election victory reaped rewards for those who had toiled. My turn awaited, and the next role was evaluated in a hopper of others who excelled on the campaign.

My eye located a "titled" job at the Department of Transportation, but that went to a Nixon inner-circle aide who, because the Watergate swath was moving quickly, soon was charged with misconduct. I went to Housing and Urban Development (HUD) as a special assistant to Secretary Jim Lynn. He had several of us, but the "senior" assistant, Dick McGraw, sat in his office, and I down the hall. Dick was the first among equals. Okay, I was being paid and had visibility and work I enjoyed. My loyal secretary, Dawn Kuhn, followed me from GSA. She was tremendous, so capable.

Both Dick and Dawn maintained friendships with me. Dick, a successful businessman and Wilmington community leader, later serving President George W. Bush's Secretary of Defense Donald Rumsfeld in the Pentagon and Afghanistan, has lived here many years. I sponsored him for membership in the Wilmington Rotary Club and nominated him for the ultimate Wilmington *StarNews* Media Lifetime Achievement Award. Dawn became a successful residential realtor in Northeastern North Carolina.

My principal HUD role was developing for the secretary a "consumer relations" plan, sort of Washington in-vogue then. Again, more national travel talking to housing officials. Not sure if my actual proposal went into action, but Secretary Lynn and his replacement Carla Hills did institute some sort of consumer feedback apparatus. I had the pleasure of working with future Reagan presidential press secretaries Jim Brady and Larry Speakes. I was strongly approached to run the campaign of Illinois Congressman Henry Hyde in 1975 but declined it and a couple other similar opportunities to remain at HUD.

LOANED TO THE WHITE HOUSE, FINALLY

Nixon of course resigned in August 1974 and Vice President Gerald Ford, who had been appointed, not elected, became president. Most of the White House staff with whom I had contact moved out, but enough survived to form a new group of advancemen. My security, ethics, morals, and other checks and clearances proved clean. For all the nearly forty-one years of government service, I earned and maintained a top secret security clearance, an essential matter of pride.

With the family at home, Fort Hunt, Virginia, 1974. From left: David, Patricia, Andrew, and Carroll.

Finally, it seemed—finally—I made it. The Ford White House trusted me to be part of a team to plan and execute the trips of the president of the United States. Mother and Daddy, you would be proud of me. In just ten years, from stuffing envelopes in San Diego, and as precinct chairman in that lopsided Democrat Los Angeles district, to the White House.

Upon request by the White House advance office, HUD Secretaries Lynn and Hills authorized me—"loaned," they called it—to advance for non-political presidential events beginning in January 1975. My first advance was in Washington, an in-towner, to get acquainted. My first out-of-towner was the president's participation in the Jackie Gleason Inverrary golf tournament near Hollywood, FL, a pleasant indoctrination. My bosses had close White House ties and legally this was fine. Scored points, and it worked to their advantage. For the next year, until I officially joined the White House staff full time, advancing when available would be a main part of my job at HUD. I was willing and usually always available as a "loaner-volunteer."

You'll enjoy reading about the Ford advance machine in Chapters 7, 8, and 9.

CHAPTER 7

LIFE WITH PRESIDENT GERALD FORD—AND, (VERY) ANCIENT ADVANCING PRINCIPLES, TECHNIQUES, AND CHARACTERISTICS YOU PROBABLY NEVER HEARD OF

So, I became an "advanceman." Okay, you don't know the term? Advancing for a president, or anybody? All right. Because what follows relate to President Gerald Ford's White House, references to the office are masculine.

Whenever the president of the United States leaves the White House, whether locally or across the globe, someone has to plan and execute the evolution and movements. This requires an extraordinary amalgamation and coordination of extremely detailed planning, absolute teamwork, and timely precision. It's an enormous, pressure-packed responsibility which must consider an agenda, security, media exposure, scheduled meetings, diplomatic protocols, accomplishment of political objectives, and more. To someone attending a campaign rally, the president just shows up and that's that. But how? While the process appears complex, the logic is quite simple.

The reader, and perhaps historians or students of the country's political processes, might like knowing how a president moved from the White House more than forty years ago. Here's the way it worked when I served President Gerald Ford for more than two years. The general public otherwise might have little knowledge or realize the impact, unless the president is headed their way and they're immediately involved.

The term "advancing" means a team of White House and federal agency staffers plan it from the intended destination, put together the pieces, get White House approval, and move into action. Then, avoid surprises, check and re-check details, communicate, be constantly alert, and follow through. The president and traveling staff know what to expect. The advance team leads them through the evolutions.

Directing this process is the White House lead political advance representative, a.k.a. advanceman: a mature, seasoned political operative who is the president's direct representative and coordinates his activities at the site. Other essential advance team members include the Secret Service, White House Communications Agency, and the White House press office.

Page 1 photo in March 30, 1976 'Washington Post' catches a glimpse of an advanceman at work. In this Pentagon ceremony, I'm visible below Defense Secretary Donald Rumsfeld and President Ford.

Although technology, communications, transportation, and potential threats have increased exponentially since the days of my forty-nine Ford advances in 1975-78 (the "Stone Age"), the basic principles probably remain the same. I'd bet there are numerous semblances of techniques and characteristics. Whenever Presidents Trump, Obama, or Bush have traveled, I look for the advanceman's handiwork, critiquing its solutions. Wish they'd invite me along.

Capsuled from both memory and my extensive personal papers collection at the University of North Carolina Wilmington's Randall Library, donated there many years ago, here are some of advancing factoids. Know that in Chapter 8 I've listed my favorite advances, and in Chapter 9 the remainder chronologically. After reading, what's your most interesting one—the one where you wish you'd been with the president?

In 1975 I was a "volunteer loaner" advance representative, okayed by my boss, the secretary of Housing and Urban Development, for non-political events. In 1976 the White House absorbed me full-time staff as a staff assistant to the president and advance representative, bringing all sorts of "bennies" and an impressive, official framed appointment manuscript which I still hang proudly.

Mixed in were some weeks on the Ford campaign committee's payroll to avoid election ethical conflicts. Crazy, but we had to play safe.

Before getting into specifics, here's an item to stir memories of old-line Wilmingtonians who've been around here more than a while.

TO COACH LEON BROGDEN

On July 30, 1976, at my request, the president sent a telegram to this local and North Carolina coaching immortal:

> Mr. Leon L. Brogden
> c/o Jerry Spivey
> Wilmington Hilton Hotel, Banquet Hall
> Wilmington, North Carolina
>
> I join your many friends and admirers in sending sincere congratulations and warm wishes on your retirement. May your coming years be as rewarding yo you and the last forty one have been for those with whom you have worked.
> —*Gerald R. Ford*

Okay, here we go.

(VERY) ANCIENT ADVANCING PRINCIPLES, TECHNIQUES, AND CHARACTERISTICS YOU PROBABLY NEVER HEARD OF

• Every time the US president leaves the White House he's going somewhere, by Marine One helicopter, Air Force One, or motorcade. The event or location he's visiting is called a "stop." His trips must be planned and executed extremely carefully, like flawlessly, both for security and mission accomplishment. No alternatives. No screwups.

• The White House advance office, working with other federal agencies—such as the State Department if it's international travel, or the Interior Department if it's to a national monument—formulate a visit package with objectives, and then dispatches an advance team to the site(s).

• There the team, headed by a White House political staff lead, who represents the president, coordinates final planning and coordination with the host organization. Once the president is on the scene, the lead staff advanceman guides him through the various evolutions. Later I'll describe that how-to.

• The scene might be for a drop-by stop of twenty minutes, or a multi-day visit to a city. Public events such as an auditorium or arena speech . . . a social event . . . a campaign rally indoors or in the open . . . a dedication . . . an award ceremony or presentation . . . a meeting with foreign leaders here or there . . . .The types are limitless—but, very controlled!

• Donald Rumsfeld, a former Illinois congressman, was the first White

House chief of staff I served under. Red Cavaney, a veteran Nixon advanceman, headed the advance office and reported to Rumsfeld.

• Rumsfeld and Cavaney laid down the advance team rules of engagement immediately after Ford became president. The Nixon Old Ways were out. Possibly reflecting public opinion of Nixon, his advance teams of political types, often heavy-handed and arrogant, landed on cities and organizations with demands and undisguised persuasion to maximize Nixon's events. Seems strange now, but it helped reelect him in 1972. Ford kept some of the Nixon advance team and recruited staff more aptly suited to his demeanor and style. In my case, I perceived, a mutual attachment..

• Ford advancemen were put on notice. Very important to the way we conducted business. Be less resolute, and more requesting and cooperative. That was Ford's style. I found it worked. For instance, when I led the team to Des Moines, Ia., in 1976, my first engagement was calling on the Republican Governor Robert Ray in the state capitol. As the president's representative, I paid my respects and discussed why we were there. Of course he offered assistance.

THE WHITE HOUSE CORE ADVANCE TEAM

• The staff lead advanceman representing the president was, a politically skilled and experienced advocate, coordinated the entire advance team. This included public relations and crowd raising, the event on the ground, and the principal coordinator with Washington and the host's principal contact. Granted wide-ranging responsibilities and decision-making authority.

• The lead Secret Service (USSS, "the Service") agent advance person. Responsible for the president's safety and security. Worked with the staff lead advance and advised on those areas, trying to accommodate political wishes with by-the-book protection. Reported to the USSS headquarters. Yes, a slightly gray area of reporting and authority, but rarely a management interface problem with the staff lead. The agents knew what the political staff wanted to accomplish, and staff totally understood the Service's responsibilities. Hiccups rarely emerged.

• The White House press office advance. One person experienced in Washington media who worked with the staff lead for maximum media coverage and availability, and arranged the traveling press corps and local media accommodations at the site(s).

• The White House Communications Agency (WHCA, or "Wock-uh" as we called them). Military personnel who set up telephone switchboard and fax operations, emergency communications, and hand-held walkie-talkie type personal radio sets.

Advance team members operated on a secured radio network, carried their instruments everywhere, and on event days attached them to clothing with cords and ear buds, a clear "giveaway" to an onlooker.

PASSKEY, THE MAIN MAN

• The White House principals had radio nickname call signs. Real names weren't used. They included: PASSKEY (The president), PINAFORE (the first lady), SHOT PUT (Rumsfeld), SUNBURN (Press Secretary Ron Nessen), TED BARON (National Security Advisor Gen. Brent Scowcroft), BACKSEAT (Chief of Staff Dick Cheney), SAWHORSE (White House doctor Adm. William Lukash), WOODCUTTER (Secretary of State Henry Kissinger). Staffers used last names on radio.

• Political staff advance members mostly were on-the-job trained and experienced volunteers from industry or the professions. They assisted as the event's magnitude required, plus other members from government agencies as required. Half of our volunteer advancemen lived away from Washington.

Advance office director Cavaney, my neighbor, reported to the White House chief of staff Rumsfeld and later Cheney. These men were superb politicians, administrators, and operators. I thoroughly enjoyed working with them. Cavaney was organized, knew his team members, made the right assignments, had our backs, but rarely actually advanced once the team was assembled except in long-range planning. He accompanied the president and thus caught up with us on site, and obviously observed our productivity.

• I had few direct interactions with the pleasant but serious Rumsfeld. The rather stoic Cheney could lighten up when pressure also lightened. We staff enjoyed time at the bar occasionally after we put the boss down for the night, like in Lawton, OK, after we drew 24,000 for a 1976 rally, when Cheney joined us. I liked the reserved Cheney and served under him again later when he was secretary of Defense under President George H. W. Bush, and I was an assistant to the under secretary of Defense (acquisition) in the Pentagon.

Dick Cheney, seen here as defense secretary with George H.W. Bush (he would be vice president under George W. Bush) was Ford's chief of staff — one of my bosses—in 1976.

• I flew on Air Force One four times, always home from an event. President Ford's aircraft was a Boeing 707 similar to President Nixon's and later President Reagan's, much-much smaller than the present 747. In those days because of limited seating capacity once we loaded the twelve-person "death watch" press pool who were always with the president, free-riders were few. Having a seat was a richly coveted reward. My most memorable trip was flying to Washington's National Airport from Newark, NJ, on July 4, 1976.

• Team members arrived separately by commercial or government aircraft. When I did non-political events, I flew either but often on Air Force aircraft (727's). For political events, until I was officially on the staff, I flew commercial. The White House made arrangements. The White House or the campaign committee reimbursed expenses depending on the nature of the event and if we were full-time staff. We rented cars and established our advance offices in the best, but not extravagant, hotels near the site with adjoining suites, the lead advance bedroom included.

DAMNED HARD WORK, REQUIRING LIMITLESS POSITIVES

• Advancing was damned hard work requiring so many personal positive characteristics looking back it overwhelms. Yes, I guess I had them. Indelible basic fundamentals learned early on. At least an authority thought so. Political acumen, alertness, wisdom, congeniality, maturity, stamina, energy, sobriety, downright political street smartness, loyalty, common sense, and decisiveness. And these abilities: To withstand mounting stress . . . To go dawn to midnight for days on end without down time . . . To work exceptionally well with people just met and won't see again.

Stamina and energy might have been the most necessary qualification. Like the advance to West Germany in 1975 out of Bonn when our motors stressfully raced for eighteen to twenty work hours a day for nine days.

• Advancing, with its myriad ways potentially to fail and having extremely high visibility representing the president, really was a young-man's-job. In 1976 I was forty-two, the oldest team member politely called the Grey Fox. The average age was probably about thirty-five. Our only female lead was Mary Fisher of Michigan, whose family business was associated with General Motors. Sharp, knew the ropes, taught me well, but could be a bit contrary. We related well on the advance on the Nation's Bicentennial in New York Harbor.

• The ability to interact successfully with an array of levels from foreign officials to state governors, local law enforcement, politicians, media, and disparate volunteers—and the White House staff and senior officials—all with varying motives, tried one's judgment and restraint. They were absolutely necessary attributes.

• Irregular sleep patterns depended upon work assignments which often were driven by schedule changes involving the president or administration officials, local political conditions, and time-zone differences. Seems as though the phone loved ringing at midnight hours.

OUR TECHNICAL (YOU'RE KIDDING, MAN?) SUPPORT EQUIPMENT

• The fact we functioned with limited technical equipment would be mind-boggling today. How on earth did we in the political staff do this highly sensitive, secretive job while limited to handheld radios, fixed-instrument land line telephones, printers, fledgling copiers ("Xeroxes") and fax machines. Of course: no computers, smart phones, internet, satellite communications, 3-D printers, and highly skilled tech support. WHCA and Secret Service personnel used their own classified communications means.

• When the president was moving on foot, although literally leading him through an evolution, advancemen did not speak to

Sometimes, like here, waiting to board Air Force One, we advancemen could speak directly with the president.

him directly, but through his constant body man, Terry O'Donnell. That meant he heard only one recognizable voice. So, if we needed to tell the president something or just alert Terry, we did it by radio or face-to-face. Terry, from a prestigious Washington law firm, was one of the nicest persons in the White House. Congenial, savvy, empathetic to us advancemen, and so easy to work with. I often thought of this procedure when watching President Obama's body man, Reggie Love, in action.

• In a static situation like waiting in a holding room, we could speak direct, but mainly only when we had information to share, not just casual chatting. See my advance report on Portland, Ore., when union officials stood up the president by missing a scheduled meeting.

• For every sub-event within an event, or within a stopover/ drop-by, we faxed to the White House hand-drawn movement diagrams. Yes, hand drawn with pencil, straight edge, and eraser. With dots and arrows, they showed all presidential movements and entrances/exits, landmarks, elevator, doors, steps, stairs, obstructions, platform/ podium dimensions and seating diagram with names, press area, people he would encounter, stops

An example of a movement diagram, this was from an October 1976 campaign event in Lawton, Oklahoma.

for restrooms/holding rooms, bands, crowd areas, location of motorcade/Air Force One. When approved, these free-style diagrams were close-held on the site.

• Motorcade vehicles listed in order with their passengers. A normal out-of-town one, July 1975 in Germany, for instance, included 17 vehicles listed in order by cars: police, protocol, pilot (Cavaney/O'Donnell/Lead advanceman Dewey Clower), honor guard, control, security, the president's limousine, Henry Kissinger and other VIPs cars, US Ambassador Schoeller, staff including myself, ambulance, minibus for press, WHCA, tail, etc. The advance team had to ensure that each was in their assigned car.

See my report on Queen Elizabeth's State Dinner aboard Her Majesty's Yacht *Britannia*, Newport, RI, July 1976, for an eye-opener.

• Advancemen were supposed to be inconspicuous and stay out of camera angles and in the background or off to the side. We didn't usually enter rooms while meetings were being held. We knew our place. Only once that I recall did I appear in a published photo with the president. Page 1A, *Washington Post*, leading him during a Pentagon ceremony.

• Advancemen didn't ride on the Marine One helicopter (a Sikorsky VH-3A), but did on its similar backup companion called Marine Two. The Nation's Bicentennial day was my most memorable trip on Marine Two twice, from New York Harbor to Newark Airport, and then from National Airport to the White House lawn.

• Because I was a commander in the Navy Reserve (Ready), I drew most all of the president's military-connected events in 1975-76. And there were many. I related and spoke their language which facilitated our interactions.

SOME OTHERWISE TOOLS OF OUR TRADE

• Our advance offices for out-of-towners were always set up in hotels. Hotel floor diagrams showed room assignments.

• For long stays, set up a White House staff lounge with snacks and beverages for senior staff (not advance team).

• Compiled a contact list of locals we would work with, plus phone numbers for Staff Office, Signal Board, WHCA Office, and hotel. Printed business cards: "To Reach The White House Switchboard, Mobile, AL, Dial —."

• For out-of-towners, I used green US Government pocket memo books to record all notes. Would draw line thru each once executed or passed. For in-towners sometimes used 8x10 note pads. My UNCW papers collection has them all. Looks like I scribbled a lot using "coded" schemes.

• Equipment included a traveling portable telephone set which could be placed on legs on the ground and was linked to the WHCA switchboard nearby.

• Always played upon the president's arrival at a site: *Ruffles and Flourishes*," then the announcement "Ladies and gentlemen, the president of

Trying on a gift jersey to be sure it would fit the president. I once failed to do this with a football helmet.

the United States", then *Hail to the Chief*, and he entered and took his position. Often we played *Hail to the Victors Valiant*, the fight song from the University of Michigan, where he played football in the 1930s. If I heard it once, I heard it 500 times. Still ringing.

• Always tried to set up the platform, podium, press area, and crowd area for maximum visual benefit: what the TV and still cameras would show. Backdrops were extremely valuable staging. See Syracuse, NY, rally in Chapter 9.

• Always had a hotel suite if he was going to be in that building long, and always a holding room where he received last-minute briefing and awaited his entrance and introduction.

• Sometimes we didn't bring enough office supplies or equipment and bought or rented others on the open market.

• The president and I were almost identical in height, stature, and a few measurements, except weight. On my events, this facilitated comprising the best angles to set up the presidential podium and for press corps photographers, and when accepting wearable gifts for him from host organizations. This worked well except in Lawton, OK Then it got rather unseemly, as you'll see in Chapter 8 how this became instant national (bad) news.

The president's measurements:

Height—6'1"

Weight—ca. 195

Suit 44L, slacks 38x32

Dress shirt 15-1/2x35

Golf shirt, jacket, sweater XL, Shoes 10 D

Hat 7-3/4

The first lady's height 5'-5-1/2"

Measurements, 36-26-34

Goodies and Thank-You's

• When not on the road, the local advance team members shared desks in the White House's Old Executive Office Building, filing expense and after-action reports, drafting thank-you letters, and sending photo requests to be filled. This required lots of follow-up. Upon returning to my office, always sent thank-you letters to host organizations and key contacts, and addressed certain follow-up issues.

• We never wanted to slight someone in the hinterland who helped us (e.g., the president) and looked forward to a goodie. We passed them out on-site to key volunteers with discretion: presidential tie clasps, cuff links, ladies brooches, writing pens, and more. Ran out of goodies occasionally, and ex-post facto provided White House staff with list of those who should be mailed. When we closed down in 1977, I came away with an attache-caseful. Still have a few.

• High school bands were the favorites for providing music and color and enthusiasm as any outdoor event, and their parents, friends, and students came to see the president.

• The advance office published for us a periodic newsletter of thanks, forecasts, expenses, guidelines, plans, and reminders for passports, etc.

• Most advancemen were volunteers. Members with whom I often worked: Pete Sorum. Bob Goodwin, Robin Martin, Larry Eastland, Greg Newell, Mary Fisher, Frank Ursomarso, Dan Slane. They were terrific.

• Twice I rode in the commercially chartered press plane back from stops. Those trips were louder, livelier and "wetter" than any I took on Air Force One or military aircraft. We all de-planed at Andrews Air Force Base in Maryland, and went separate ways to gather again at the next big Ford event. I had slight working encounters with some of the young lion media luminaries of the day: Sam Donaldson, Cokie Roberts, Lesley Stahl, Ann Compton.

• Advance team members also

```
        Fri., Oct. 8, 1976              page 2   Fri., Oct. 8, 1976
3:30 pm  AF 1 dept. L.A.                 8:45 pm  Meeting concludes
6:15 pm  AF 1 arr. Lawton                8:45 pm  Pres proceeds Caribbean
6:20 pm  Pres. arr. platform                     room
6:30 pm  Pres. remarks                   8:50 pm  Meeting begins
6:40 pm  Remarks conclude                9:30 pm  Meeting concludes
6:45 pm  Pres. depts. platform &         9:30 pm  Pres. proceeds to suite
         greets crowd                    9:35 pm  Pres. arr. suite
7:05 pm  Motorcade depts.                         Sat., Oct. 9, 1976
7:15 pm  Motorcade arr. Montego Bay      5:00 am  Baggage call
7:20 pm  Pres. arr. suite                7:50 am  Pres. depts. suite
7:50 pm  Pres. proceeds Royal Med-       7:55 am  Motorcade depts. for air-
         iterranean room for pro-                 port
         clamation signing               8:05 am  Motorcade arr. airport
8:00 pm  Pres. proceeds Royal Med-       8:10 am  AF 1 depts.
         iterranean Room South
8:01 pm  Meeting begins

         MOTORCADE                       page 2   MOTORCADE
Pilot            R. Cavaney              Guest & Staff Bus   K. Berger
                 W. Jones                                    N. Yates
Spare            Dr. Lukash                                  J. Bull
Lead                                                         M. Meinking
President's Car  The President                               K. Nordstrom
                 Sen. Bellmon                                F. Chanock
                 Sen. Bartlett                               P. Rousel
                 Rep. Steed                                  A. Bautista
                 Rep. Jarman                                 C. Gerrard
Follow-up                                                    R. Thomas
Control          D. Cheney
                 T. O'Donnell            WHCA
                 Maj. Barrett
Camera 1                                 Tail
Wire 1
Wire 2
Camera 2
Camera 3

Guest & Staff Bus  Sen. Laxalt
                   R. Hartmann
                   R. Nessen
                   B. McFarlane
                   J. Baker
                   P. Butler
                   D. Penny
```

This is the pocket schedule for President Ford's October 8, 1976 airport rally in Lawton, Oklahoma.

departed right away either on Air Force One or commercial aircraft. Carroll often met me at Andrews on arrival, or if not, I rode home in a government car.

• As soon as the president departed the platform, one of us would retrieve the speech and papers from the podium. We turned them over to other staff, but I kept photocopies of some speeches.

• Some arrivals to a site were "closed," meaning no greetings or crowd. Press pool coverage and crowd situation would be allowed and stated on schedule.

• The schedule was super-compressed into times and brief evolution names the size of index cards which we placed in plastic pocket holders. Very handy for moving quickly. We also carried detailed schedules in notebooks with us at all times of event days. Reminder: everything was paper—no hand-held electronic devices, apps, and beeps.

• Schedules allowed for the president's personal and staff time. We always provided a suite and staff offices. Schedule times were written in hours/minutes. When staff controlled movements and evolutions, the schedule was followed. When out of our control, we made the best of it.

• Members of Congress, governors, and other local elected officials often were included in greeting party and at receptions. Members often flew on Air Force One.

• Many of my advances were black tie events, meaning same for me. Got a lot of wear out of mine, which continues to this day, same one, but a bit "tighter."

WHERE/WHAT DID WE EAT? CAN'T REMEMBER

• Can't remember what I ate anywhere on any advance, except that it was consumed quickly. No time to lollygag. On out-of-town events I took most meals in the staff office or my hotel room. The idea was to work hard and long, and not take notes for a Michelin restaurant travel guide. Consumed very little alcohol until after the president departed when we could relax a bit.

• Expense reports showed unimaginable (today) small meal costs, indicating that I ate a lot of fast food crap and sandwiches in the staff office or my hotel room, and rarely a sit-down restaurant meal unless meeting with local contacts. For two-plus years my fitness workout routine turned upside down. I burned calories through working but not in the gym.

• Often I received a thank-you letter from the host organization, and from persons I worked with—always complimentary. Usually there was follow-up from either them sending clippings or me sending thank-you letters, mementoes or signed photos. Advancing created exceptionally brief, whirlwind close working relationships, soon to be forgotten, and never any lifelong best friendships.

• Sometimes a staff secretary came along, but in all cases we staffed our offices with local Republican volunteers. Virtually all were women experienced in a high pressure environment with fine tuned administrative skills who considered this duty a payback for party service, and wanted only photos with the president. We recruited in advance local volunteer office assistance. Previous campaign or high-level work experience was important, including reliability and trustworthiness. Absolutely essential to operating our high-intensity office. They were truly indispensable, like my ladies in Mobile, AL: Marilyn Rohmer, Barbara Wattrick, Rhondi Turner, Helen Vulevich.

See and Greet

PRESIDENT GERALD FORD

SUNDAY, SEPTEMBER 26
MOBILE MUNICIPAL AIRPORT
(BATES FIELD)
GATES OPEN 5:30 P.M.
FREE ADMISSION No Ticket Required

Plenty of Free Parking

• See Air Force One
• See Presidential Motorcade
• Entertainment Starts 6:45 p.m.

Ad for a campaign event in Mobile, Alabama, where I worked with a crew of oustanding local volunteers.

Three key advances went without me:

• The Republican National Convention in Kansas City, Mo., during which I headed to Yellowstone National Park to prepare for Ford's visit there after the convention and his rest in Vail, Colo.

• The attempted assassination attempts on the president, by Lynette "Squeaky" Fromme, a Charles Manson follower, in Sacramento, CA, on September 5, 1975, and by Sarah Jane Moore in San Francisco, on September 22, 1975. Fromme (who fired two shots) served thirty-four years in prison before being released, and Moore, who later fully regretted her actions (she fired no shots), served thirty-two years. When Manson died in November 2017, Fromme came to mind.

GERALD R. FORD, THE MAN

President Ford was the nicest boss I ever had. Considerate, cool, amiable, down-to-earth, moderate in ways more than just political philosophy, with an immediate grasp of issues, he cared for his country and staff. He had good friends on both sides from his years in Congress and engaging personality. We overcame a nearly 30-point polling deficit in August to close fast to within two final points.

Those of us deeply involved knew why he lost to Jimmy Carter: The Nixon pardon, one of two courageous acts he made to get America back on track and cut severe past national wounds. The Left and Democrats wanted blood but he removed Nixon from the sour public discourse. The consensus of history since has agreed with us.

Another reason. In October I was leading the advance team in Mobile, AL, where we planned a huge rally to conclude the president's day-long motorcade

Our staff farewell with President Ford in the Oval Office, January 1977.

He's making us proud again.

Ford campaign brochure made an indirect reference to Nixon and Watergate.

along the Gulf Coast, beginning near New Orleans. One night while watching his debate with Carter on my hotel room TV, I was stunned to hear him say something in a topic on the Soviet Union and communism about Poland being free. At first I doubted hearing that. Carter lashed on to it because, of course, Poland was a Soviet Communist Bloc nation. Anything but free. The post-debate analysts pointed out the statement, the media pounced, on the next day that was all one knew about the night before (when Ford actually had done quite well.) Voters who paid attention could use that rationale against him.

Never mind Carter's "I lusted in my heart" for women comments in the latest *Playboy* Magazine issue. Guess that just didn't matter as much because he was known as such a devoted Christian regardless.

Ford's other courageous act was pardoning the Vietnam War draft dodgers and those who went elsewhere such as to Canada. That stigma was gone, along with the draft he terminated.

Ford presided over the final pullout of US forces and civilian staff, along with loyal Vietnamese, in early 1975, to end that adventure. Protests, marches, and editorials against the war subsided. He showed guts and decisiveness in handling the SS *Mayaguez* terrorist attack.

His accomplishments and mishaps as a place holder between Nixon and Carter aren't really debatable, but he was the right person for the job at the time. America was gifted.

POSTSCRIPTS

Letter from the president to me, November 22, 1976:

Dear Wilbur:

One of the greatest sources of inspiration for me during the 1976 Presidential campaign was the people who worked in my behalf. Enthusiastic and dedicated, you will always be remembered in the Ford family as the finest team that we ever knew.

In future years, as you look back upon your experience during this campaign, I hope that you will remember the days when we were more than 30 points behind in the polls and political observers had written off our campaign. We never gave up.

Together we managed one of the greatest comebacks in American history . . . . We gave it all that we had in a cause that we believed to be best for the country. Let us walk away from this struggle with our heads held high, pledged to continue working for our beliefs while also giving the new President-elect the same generous support that we would have asked of all Americans.

You have my deepest gratitude for the contributions that you have made. It was a privilege for me to have served as your president and to have worked with you on this campaign effort.

—*Jerry Ford*

Advance Office Director Red Cavaney's letter to me, November 29, 1976:

A long overdue "Well Done" is yours for your tireless and unselfish efforts on behalf of the President . . . . You have every justifiable right for feeling proud at having served as one of the key ingredients to the 'comeback of the century.' . . . . You were superb!!!

Thank you both. What an honor, a privileged experience.
Now on to life's next stage.

GERALD RUDOLPH FORD, JULY 14, 1913-DECEMBER 26, 2006

When President Ford died, the *StarNews* interviewed me for a page A1 piece on December 28, 2006, headlined, "Ford lauded as 'exceptionally genuine' man." I was emotionally moved and proud to be asked. The story opened with the Bicentennial event in New York Harbor covered in Chapter 8. "It was probably the first time in history the president had been lost," I said, but "my concern was quickly dispelled" by his positive, accommodating manner.

I continued.

> He made a point of knowing the staff, knowing something about us, calling me by my first name. Because he had served in the House [of Representatives] for so long he got along with everybody. He had a wonderful reputation, lots of friends across the aisle. It was hard, if not impossible, to dislike Jerry Ford.

> I'm not sure we will ever have another person in the White House like him because he tried to, and I think he was successful in lifting the office to where it should be after Nixon defamed it. He brought hope to this country in extremely bad times," moving on "from that whole Watergate experience. He was not concerned with polls or focus groups. He would not have pardoned Nixon if he had been. He was not the typical politician because he would never knowingly be associated with anything immoral, unethical, illegal, or unfair. Ford was exceptionally genuine.

In 2000 declining health and inability to travel from his California home had caused him to decline UNC Wilmington's invitation to appear during an exhibit of my personal papers at Randall Library about the 1976 campaign.

On January 12, 2007, I wrote this *StarNews* op-ed follow-up piece.

> President Ford's death created a sizeable cavity in my life. It dominated my thoughts for a week, replaying the countless hours and high-stress moments of serving from 1975-1977 as an advance representative on his personal staff.

> I had contemplated his anticipated passing. How would I react? What would I remember? Other than when my parents died, I never grieved so hard," but could not attend the Washington funeral. "From such tumultuous times, so much resurfaced. What struck me then, and indelibly remains, is Jerry Ford the man. I realized again after 30 years that in this small role I performed my greatest service to our country.

> The media asked me what would be the Ford legacy. It's accomplished. Long ago his healing the nation and restoring

decency to the presidency established his mark on history. For many years our Nixon and Ford alumni gathered for annual reunions until recently petering out. Like Jerry Ford, it too has passed.

My White House credentials are a memento of the greatest honor of my life: serving President Gerald Ford.

    Many pleasures and achievements mark my devotion to my community, state, and country, but none could possibly surpass the honor and profound effect of associating with and serving President Ford and his White House. Why me? How did I get there, and who took chances I would fit?

CHAPTER 8

WITH FORD MAKING HISTORY: FORTY-NINE ADVANCES SAVORY EXPOSES ON 'THE FOOTBALL,' 'THE ATTACK OF THE ZERO,' GEORGE WALLACE & BEAR BRYANT, THE 'HEISMAN TROPHY HELMET,' AND THE DAY I LOST THE PRESIDENT

Listed Chronologically from May 1975 on. Purloined from Memory and My Personal Papers Collection in Randall Library, University of North Carolina Wilmington.

Presented to Readers in Pseudo-Note Style as if Lifted Straight off of My Ubiquitous Scratch Pads

• **The president's visit to the commissioning of the USS *Nimitz*, Naval Station, Norfolk, Virginia—May 3, 1975**

Out of a possible 125 working hours I worked 86 (70%). Flew home on both Marine Two and Air Force One. Billed as "Chief Executive" and "Commander-in-Chief"—at the commissioning of the world's largest fighting ship, the nuclear powered attack carrier *Nimitz* . . . . President arrived by Marine One on to flight deck. 15,000 at least attended. Mentioned Vietnam only once. *Navy Times*, May 21: "Ford Puts Nimitz in Commission—'Nothing Like Her in the World' . . . "A solid symbol of US strength and US resolve." (Reminds me of President Trump's remarks in commissioning carrier USS *Gerald R. Ford* in 2017).

• **The president and Mrs. Ford's visit to Bonn, Federal Republic of Germany—July 26-28, 1975**

My only foreign advance and first visit to Germany since 1959. President en route Finland to sign Helsinki Accord ending European Security Conference. Advance team met on arrival at Cologne Airport by Mercedes and German driver for each. Mine hit the autobahn to Bonn at 130 km. Fast lane. Hold on. Embassy military officer or civilian official worked with us for each major evolution. All contacts made by telephone, two-way radio, or face-to-face.

I handled president's arrival/departure at Cologne Airport; motorcade from Embassy; state dinner hosted by Germans on board Rhine cruise ship MS *Drachenfels*, and official meetings in Chancellor Helmut Schmidt's office and complex at the Palais Schaumburg where I met him. Children Jack and Susan Ford and Secretary of State Henry Kissinger attended. When we moved, I flew on German air force Puma helo.

DELIGHTFUL DRACHENFELS CRUISE

Black tie dinner, July 27. Cabins reserved lower deck for president and first lady and staff. Boarded at Bonn. Stopped at Linz (city since year 874), 16 miles upstream for entertainment, which I advanced. Among attractions, foundations of World War II Remagen Bridge. Host: FRG President Walter and Frau Scheel, Chancellor and Frau Hannalore (Loki) Schmidt. Entertainment: The Big Band of the Bundeswehr. Lots of German media coverage. Menu, nothing special: Crab meat in special sauce, assorted mushrooms, coated veal fillet, chef salad, cheeses, ice cream "cassis" with raspberries. Advance team ate in the corner, same menu.

After president departed Bonn, I took train south to Mainz and Wiesbaden to visit Carroll's residence in early 1950's. Found their villa in Eltville, and German navy patrol boat base in Schierstein, where Captain Robbins commanded Rhine River Patrol. Received tour from sergeant who served under Robbins and would retire in few weeks. Returned to Cologne for flight home on Air Force C-5 cargo aircraft.

SEPTEMBER 24 THANK-YOU LETTER FROM PRESIDENT TO ME:

> The schedule could not have been more professionally handled during my recent visit to Bonn, and I know you deserve a great deal of the credit for this. I am deeply grateful for all that you did to ensure the success of this visit.

• **The president's visit to Jacksonville, Florida, for meetings with**

I worked with these members of Egyptian President Sadat's delegation in Jacksonville, Florida, 1975.

President Anwar Sadat of Egypt—November 2, 1975

This note is gonna be Long. The experience was rather earth-shaking, mine and everybody else's.

Nine-day advance. Hah—meals daily expenses less than $10 each. I advanced the Naval Air Station and boatorcades across St. John's River for president and later Sadat. Airport crowd 7,500. Wolfson High School band played Egyptian national anthem on arrival of His Excellency Mohamed Anwar Al Sadat, president of the Arab Republic of Egypt.

Egyptian party: HE Ismail Fahmy and Mrs. Fahmy, Deputy Prime Minister and Minister of Foreign Affairs, and Ambassador to the US HE Ashraf Ghorbal and Mrs. Gorbahl; a son, daughters and sons-in-law of Sadat. When the huge Egyptian party deplaned, my eyeballs exploded. What absolutely gorgeous women, maybe most beautiful I'd ever seen. Mrs. Jihan Sadat strikingly so. Seeing them up close at the evening reception enhanced visual treat. But, unwritten protocol says I can't linger long sensing eye contact. Shook hands with both Sadats. An impressive man, so stately. Never forgot, and deeply saddened when hearing of his assassination in 1982.

President Ford greets Egyptian President Anwar Sadat after boat ride on the St. John's River in Jacksonville, Florida. At left is Secretary of State Henry Kissinger.

Visit generated political overtones. The *Florida Times-*

Union/Jacksonville Journal of Nov. 2 stated: "Some political observers believe if the president can win [Florida Primary] . . . it will effectively eliminate former California governor Ronald Reagan, Ford's most serious challenger."

THE ST. JOHN'S BOATORCADE

Boatorcade "flotilla"of Navy boats a one-of-a-kind advance. Sadat party went first. I ushered them into boats and remained on station. On return from private Epping Forest residence across St. John's River, those boats transferred Ford party, and I rode along. Eleven boats, similar to World War II convoy diagram, spread out in 25-yard intervals on designated course, speed (six mph), transit time twenty minutes. Ford's boat from USS *Yosemite* astern of lead boat. Seventy passengers all told. I diagramed all positions and departure and arrival times. Sideboys piped Ford aboard presidential boat.

Epping Forest was Sadat's residence. He met Ford and Kissinger on arrival there for head-to-head meetings in Venetian-styled boathouse astride river. No public appearances. The two presidents talked at White House day before. Luncheon table: Ford at head, Sadat to his left, three Egyptian officials. To Ford's right were Secretary of State Henry Kissinger, national security advisor General Brent Scowcroft, two more Egyptian officials. Staff waited on the pier adjacent to the boathouse.

EARTH-SHAKER NO. 1.

Air Force presidential aide Captain Mead carried briefcase containing nuclear launch codes ("The Football"). Placed it on the edge of the pier and walked away. I saw it. What are you doing!? I was terrified it might fall into water, and then . . . ? I picked it up and held on until he returned. Later I was scolded politely for doing it because no one else is supposed to touch the briefcase. Okay, if it's left there and falls overboard, do we all shout? Not sure whatever happened to Mead, but could hardly see him escaping serious reprimand. Saw him on advances later but his thanks I never got.

Reception and dinner held in San Jose Country Club. No alcoholic beverages served in deference to Sadat. Florida Governor Reuben Askew hosted. His press secretary promised: "Not going to be a bash . . . .Very informal, very low key." NBC's Barbara Walters interviewed Sadat. Mrs. Ford traveled separately and joined at the reception.

EARTH-SHAKER NO. 2.

Volcanic house cleaning. Get a load of this. Earlier that day president fired Secretary of Defense James Schlesinger and Central Intelligence Agency director William Colby . . . Removed double-hatted Kissinger as secretary of State, leaving him as national security advisor . . . Named George H. W. Bush as CIA director . . . Replaced Schlesinger with Ford Chief of Staff Rumsfeld . . .

Moved Deputy Chief of Staff Cheney as his replacement ("a heady job for a boyish 34-year old with little political or managerial experience. This was his desire to put his personal stamp on his administration, to demonstrate to the country that he was a decisive and forceful national leader."—per *The Washington Star*, Nov. 6).

After Vice President Nelson Rockefeller bowed out as Ford's 1976 running mate, the president chose Kansas Senator Bob Dole as candidate for VP.

There's more: Vice President Nelson Rockefeller announced he would not be Ford's running mate in 1976. Needless to say, shuffle was sizzling-red hot overshadowing Sadat meeting. Media called it "Saturday Night Massacre." What a day of scrambles and shambles submerging us lowly staff types not on "the inside." Who's next? we whispered.

President Ford's letter to my day-job boss, Secretary of Housing & Urban Development Carla Hills, of Dec. 16:

> I wanted you to know of the outstanding which Wilbur Jones did in assisting our Advance Office recently. His efforts were invaluable in planning for President Sadat's visit to Jacksonville, FL, on November 2. You are fortunate to have someone of his caliber on your staff, and he is to be commended for his professionalism, his organizational ability and his leadership. I appreciate his willingness to volunteer for this important assignment.

At least I survived this earth-shaking day to live on and advance again. Whew.

• **The president and Mrs. Ford's visit to Honolulu, Hawaii, and the USS *Arizona* Memorial in Pearl Harbor—December 7, 1975**

President en route home from China, Indonesia, and Philippines. Expense report shows Honolulu dinners ranging from $7 to $14. Today, that much for a bagel. Stayed Hale Koa Hotel which catered to military personnel, right on the Waikiki beach with a nice view of Diamond Head. For the first couple of days we could unwind in the hotel lounge where we got ears full of *Feelings, Listen to*

President Ford arrives at USS 'Arizona' Memorial in Pearl Harbor for the anniversary ceremony on December 7, 1975.

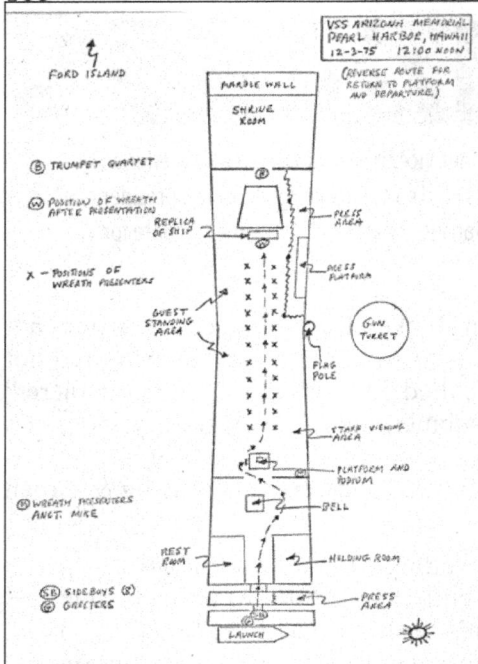

My diagram of the USS 'Arizona' memorial for the 1975 Pearl Harbor commemoration ceremony.

What the Man Said, Paul McCartney and Wings; and Blood, Sweat and Tears on the overhead sound system.

My event was president's visit to the *Arizona* Memorial by five-boat boatorcade to memorial, arrive by 7:45 a.m., speak at 7:52, including boatorcade. My expertise. Thirty-fourth anniversary of Japanese attack which launched USA into World War II. Guests on president's launch included Admiral Noel Gaylor, commander-in-chief, US Pacific Fleet, Senator Hiram Fong, Governor George Ariyoshi. Spoke for eight minutes, then laid wreath. "We will hold our course for a peaceful Pacific, remembering that vigilance, the price of liberty, must be paid and repaid by each generation . . . as we thank those fallen heroes we honor today. Their duty is done, let us do ours." Rear Admiral R. S. Wentworth presented me with a flag flown over *Arizona* and framed ship memorial photograph.

'THE ATTACK OF THE ZERO'

I waited on Memorial's landing platform for arrival, now two minutes late. As President and Mrs. Ford disembarked, suddenly from west aircraft zoomed very low overhead toward submarine docks. Clearly it was a WWII Japanese "Zero" fighter (obviously restored). Holy Toledo! Secret Servicemen reached for pistols. How useless, but natural reaction. The rest of us jerked heads skyward in stunned amazement. We're under attack? Such irony on the 34th anniversary, reminder of 1941. Later heard aircraft's pilot encountered trouble with authorities.

Visited Comstock Apartments where Carroll and family resided on Dec. 7, 1941, across from Royal Hawaiian Hotel. Timely, because its destruction planned for following week. My second very close call on an advance visiting her former residences. Los Angeles aunts Muriel and Katherine O'Meara in town. I arranged Navy boat tour for them around Pearl Harbor. Passed Drydock #1 which on Dec. 7 contained Carroll's father's ship, destroyer USS *Shaw*, blown up by bomb, second-most famous photograph of attack.

From president through Red Cavaney: Dec. 16:

> On several occasions, the President relayed to me how pleased he
> was with every aspect of the visit and asked that I pass along his
> thoughts to all advancemen . . . I have never seen as entire trip go
> so smoothly, and the credit for this must go to the dedicated efforts
> of advance teams in each stop.

• **The president and Mrs. Ford's whistle stop campaign train in the Michigan Primary, Lansing, Michigan—May 15, 1976**
Prior to May 18 Michigan presidential primary election. "Old fashioned whistle stop" began in Flint at 9:00, will stop in Durand, Battle Creek, Kalamazoo, and Niles, where the president will join a motorcade to Grand Rapids. Engine and seven cars. *Lansing State Journal*, May 12: "Ford decided on the unorthodox railway

Ford's rainy day 'whistle stop' in East Lansing in advance of 1976 Michigan primary election.

campaign in an attempt to counter inroads by Ronald Reagan. A Reagan victory in Ford's home state would be a damaging blow . . . ."

Worked with Michigan State University Ford students. President spoke briefly inside station restaurant and from rear platform car. Sorta fun putting this together. Could see Teddy Roosevelt, Harry Truman back there talking for hours. Estimated 3-4,000 people outside. Steady drizzling rain.

Ingham County Republican Party Chairman Ms. Dee Kinzel wrote me a note to the president on May 19:

> I must say an extra word about Wilbur. Whether dealing with party,
> young volunteers, VIP's or a waiter in a restaurant, he was always
> aware of making and keeping friends for you, Mr. President. He
> was also keenly sensitive to the needs and desires of the local area
> and our county organization, making sure that his actions enhanced
> a good relationship between us and the White House.

Obvious different attitude and approach Ford advancemen had vis a vis old Nixon teams.

• The president and Mrs. Ford's visit to the USS *Nashville* on the 200th birthday—the Bicentennial—of the United States of America, Hudson River, New York Harbor, New York City—July 4, 1976

Can the president of the United States get lost? What's that? Think not? Just wait.

USS 'Nashville' and its commander, Captain Herbert Dowse, Jr., were president's hosts for Bicentennial celebration in New York Harbor.

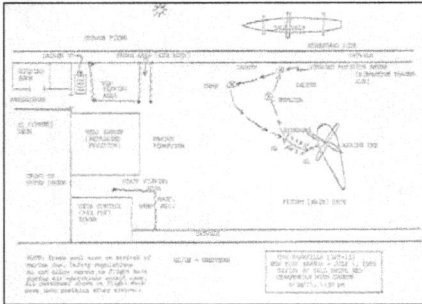

High profile July 4, 1976 event, like all others, required detailed diagrams. This shows presidential helicopter's arrival on 'Nashville.'

I helped shepherd this International naval delegation, sailors from from visiting tall ships in the 'Operation Sail' review.

Other than wedding day, today most memorable of my life, certainly most favorite Ford event, for hundred reasons. Professionally honored, personally privileged for opportunity. Our nation's Bicentennial, the grandest day of 1976.

Operation Sail, tall ships from all over the world, and International Naval Review, global warships gathering. Vessels passed *Nashville* in review from Verrazano Narrows Bridge up Hudson River to George Washington Bridge, then retraced course. *Nashville* my site. Captain Herbert Dowse, Jr., ship's commanding officer, logged: "Ship's heading is SSW downstream because of flood tide conditions at anchor at time of arrival." Stayed at the Waldorf-Astoria, spent July 3 on board.

Advanced *Nashville* in Roosevelt Roads Naval Station, Puerto Rico, two weeks prior. Flew there on Air Force Two (president's backup 707) with only Secret Service and White House Communications Agency advance persons—we three plus crew. Traveling real cool.

Earlier in day Fords started at Washington's St. John's Church, then to Valley Forge, PA, Philadelphia, PA, USS *Forrestal* ceremony off Staten Island, flew

It was my job to keep the president dry during the Bicentennial. But aboard USS 'Nashville,' possibly with help from the ship's captain, he found a place out of the rain . . . that I didn't know about.

to *Nashville* in Marine One helo. Accompanying: Susan Ford, Secretary of the Navy J. William Middendorf, Bicentennial Commission Chairman John Warner. President reviewed ships' company formation on flight deck, met Operation Sail international cadets, one from each country, viewed passing sailing ships, cut traditional national birthday cake with assist from Danish cadet.

RAIN-RAIN, AND HOLY TOLEDO! WHERE'S THE PRESIDENT?

Advanceman's first cardinal rule. Hang on to the president.

Rained before and during visit. My jobs: hold the umbrella over him, check my notes, initiate his movements, keep him on schedule, receive all the items given him, drop nothing, stay dry. All were possible, save for dry, because God gave me four extra hands that day.

Let's get inside out of rain, Captain Dowse must have told president, meet crew on mess deck. Okay, he must have replied, and zip—gone. While three normally reliable staff persons momentarily preoccupied: body man Terry O'Donnell, Secret Service, myself. Stunned, we turned around ten times, where is he? Still raining, soaking wet. Gone for minutes, fifteen, twenty. Holy s—! Where's WHCA, are they with him? Radio check, radio check. Steel ship interference.

Despite the rain and despite briefly losing track of the president, the Bicentennial celebration in New York Harbor was a career high point.

Hey, you guys seen PASSKEY? (More formally, of course.) Mild scrambling, searching, rapid heartbeat. I just knew my career was toast.

Today I lost the president.

Eventually, White House Communications Agency agent found him in captain's cabin having coffee. Got him, they radioed. Soon here comes president on deck with captain. Rushed over with umbrella. "Mr. President, where have you been? We were worried about you," I asked with controlled-frantic. He said, "I was in the captain's cabin. All is well, Wilbur. We were having some coffee out of rain. You all right? You're doing a good job." With that, lifeblood gushed to weary legs, I forgot I was soaked, and regained some composure.

You comprehending this? It did happen. They kept me on payroll.

GLORIOUS FOURTH ON WHITE HOUSE LAWN

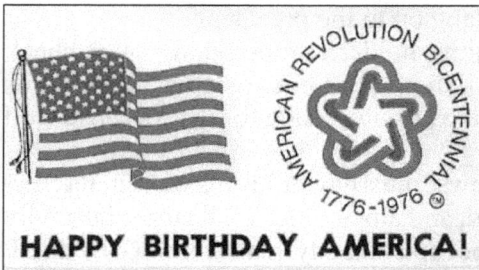

HAPPY BIRTHDAY AMERICA!

The nation's 200th birthday was a 'Glorious Fourth' and was my life's most memorable day.

Drenched, departed *Nashville* on Marine Two helo to Newark airport, circling Statue of Liberty and countless small craft and ships dotting harbor, sight to behold. Flew Air Force One to National Airport, then helo'd to White House lawn, circling immense thousands on National Mall. Glorious hot day for weather, for America, to be alive . . . Barely. The aircraft freezing, sinus mutated into cold, head swelled, nose running, stuffed up. Congressman Murphy (D-NY) sitting across in the aircraft provided Contac. Didn't work, but don't let that spoil what's next.

President and Mrs. Ford hosted picnic and fireworks on South Lawn for staff and families. Carroll and kids joined me with dry clothes. Still have red necktie, now dried, as memento. Won't wear it. Home after midnight. Message from Cavaney: pack bag (one always ready), head to Hoboken, NJ, early tomorrow to board Her Majesty's Yacht *Britannia* for advance meeting with British staff. Queen Elizabeth hosting Fords on board as return state dinner on July 10 in Newport, RI Your event (their go-to guy for ships). Oh yeah, sleep tight.

• **The president and Mrs. Ford's visit to Her Majesty's Yacht *Britannia* for the return state dinner, US Naval Station, Newport, Rhode Island—July 10, 1976**

Previously only brief, slight interactions with now just National Security Advisor Kissinger, but nothing like Newport.

My sites Naval Education & Training Center, residence of Naval War College president, and assist at *Britannia*. Fords hosted Bicentennial celebration White House state dinner for Queen Elizabeth on July 7. *Britannia* official and private residence for the Queen and royal family. Met for planning with her staff and ship's officers on board in Hoboken.

On arrival, Prince Philip escorted Fords to Queen's quarters for refreshments, then to main dining salon. Vice President Rockefeller and Kissinger attended. Black tie, late serving European style. President wore white dinner jacket. Staff

First Lady Betty Ford and daughter Susan Ford head down the gangplank of royal yacht 'Britannia' as Britain's Prince Philip bids farewell to president.

remained on pier. The menu? *Providence Sunday Journal*, July 11—"A British embassy aide circulated a copy of the menu, which described in French a dinner of scampi, chicken, and vanilla ice cream. 'A fund-raising dinner,' sniffed a French correspondent."

Providence Sunday Journal: By protocol, Fords were first to depart the yacht, "but they were obviously reluctant to depart . . . Looking back once to nod and smile to the Queen" who had remained at salon door. Queen, by protocol, remained inside. "Mr. Ford led his family down the gangplank. 'Delightful.

Couldn't have been nicer,' he said." Dinner concluded at 10:45, and motorcade prepared to depart.

Not yet. Separate car for Kissinger and wife behind Rockefeller's. Kissinger wouldn't stop talking to British or board car. Held up motorcade. President ready to leave. Secret Service told me they must leave now, get Kissinger into car. I asked him, ignored. Got yelled at again. Told him again politely but genuinely. Refused. I told agent to depart without Kissinger, would deal with him later. Unique advancing situation. President departed. Kissinger glared and grumbled at me but I'm on solid ground. Told him we'll send a car back for you, and ended conversation. So we did. Kissinger rather difficult to deal with, as we smallish staff people experienced. Advancemen didn't wear name tags so maybe he can't remember to this day who the hell I was.

• **The president's motorcade visit and rally at the Municipal Airport (Bates Field), Mobile, Alabama—September 26, 1976**

Was staff Lead. Alabama Governor George Wallace and football Coach Bear Bryant. 25,000 people, and totally exhausted. Really deep into campaign now. Extremely heavy media coverage. Inviting Bryant my idea. Some local told me, if you want to raise a crowd, invite Wallace. If you want to raise a damned huge crowd, invite Bear. A once-in-a-career-type of event. Full of good notes. Was staff Lead.

University of Alabama football coach Bear Bryant gave Gerald Ford this hat at Mobile campaign rally.

Alabama Governor George Wallace graciously took me into his car to rest my feet during a long day in Mobile, 1976.

Mobile final stop on day-long campaign motorcade originating in New Orleans via Bay St. Louis, Gulfport, Pascagoula, Biloxi, Miss. Expense report: meals $55 for nine-day stay, one of my longest advances. Public relations firm budget: $2,659 for radio, newspaper ads and posters/ circulars. Today's tab for that work would be out of sight.

Congressman Jack Edwards invited Wallace on president's behalf. Notes to Cavaney, Sept. 25: "Governor Wallace and Bear Bryant both indicated to me that they would be glad to make remarks from the speakers platform." Spoke to both on phone. Governor's aide later told me "governor did not want to do anything that would embarrass the president." Wallace will be first greeter. "We have constructed a special ramp for his wheelchair."

Bryant and Edwards arrived with president. Also on platform: Congressmen Bill Dickinson and John Buchanan. Scheduled to arrive at 7:15 p.m. Arrival delayed for an hour—crowds. My feet, on hot tarmac for hours without respite while organizing, directing, sweating, were almost dead. Wallace generously had me sit in his sedan to rest for a while and chat. Treated me cordially, nice man.

ACKNOWLEDGE LOCALS, THEN CLASSIC STUMP SPEECH

President to crowd:\

> You don't know how pleased I am or honored I am with the comments by my long-time friend, Bear Bryant. He graduated from the University of Alabama and I from the University of Michigan. He got into coaching, and I did. He did a lot better in coaching than I did, but let me say that I am a good Monday morning quarterback when it comes to reading the paper and seeing what ball teams win and what ball teams lose . . . . I want to commend all of you here in the great State of Alabama for not only having a great university at Auburn, but I want to commend you for having, I think, one of the outstanding coaches not only from the point of view of technically being a great coach but being a great leader of men, and that is what really counts.

They coached North Carolina Navy Pre-Flight team together during WWII. Received mementoes from Wallace and Bryant, and note from Bryant. He endorsed Ford from platform and was very cooperative and receptive in helping the president.

Thrust of president's campaign stump speeches, which I came to nearly memorize:

> As Coach Bryant said on August 7, 1974 when I became President, there was a pretty dark cloud in this country. We had gone through some traumatic experiences. The people were divided. There was great unhappiness. We had riots in the streets and riots on our campuses. We were facing a serious economic problem. There had been a loss of trust and faith in the White House itself. We were still involved in Vietnam . . . .As Coach Bryant said, we were back about on our own goal line . . . .What has happened? We have restored faith and trust in the White House. We have turned the economy around from inflation of over 12 percent to under 6 percent.

> We have added four million jobs from the depth of the recession in the last 17 months . . . .I won't be satisfied . . . until we get a job for everybody who wants to work . . . .We have extricated ourselves

from Vietnam,. We have peace. We have military strength and the diplomatic skill to keep the peace. We don't do it through the draft, we do it through an all-volunteer military force . . . .We have a big election November 2nd. I want your support. Can I have it?

THE BEAR'S HAT

Mobile Press, Sept. 27—"The president's 'southern strategy' was apparent from the start . . . .Jerry Ford played football without his helmet last night. But he had something much, much better. He wore the Bear's hat . . . It was somewhat of a political coup in this Deep South state . . . ."

Mobile Register, Sept. 27, page 1: Big photo of Ford wearing Bear's checkered hat, with Bryant . . . ."Welcome here fitting climax to 'super day'." . . . . "Ford fever grips city; South gives welcome." . . . . "Tired but exuberant Ford received a tremendous welcome . . . and thousands of other persons greeted him and his motorcade . . . who lined the airport runway ramp for as long as five hours to greet him . . . . No one got the chance to ask Ford if he ever lusted after other women, as Carter said in a now-famous interview with *Playboy* Magazine."

Cavaney note, Oct. 6: ". . . The President was ecstatic over the results . . . . Rarely, if ever, have I been more proud of my association with the Presidential Advance Team! My flaming feet still hurt.

I prepared this schedule for the Mobile rally, a high point of a long, nine-day Gulf Coast campaign trip.

• **The president's visit and airport rally in Lawton, Oklahoma— October 8-9, 1976**

Oh boy. Another "football" incident, another hat to wear. This one burned up the wires. How many lives (nine?) does this advanceman have?

Was staff Lead. Eight-day advance. Overnight stop. Several events. We had two advancemen at these sites: Municipal Airport, Cameron University Stadium, Montego Bay Motor Hotel. Lawton is home to Fort Sill Army base in Southwest Oklahoma. Locally called "the Lawton-Fort Sill community." Only Oklahoma campaign stop. First presidential visit to Southwest Oklahoma since

Teddy Roosevelt in 1905.* Lead's room customarily connected to staff lounge and offices, and here eight doors from president's suite.

 * President paraphrased Roosevelt: "Mr. Carter speaks loudly and carries a flyswatter."

 Public rally announcement stated: "The event should be completed in adequate time for the public to later attend the local football games and sheriff's circus." President dressed in three-piece vested suits both days. He liked them. Besides US senators and congressmen, airport platform included: former Oklahoma University quarterback of national champions 1974-75 Steve Davis; actor Dale Robertson; Nelson Big Bow, Kiowa Tribal Chairman; Steve Owens, former OU Heisman Trophy winner; Indian princess; Jim Stanley, Oklahoma State University football coach; country and western star Roy Clark.

 Original sign spelled: F-orthright, O-bservant, R-ealistic, D-ecisive.

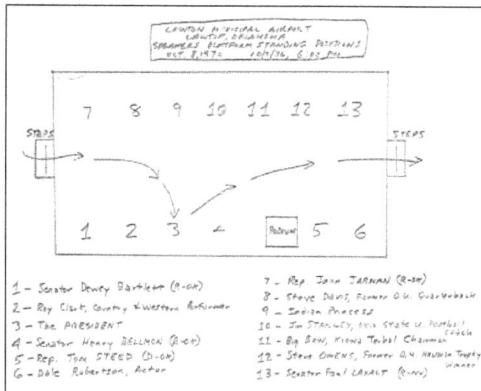

Diagram for Lawton, Oklahoma event shows range of personalities an advanceman deals with: actors, athletes, musicians, politiciams, even Indian chiefs.

NATIONAL MEDIA SAY: ONE-SIZE HELMET DOESN'T FIT ALL

When Owens presented president an OU football helmet, became my most embarrassing moment, and did president no good. Tried hard to put it on—tuggg, oooohh, tuggg—no way. National media pounced. Mr. President, here, let me have it. Took it from him, prayed the damn thing would just disappear. Media got their shots. Potential dagger because false myth of president was as a stumbler.

Washington Post, Oct. 9—Photo of president struggling with the fit. Caption states: " . . . That proves to be a tight fit." *Oklahoman & Times*, Oct. 9: Similar page 1 photo with his eyes closed, having trouble. *Lawton Morning Press*, Oct. 9: "Much too small . . . Ford struggled

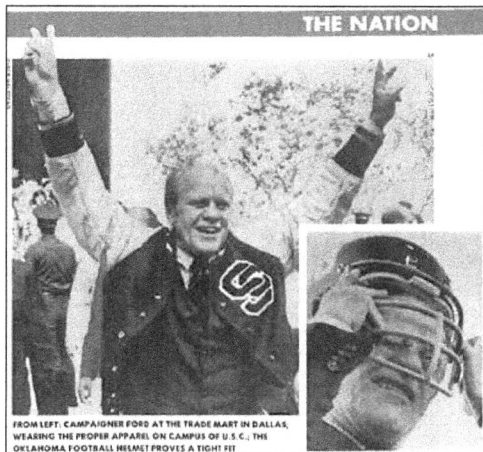

Oops. Oklahoma football helmet presented as a gift turned out to be too small. Why? I didn't check it.

unsuccessfully to get on." *Oklahoma Journal*, Oct. 9—Photo of Owens [sic] joking with Ford as he starts to try on helmet. Struggling photos also in *Time* Magazine, *Newsweek* Magazine, *Atlanta Journal-Constitution*, and goodness knows how many more. Embarrassed, I stopped collecting them for files.

Another view of the infamous helmet incident. The president's body double (me) didn't try it on first.

Why this ungodly screw-up? Because I failed to try my own head first. Always, presidential gifts given to advancemen who examines, then over to Secret Service for dog-sniffing and examination. Then gift return to giver. Simple 1976 satisfactory security. President and I almost identical size. I try on jerseys, war bonnets, ball caps (but not the Bear's, was ad-libbed), you name it. Fit me, fit him. This day, tired, rushed to assemble a ton of platform guests and count the 25,000 or so folks, gave helmet direct to agents, then back to Owens. No excuses. Ex-treme Em-barrassment.

President kidded me about that in hotel elevator as we "put him to bed" for overnight. Was so polite and thanked me for doing good job. Must have been talking about the 25,000. Later in hotel bar received forgiveness from Chief of Staff Cheney and advance boss Cavaney. We were exhausted and cold beer hit the spot. (But they hadn't read tomorrow's newspapers yet. Gulp)

GENUINE OKLAHOMA BUFFALO CHIPS

Two gifts were one-sized for each president and me—mounted, spray painted silver, Buffalo Chip Plaques from Cache, OK, Chamber of Commerce, home of southwest championship Buffalo Chip Throwing celebration.

Attorney Donald Van Meter, our principal contact, to White House, Oct. 13:

> . . . Commend to you his [Wilbur's] fine work in Lawton . . . . A major event . . . is certainly a task upon an advance man to handle the many matters which will arise. Wilbur not only met those by was a pleasure to work with in resolving the many items that brought about an exciting rally with more than 25,000 people attending . . . .Our sincere appreciation of the talents of Wilbur Jones in making the President's visit to the Great Plains of Oklahoma a memorable event . . . .

Another Jones credo: "All's Well That Ends Well." Kept that buffalo chip many years.

CHAPTER 9

PRESERVING MORE HISTORY: THE OTHER FORTY ADVANCES

Purloined from Memory and My Personal Papers Collection in Randall Library, University of North Carolina Wilmington, Presented to Readers in Pseudo-Note Style as if Lifted Straight off of My Ubiquitous Scratch Pads

• **The president's visit to the National Collegiate Athletic Association Honors Luncheon, Sheraton-Park Hotel, Washington, DC—January 7, 1975**

My rookie advance, an in-towner. President received the Theodore Roosevelt (Teddy) Award, "highest honor the NCAA may confers on an individual."

• **The president's visit with the Alfalfa Club men's dining club, Washington, 62nd anniversary dinner—January 25, 1975**

• **The president's participation in the Jackie Gleason Inverrary Classic Golf Tournament, Diplomat Resorts and Country Club, Hollywood-by-the-Sea, Florida—February 25-26, 1975**

First out-of-towner. Met Jackie Gleason briefly. President played golf. Training must have been thorough—looks like I knew exactly what to do before, during and after the event, including filing expense reports. Still possess my only purloined souvenir from an advance: wood coat hanger from hotel. First flight on Air Force One—a plum and extra incentive. President sent nice thank-you letter. "From all reports, you did a splendid job as a member of the advance team, and I sincerely appreciate your fine efforts . . . ." Nice start.

• **The president's visit to New Hampshire for joint convention of the New Hampshire Legislature (General Court of the State of New Hampshire)—April 18-19, 1975**

Joint convention (600 attended) of the third largest legislative body in the English speaking world. My return to the state after directing President Nixon's reelection campaign in 1972, re-connected with friends. *Manchester Union-Leader* gadfly publisher William Loeb tweaked "Mr. Ford": "If the visit is . . . a political visit designed to build up his support on the first-in-the-nation New Hampshire Primary next March, we would say it is probably an exercise in complete futility . . . . Seems HIGHLY UNLIKELY that President Ford would find the Republican nomination for president worth very much in next year's national election."

• **The president's visit to Milwaukee, Wisconsin, for the White House Conference on Domestic and Economic Affairs—August 25, 1975**

• **The president's participation in the US Navy's 200th Birthday, Leutze Park, Washington Navy Yard, DC—October 9, 1975**

Twenty-one-gun salute. President spoke for ten minutes. Navy presented him with wood block of wood from original keel of warship USS *Constitution*. Carroll and children attended, I think the only one she ever attended. *Washington Post*, Oct.10—"President Ford, criticizing Congress for cutting his defense budget, yesterday deplored what he called a 'misguided notion' that new domestic programs can be created by trimming spending for military hardware. This is not the time to dismantle our defenses."

• **The president's participation in the Marine Corps' 200th Anniversary Observance, Marine Corps War Memorial, Arlington, Virginia—November 10, 1975**

Commandant Gen. Louis H. Wilson (Medal of Honor, Guam, 1944) introduced president, who laid wreath at memorial and spoke: "My aim is to train America's youth for war, not to develop weapons to kill . . . the military strength which is our mightiest hope for peace." I met Iwo Jima Flag Raiser Rene Gagnon, lone Marine survivor. Sculptor Felix de Weldon attended. Marines paraded.

Gagnon: "You don't think about the big things, that's for the generals . . . .The little things—the ground was all volcanic ash, you couldn't dig a foxhole because it would all fall in. You think about the guys. I was a battalion runner and I wasn't with them all the time. I would come back and find a guy that I had known . . . had been killed."

Per the White House on Nov. 1: "The program was well organized and timely and had the appearance of a typical Wilbur Jones production."

• **The president and Mrs. Ford's participation in the swearing-in of Donald Rumsfeld as secretary of Defense, The Pentagon, Washington, DC—November 20, 1975**

• The president's speech before the National Association of Secondary School Principals, Sheraton Park Hotel, Washington, DC—February 16, 1976

• The president's speech at the dedication of the Disabled American Veterans National Service Headquarters, Washington, DC—March 3, 1976

• The president's drop-by at the reception honoring Sen. John McClellan sponsored by the Oklahoma Congressional Delegation and the Tulsa Economic Development Commission, Capitol Hill, Washington, DC—March 3, 1976

• The president's attendance at the Associated General Contractors of America Annual Convention, Washington Hilton Hotel, Washington, DC—March 9, 1976

• The president's drop-by at the Veterans of Foreign Wars annual congressional dinner, Sheraton Park Hotel, Washington, DC—March 9, 1976

President lifetime member of VFW. His Florida Primary victory announced that evening. "He was obviously in good spirits," my wrapup report stated. "Cooperation from VFW was far from the best I have received, with Executive Director Cooper Holt being downright blase about the president's appearance. We were blitzed on several items, none of which was major or embarrassed the president. No problems developed—except the slight difficulty in getting it straight with VFW's permanent staff."

An anomaly, for certain. Everywhere else received nearly ninety-nine perent attention and cooperation, except for AHEPA event below.

• The president's attendance at the National League of Cities-US Conference of Mayors Annual Congressional-City Conference, Washington Hilton Hotel, Washington, DC—March 15, 1976

• The president's appearance in the Joint Military Ceremony for Presentation of Department of Defense Medals of Distinguished Service, River Entrance, The Pentagon, Washington, DC—March 29, 1976

• The president and Mrs. Ford's drop-by at the Bicentennial Congressional Dinner of Order of American Hellenic Educational Progressive Association Washington Hilton Hotel, Washington, DC—April 5, 1976

A potential sensitive foreign policy affair, closely avoided big problems. White House Memo, March 23: "From the viewpoint of foreign policy, the president's attendance could be misinterpreted by the Turks, especially if it will be followed shortly by a State visit by [Greek] Prime Minister Caramanlis . . . .It is felt important for domestic reasons for the president to attend, the negative foreign policy aspects could be minimized by scheduling his attendance in the form of a brief drop-by and greeting We believe this would be entirely appropriate for the occasion and would be welcomed by the AHEPA membership."

MY POST-EVENT REPORT

"We had anticipated several problems which essentially did not develop: outside demonstrations against US Cyprus/Turkish policies, and a walkout by protesting AHEPA members during the president's speech. Because of tight control by AHEPA's president and basic support of AHEPA for at least a courteous welcome of the president, the demonstrations broke off prior to the arrival and only a minor scuffle inside the ballroom developed during the speech which was handled by their own members. The greeting was polite but not overwhelming. Preparation of remarks and negotiations were more acute because of sensitive diplomatic problems, requiring an almost 'international event' approach in some regards. "

"The AHEPA contact could not make any decisions. They organized the event out of their hip pocket—took no notes, etc., changed the program constantly, blitzed us on allowing the Greek Deputy Foreign Minister to speak right after the president with a 'message for US Policy.' The hosts were pleasant and agreeable but almost seemed to never get organized . . . . Mrs. Ford was received very warmly in receiving the 'Salute to Women Award.' Overall, planning and execution of this event took more time and care than the usual in-towner."

• **The president's participation in the dedication of the Lyndon Baines Johnson Memorial Grove, Lady Bird Johnson Park, on the Potomac River west bank, Washington, DC—April 6, 1976**

Vice President Nelson Rockefeller and Mrs. Johnson greeted president. Dedicated LBJ memorial of forty-five-ton granite from Texas hill country. Fifteen-acre site, living memorial of white pines and flowering trees and shrubs. Lynda Johnson and husband Chuck Robb and Mrs. Johnson's longtime aide Liz Carpenter present. Luci Johnson and Pat Nugent unable. President spoke one minute.

Escorting Lady Bird Johnson was a delightful duty. Former first lady dedicated a memorial to her late husband LBJ along the Potomac River in April1976.

Enjoyed meeting delightful, pleasant former first lady who appeared to appreciate my work in arrangements and schedule making successful event, verified by Carpenter later: "Liaison between Mrs. Johnson and Jones. Most cooperative. Delightful person interested in negotiating both the president's interest and Mrs. Johnson's." Mr. Nash Castro,

Chairman the memorial committee: " . . . Ceremonies went off flawlessly only because of your outstanding leadership in providing for the arrangements . . . .Mrs. Johnson, Lynda and Luci were particularly impressed with the splendid arrangements, as was our committee." Mutual quick affection. Mrs. Johnson was a gracious, cultured lady.

• **The president and Mrs. Ford's attendance at the Good Friday services, St. John's Episcopal Church, Washington, DC—April 16, 1976**

• **The president's participation in the 33rd annual celebration commemorating the birth of Thomas Jefferson, Jefferson Memorial, Washington, D. C—April 13, 1976.**

Daughter Patricia accompanied me, later got autographed photo from president. Nice.

• **The president's visit to Peachtree High School, DeKalb County, Georgia,—April 23, 1976**

President spoke before 2,300 in gymnasium. Large student banner in

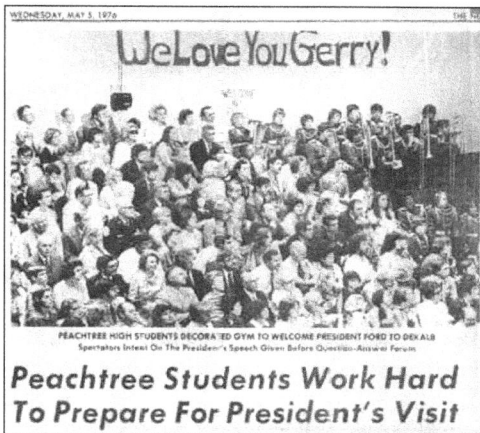

WEDNESDAY, MAY 5, 1976

We Love You Gerry!

PEACHTREE HIGH STUDENTS DECORATED GYM TO WELCOME PRESIDENT FORD TO DEKALB
Spectators Intent On The President's Speech Given Before Question-Answer Forum

Peachtree Students Work Hard To Prepare For President's Visit

What's in a (nick)name? Enthusiastic Atlanta area students assumed, wrongly, that informal version of Gerald was 'Gerry.' Nope. The president was 'Jerry.'

balcony read "We Love You Gerry!" not "Jerry." My boss didn't catch that mishap. President greeted school cafeteria overflow crowd of 700. Assistant Principal Mary Rivenbark, my school contact, exceptionally proficient and cooperative. Blockbuster event. White House press office sent her dozen red roses.

KUDOS FROM THE KIDS

Get a load of this from the students. Rivenbark's April 27 letter read: "We love you here." Students' comments: "Mr. Jones is super cool!" . . . "Did Mr. Jones really like us or wa s he putting us on? We like him!" . . . "Mr. Jones is like you sometimes in making his requests—overbearing but in the end admiration, appreciation, and praise for our efforts. That's what counts. At least you two get the job done well." . . . "We did not like Mr. Jones when he spoke mean to you, but you held your own." . . . "He actually ate in the cafeteria and said the food was good." . . . "Miss Rivenbark, when you accept a principalship, choose an A.P. like Mr. Jones. Gosh, what a school it would be—two wheels going full speed for kids! He would take time to listen too. What a blast! You two at a school dance." . . . "Would you please invite Mr. Jones to visit us?" . . . "May we send Mr. Jones a graduation invitation?" . . . "By the way, we liked President Ford, too."

Rivenbark added:

> You have it in writing as taken from a recording. Words and facial expressions say you made a hit! Several hundred home runs in five days is a darn good batting record for a Jock like you. The students, faculty and parents . . . were very much impressed with the president's comments . . . Thanks to your expertise in planning a program.

Never in my Advanceman Life could I imagine . . . Those seniors are sixty years old today. How would they at eighteen react to this visit in 2020s America?

• **The president's visit with the Fort Worth-Tarrant County Bar Association, Fort Worth, Texas—April 28, 1976**

Now full-time in White House staff as staff assistant and advance representative to the president. Advance team watched rodeo in the Cowtown Rodeo, the first such indoor arena. My first rodeo, and only.

Washington Post, April 29, dateline Fort Worth: Ford "challenging Reagan to abandon his 'superficial arguments' and 'talk seriously about his policies and the consequences of his policies,'" President Ford "charged that the Reagan presidential campaign so far has been 'fundamentally harmful' to the country." *Wall Street Journal*, April 29, from Texas: "Fight For the Right. How Conservative is Ford? That's Key Issue in Texas GOP Primary. Reagan's Challenge Causes Subtle Changes by Ford in His Foreign Policies, Adding a Dash of SALT."

• **The president's visit to Archbishop Bergan Mercy Hospital, Omaha, Nebraska—May 7, 1976**

• **The president's visit to Pendleton, Oregon.—May 23, 1976**

Idaho residents among 5,000 who attended agricultural reception and Ford remarks in Happy Canyon Arena—Oregon National Guard Armory, plus GOP reception. President there ninety minutes. Snapshot shows me with shovel digging out mud at arena arrival area. Huge sign hanging behind the podium on the wall "Pendleton, Ore., Round-

Politics sometimes involves slinging mud. Here, in Pendleton, Oregon, it required shoveling the stuff. An advanceman's duties call for widely varied skills.

Up Capital of the World, Welcomes . . . President Ford."

East Oregonian, May 24—"Security was limited to a quick search of hand bags and packages and cold stares from men in dark sunglasses and herringbone suits . . . . Local pageantry, Indian royalty" and four bands "provided the sparkle . . . . Crowd was polite and responsive, but not overly so." I placed "Indian royalty" in camera range with president. Nice shots.

With Betty Ford in Dayton, Ohio, I demonstrate the umbrella skills that would prove essential with the president at the Bicentennial in New York Harbor.

Gerald Ford works the crowd in Dayton, May 1976. These sorts of encounters could be nerve-wracking for both advancemen and the Secret Service.

• **The first lady's visit to Dayton, Ohio—May 28, 1976**

My first advance with only Mrs. Ford. Umbrella holder, quiet guide, comfort aide. Team performed all advance requirements except more down-sized. Pleasant to work with, and mutually respectful. Flew back to Andrews Air Force Base with her.

• **The president's motorcade from Dayton to Toledo, Ohio, via Springfield, Lima, Findlay, Bowling Green, Middletown—June 7, 1976**

On I-75 via these city campaign stops, veritable exhausting marathon of 250 mile. He began the day in Cincinnati with local GOP breakfast. Overpasses and highway cleared. Hundreds of officers from fourteen state and local law enforcement agencies.

I worked Dayton, then drove fast up I-75 staying ahead of motorcade to reach Toledo to assist with rally and Air Force One departure. White House alerted the Ohio State Highway Patrol that I would be driving over the speed limit. Expense report showed meals cost $59 for five days saving taxpayers money. How did I survive eating so little?

• **The first lady's visit to the Iowa State Republican Convention,**

Des Moines, Iowa—June 18, 1976

Veterans' Memorial Auditorium: Salute to Mary Louise Smith Dinner—3,495 attended. Big, ugly state politics today. My quick thinking scored significant tactical victory regarding Governor Reagan. Each of us sought same voters. Originally president scheduled to attend, because of Lebanon crisis remained in Washington. Mrs. Ford and son Jack came. Firestorm among Reagan supporters and media. My site convention dinner

Des Moines Register, June 18:—"Ford Orders US evacuation from Lebanon" . . . . From, war-torn Lebanon. Less than 48 hours earlier Ambassador Frances Meloy, Jr., an embassy counselor, and their bodyguard-driver were kidnaped and shot to death in Beirut's no-man's land on peace mission.

Washington Star, from Des Moines, June 19 : "Ford Skips Iowa Showdown; Opponents Whisper Chicken" . . . "Reagan supporters contended that the president was reluctant to face Reagan head on as he did in Missouri last weekend . . . ."

TACTICALLY BLOCKING REAGAN

At this Iowa GOP event, I prevented Ronald Reagan from upstaging Betty Ford. Reagan was Gerald Ford's rival for the 1976 Republican nomination.

En route to her table, Mrs. Ford greeted Mrs. Smith and Reagan. He spoke, then she for four minutes. Somewhere in these movements, I saw Reagan make a move back to platform to interrupt recognition underway for Fords, quickly stepped in front to block his access to platform. This kept him from trying to capitalize on media and delegate attention. Reagan stopped, stared me down, backed off. I didn't. Doubt many people saw this.

My post-event report: note to Cavaney: "An extremely tough stop because of the delicate political maneuvering, the lateness in getting there, the fact that we had little control over the dinner events as we normally would. On top of that, the cancellation by the president and the substitution of the first lady in his schedule was another tough one to handle."

Meanwhile. *Washington Post*, June 18: "The first lady . . . said today that she 'could not understand why Republicans 'should want to make changes . . . when things are going so well.'" Ford won most Iowa delegates to national convention.

- **The president's drop-by at the National League of Families of**

Prisoners and Missing Americans in Southeast Asia Dinner, Statler-Hilton Hotel, Washington, DC—July 24, 1976

• **The president's attendance at the Good Guys Dinner, Capitol Hill Club, Washington, DC—August 4, 1976**

• **The president's participation in the Catholic Church's 41st International Eucharistic Congress, John F. Kennedy Stadium, Philadelphia, Pennsylvania—August 8, 1976**

Arrived for advance late, given "utility" assignments at Spectrum, home of the Flyers National Hockey League team, JFK Stadium, and airport. Spectrum reception with Catholic leaders, received Flyers jersey with "FORD" on back and No. 1, for all-star goalie Bernie Parent. Flyers Stanley Cup champions in 1974-75 and runners-up in 1976. One of many souvenirs/mementoes I brought back to White House. Rode Air Force One back to Andrews.

One hundred thousand attended in JFK. Introduced by Archbishop of Philadelphia John Cardinal Krol for three-minute remarks. *Washington Post*, Aug. 9—"The final mass was served by more than 2,500 priests, the largest single contingent of clergy to perform the principal rite of the church at one time . . . . Received communion within 20 minutes, faster than it usually is celebrated in individual churches."

And *Washington Post*:—"Ford Gives Catholics Some Comfort on Abortion." Ford "shares with them their 'deep appreciation about the increased irreverence for life,' an obvious reference to the politically explosive abortion issue. Ford's reference to a 'rising tide of secularism' which he intimates fosters and irreverence for life, was the political note in his speech, and although he never mentioned abortion outright, the significance of his remarks was not lost on the crowd . . . The supreme value of every person to whom life is given by God is a belief that comes to use from the holy scriptures, confirmed by the great leaders of the church.'"

SCHEDULE	
3:25 pm	Air For One Arr
3:30 pm	Pres Boards Motorcade
3:35 pm	Motor Arr Spectrum
3:40 pm	Pres Arr Reception
3:45 pm	Liturgical Procession Begins
4:05 pm	Pres Departs Reception
4:10 pm	Pres Arr Holding Room
4:20 pm	Staff To Motorcade
4:27 pm	Pres Departs Holding Rm
4:32 pm	Motor Dep Spectrum
4:34 pm	Motor Arr JFK Stadium
4:35 pm	Pres Arrives Altar
4:36 pm	Pres Proceeds To Seat
4:38 pm	Introduction Of Pres
4:40 pm	Pres Remarks
4:43 pm	Remarks Conclude
4:45 pm	Bless & Sprink Holy Watr
4:50 pm	Message of Holy Father
4:53 pm	Mass Begins
6:05 pm	Distribution of Holy Communion Begins
6:16 pm	Pres Proceeds Elevator
6:17 pm	Pres Arr Elevator
6:20 pm	Pres Proceeds To Motor
6:25 pm	Motor Dep JFK
6:30 pm	Motor Arr Airport
6:35 pm	Air Force One Dep

Schedule for Catholic Church event shows importance of sensitivity to both political and religious beliefs.

• **The president's attendance at a reception honoring members of the Professional Golfers Association at the residence of John and Jean Pohanka, Bethesda, Maryland—August 10, 1976**

• **The president's visit to Yellowstone National Park, Wyoming—August 29, 1976**

A former park ranger himself, President Ford gets a VIP tour of Yellowstone National Park, August 1976.

Missing GOP convention, I went to Yellowstone. Stayed Old Faithful Inn. President came from a nine-day vacation in Vail, Colo. My site Canyon Artist Point. Drove through park's moose and bison to Jackson Hole, Wyo., and the Snake River—one of loveliest sights I've seen. Only time ever in Wyoming and Montana.

Air Force One arrived in West Yellowstone, Mont. To get to the Point, president traveled from Old Faithful by Marine One and motorcade for barbecue picnic with park employees in observation area. Accompanied by retired ranger Wayne Replogle, president's roommate when both worked Yellowstone in 1936. Replogle trained "buck ranger."

Billings Sunday Gazette, Billings, Mont., Aug. 29—Ford "has called the site the greatest summer of my life . . . . One of his duties was to ride, gun in hand, on the back of a ranger truck that drove into the park garage pit to feed the bears . . . . Because Ford was a handsome young bachelor . . . , he often was assigned dance duty." *Salt Lake City Tribune*, Sept. 13: Cartoon: Old Faithful, with sign: "Old Faithful—10% Steam, 90% Hot Air. Ford Promises Massive Expenditures for National Parks—News Item."

• **The president's attendance at the 98th General Conference of the National Guard Association of the United States, Washington Hilton Hotel, Washington, DC—September 1, 1976**

• **The president and Mrs. Ford's attendance at the Washington Cathedral service performed by the Archbishop of Canterbury, the Washington Cathedral, Washington, DC—September 12, 1976**

• **The president's drop-by at the National Shrine of the Immaculate Conception reception, Washington, DC—September 16, 1976**

• **Daughter Susan Ford's participation in the annual Steuben Parade, New York City, September 18, 1976**

Only advance for one of the children. Yes,

Miss Ford Likes Steuben Parade, Sees President Doing Well Here

'New York Times' on Susan Ford's visit to NYC, my only advance for one of the president's children.

walked down Fifth Avenue, too. *Time* Magazine, Oct. 11: "Susan Ford does not like—or excel in—public speaking, and can be pouty about campaigning, but she is fond of parades. So, smiling like a homecoming queen, Susan is dispatched to march down Main Streets at the first roll of a drum."

My report to Cavaney: "She was very pleasant and easy to work with. It was a fun day and she did quite well."

• **The president and Mrs. Ford's visit and rally in St. Louis, Missouri— October 16, 1976**

Staff Lead. Night rally at Northwest Plaza Shopping Center. Designed around stores, trees and plazas, rather unusual, but worked. Celebrities on platform: Olympic Gold Medal boxer Michael Spinks; astronaut Alan Sheppard; Olympic gymnast Kathy Rigby Mason; poet Rod McEuen; actors Hugh O'Brien, Peter Graves, Chuck Connors; Governor Kit Bond. Four high school bands. Crowd 10,000. *St. Louis Post-Dispatch*, Oct. 17—Ford said Carter "wanders, wavers, waffles and wiggles . . . . In some of the harshest terms he has used so far in the campaign."

• **The president's visit to meetings of National Association of Broadcasters Northwest Regional and Northwest labor leaders, Portland, Oregon—October 25, 1976**

Staff Lead. Direct from St. Louis, commonplace to go from one site to next without via home to exchange laundry. Large economic issues. My intelligence memo to White House, Oct. 22—"Reliable sources have indicated to me that the president can make a major positive impact on Eastern Oregon, where he now trails by 2 to 1, by announcing his support for the construction of an aluminum plant in Umatilla County . . . ." Also, nuclear energy, public works housing, hospitals, wheat and cattle.

President scheduled to meet privately (no press) with union leaders. However . . . *The Oregonian*, Oct. 26: Page A1, Headline: "Labor snubs Ford at Portland Meeting; One out of seven talks to president." . . . "Organized labor snubbed President Ford during his brief three-hour visit to Portland Monday as only one of several expected top union leaders appeared at a schedule meeting with the president. A disappointed Ford said he did not know why the labor leaders ignored an invitation to meet with him. But Nellie Fox, legislative and political director of the Oregon AFL-CIO, said labor avoided the meeting because 'we believed we were being used to make the Jimmy Carter campaign look bad.'"

Very unprofessional, rather childish. President, Senator Bob Packwood, former Congresswoman Edith Green, and I huddled. He asked me what to do. Be cordial to media and don't disparage unions: "Too bad they didn't show up. I was looking forward to a dialogue about the area issues," etc. Later apologies and reassessments, and episode amounted to little. Because: Gallup Poll, Oct. 24: "An increasing number of voters see Democratic challenger Jimmy Carter as politically left of center, which may help explain why he has not been able to maintain his wide lead over President Gerald Ford . . . .History has shown that presidential candidates who veer too far to the left or right of the political ideology of the electorate have failed to win elections."

President's black raincoats negative-ized his appearance. I suggested tan, but it was too late for campaign changes. Anyway, Ford was closing fast.

• **The president's visit and rally in Onondaga County War Memorial Auditorium , New York—October 30, 1976**

EVERYTHING'S OK. President term. Ford predicted a Tuesday vic- Ford gives the high sign that every- tory before a screaming War Memo- thing is under control in the final rial Auditorium crowd last night. As- days of his campaign for a four-year sociated Press Photo.

UPSTATE IS UP BEAT FOR FORD

After a long day of speechmaking and which turned out to cheer him, before traveling, President Gerald Ford had embarking for an overnight stay in enough energy to mingle with the Buffalo. War Memorial Auditorium crowd

Syracuse 'Herald-American' on Ford rally in late October, two days before 1976 election.

Staff Lead. Flew from Oregon via Pittsburgh. Staff Lead. Platform: Senator Jacob Javits; Dolph Schayes, Syracuse Nats all-time, all-pro player; Lionel Hampton; Ben Schwartzwalder, former Syracuse football coach; Joe Garigiola, former baseball player and national TV personality. Hanging backdrop banner: "Upstate is Upbeat for Ford"—From press area with president at podium, photo angle might show "beat Ford." We moved it. 9,500 people packed house; 6,000 lined streets. Had basketball scoreboard show Ford 41, Carter 0 (New York electoral votes).

Syracuse Post Standard, Nov. 1—"'I am the first president since president Dwight D. Eisenhower who can go to the American people and say America is at peace. Not a single young American is fighting or dying on foreign soil tonight and they won't under a Ford administration . . . ." Stump speeches basically same the last two months. Sense president gaining strength and momentum: crowd enthusiasm, attitude, and spirit.

Post Standard, Nov. 1—"We've seen a good many president election rallies lover the past half century, but we can't recall one that stirred up more spontaneous evidence of loyalty to a candidate than did that Syracuse turnout Saturday night . . . ." *New York Sunday News*, Oct. 31: Page 1 banner headline: "Ford Gaining, May Pull Upset."

• **The president's visit and rally at the Ohio State Capitol, Columbus,**

Ford rally in Columbus, Ohio, November 1, 1976, would be my last before his defeat by Jimmy Carter. But I wasn't entirely done with advancing . . . .

Ohio—November 1, 1976

Took commercial flight to Columbus from Syracuse. Two-day advance as utility and handled crowd at Capitol. Incredible: eleven high school bands performed. Twenty or so thousand attended noon rally.

Washington Star, Nov. 1—"How Ford Strategists Made It a Horse Race; Five-Point Plan Gave President The Late Surge." Ford trailed by 30-odd points three months ago. If Ford wins, "it would rank as one of the most dramatic comebacks in American political history . . . .The president deserves little personal credit for the success of the campaign plan, for it was one that relied more on what he didn't do than on what he did . . . based on the notion that Ford was an electable candidate in spite of himself, and on the possibility that Carter would make some egregious errors . . . .

". . . Ford has to be given credit for agreeing to a campaign blueprint—and then sticking to it—that was hardly flattering to his view of himself as an able stump performer . . . .Perhaps he . . . learned a lesson from the nomination fight with Ronald Reagan . . . .This time, against Carter, it had to be different."

Presidential election next day. Final Gallup Poll: Ford, 47-46, 4% undecided. Went home and nervously collapsed.

All to naught. We lost.

AND THE FINAL ADVANCE

• **Former President Ford's appearance at the John Warner for US Senate rally, Robinson Secondary School, Fairfax, Virginia—October 8, 1978**

President's staff resurrected me for one more. My job, coordinate with his staff and prepare GOP hosts on what to do. Teacher. Old Pro. Lead him through it. Warner served as chairman of the Bicentennial Commission and was Ford's secretary of the Navy. I liked him, good man. Chatted with Liz Taylor (Mrs. Warner).

My notes to the hosts: No *Ruffles and Flourishes* or *Hail to the Chief*. After announcement—Ladies and gentlemen, President Gerald R. Ford. Then *Hail to the Victors*. My requirement: "The MC for the pre-program should be dynamite! No shrinking violet. Not afraid to stir up the troops. No admission charge. The more COLOR the better." I remembered what turned rally into Huge Rally: Music, high school bands, pre-program entertainment, signs/banners, posters, hats/pins/stickers, ushers, parking arrangements, decorations, crowd raising. 3,000 attended.

People Magazine, Oc. 23—Cover: The Warners, "Liz stumps for John; But her past troubles Virginia voters." Liz sat next to Ford on the platform. I chatted with her backstage. *Northern Virginia Sun*, Oct. 9—Page 1, UPI: "It was almost like 1976 all over again. The national Republican ticket from that year, Gerald R. Ford and Kansas Senator Bob Dole, verbally lashed the Democratic party's performance on inflation and national defense."

Warner won. President thanked me by letter. And that was that.

—o—

49 White House advances = 46 for the president, 2 for the first lady, 1 for Susan Ford; 22 were "in-towners."

How fortunate and honored I was to serve this man, his family, the White House, our country.

CHAPTER 10

MOVING ON AFTER FORD'S DEFEAT:
HEY, DOES ANYBODY OUT THERE NEED AN OLD ADVANCEMAN?
THE PENTAGON PROVIDED REFUGE

The election of Jimmy Carter crushed me. Or, more appropriately stated, the loss of Gerald Ford. Election night as Carroll and I watched the TV results, I knew it was bad news when New York went down, where I had just spent five days leading his rally's advance in Syracuse's Memorial Auditorium. Then Ohio, where I had closed the last two campaign days playing utility, which we had to take, was extremely close.

Carter won by .27%, yes .27%. Damned awful news. When Texas, supposedly a Republican bulwark, went for Carter, I turned off the set and went to bed, telling her that I had lost my job. I hung on to a paycheck for several months, then it was up and down, mostly down.

Sadly, the Ford White House shut down a few days before the January 20, 1977, Carter inauguration. The president kindly met in the Oval Office with the various staff officers for a final thank-you and photo. I treasure that of the two of us shaking hands. It's been on my home office wall since.

And there was the Carter inaugural parade down Pennsylvania Avenue. That morning I took my car to Springfield Mall for some maintenance and had to wait in their claustrophobic lounge area for two hours while the TV blared.

Both wife Rosalind and he walked holding hands. How sweet, and to remind everyone of their public piety, the bands played their love song "Amazing Grace" repeatedly. Two things: I fought off: deep sickness-to-the-stomach, and vowed to avoid that hymn forever, especially when played by bagpipes. To this day I try shutting my mind and ears in church and at funerals and ceremonies. An extremely unpleasant time for my family and me.

ANOTHER OBSTACLE: OUT OF WORK AGAIN.
ANYBODY NEED AN OLD ADVANCEMAN?

The Nixon-Ford crowd scattered, looking out for themselves, and were less inclined to help each other rebound. Some of them moved on, others with stronger or long-connected ties stayed in Washington with private positions. Now up to each of us individually. Fortunately, "The House" pulled some strings and got me assigned to the Department of Transportation's National Transportation Safety Board. I did some decent staff work for the director until the Carter team gave me the door in mid-1977.

When out of work, as I was four times in my life, one must approach each day as if it's a regular work day. From 1969 until 1995, we lived on Yardley Drive in the Fort Hunt-Mount Vernon area with an Alexandria postal address. By 1977, Carroll (we were both forty-three), to her everlasting credit, had earned her residential Realtor's license with Shannon & Luchs, a prestigious Northern Virginia company. In one of the country's hotbed, dog-eat-dog competitive home markets, she was learning the ropes by working hard and long but earning little. Patricia was sixteen and David fifteen in Fort Hunt High School, and Andrew eleven in Fort Hunt Elementary. For several months we survived mostly on a little savings and unemployment compensation. Looking back, I can't figure out how we did it.

Best as I could, daily I worked the phone and typewriter at my desk, coat-and-tie ready for any trip into town, and prayed a lot. Discipline: Approach each day as if it's a working day; dress and get moving. What kept my morale and sanity was our family participation in baseball and basketball with the Fort Hunt Youth Athletic Association, which I served in those days as chief umpire and chief basketball official. I recall instances rushing home from appointments (also later on from duty in the Pentagon and at Fort Belvoir) to doctor rain-swept baseball fields to ensure we'd play that evening. Enjoy reading about my officiating career in Chapter 12.

AIM: STAY IN TOWN

The aim was employment in Washington or Virginia suburbs Arlington or Alexandria. This meant distributing resumes everywhere, phone calls from DC's Mayflower Hotel phone booth, pounding K Street and Capitol Hill, meetings with contacts, post office for stamps and mailings, interviews all over town, trade association lobbying for administrative, hard-charger jobs— whatever you need me for. I am experienced, know people and can do it. But DC was no longer a Republican town. I was out of politics after thirteen tumultuous years, now competing for similar possibilities with displaced Nixon-Ford colleagues.

K Street, DC's lane of lobbyists, proved to be a hard nut to crack when I was looking for work.

Staff politics then had no matrix, no how-to manual, or check list for moving up a ladder. One made his own. In my case, through ambition and controlled self-assuredness, I grabbed opportunities. Some turned out better than others. Be alert for opportunity and timing, and know people in the right places of insurmountable importance while refusing to hang-on or kiss butts. If I could continue producing and "keep my nose clean," I could devise my own upward mobility, helping while perhaps being helped, but remaining competitive and ahead. Never Give Up.

To illustrate the foregoing, here are some attributes of 1970's Washington political staff work. Ergo, how to stay afloat.

• Know when to lift one's head or keep it down came following years and experiences on the "front line," and keep learning.

• Stay vigilant, paying strict attention to duties, follow instructions, be loyal, know who's around and listening, and guard the flanks and back.

• Develop a "leather ass" self-protection backside. In this whirlwind profession, especially in volatile times such as the Watergate investigation, it's mandatory. Leather-izing staunches the bleeding and numbs attempts to be chewed on.

So mine would become when eventually in 1997 I departed the Washington circus with my reputation intact. My ass, pummeled hard and often, proved storm-worthy and toughened. Yes, through the mill. Risky business, but I won and got out of town unscathed. Call it Super Experience and Maturity. Does this sound like the corporate world, or anything you've endured? Is this a career? What did I accomplish? Mother and Daddy, how I wish you lived long enough to be proud of me.

All right, now let's get to the next phase, with optimism, confidence, and faith remaining exceptionally high, particularly realizing from whence I came.

TRYING AN UNCONVENTIONAL APPROACH

And so I continued on a checkered kind of career, or careers: Staff politics, Navy duty, Federal Government positions, brief flirtations in private business, and finally "Armed Forces Academia." Imagine this: I progressed in academia to professor and associate dean positions without an advanced degree. And without breaking rules or appealing to the Supreme Court. Book-ended from beginning in 1956 to eventually ceasing in 1996, nearly forty-one years of service to the Department of Defense.

In 1977 I tried something rather unconventional: Not asking for a job while asking for guidance. Headhunters offered flattering bromides but their objectives reversed my needs. They sought candidates for client organizations, and allowed how they were not employment agencies. But, their interesting advice suggested a new method for approaching potential sources. Seek interviews with key persons in areas of interest, do not ask for work, tell them what you're qualified for, and ask for hints on how to enter those fields, and contacts. Maybe that produces job leads. What's to lose?

Okay, so I explored sports management and university development. For several months this procedure brought surprisingly positive and confidence-building results, but not without having spent significant time and money. No solid job offers. I received appointments with a number of senior officials offering advice and lovely conversations. They included sessions in New York City with:

• Major League Baseball Commissioner Bowie Kuhn and his associates, Hall of Famers Ernie Banks and Monte Irvin;

• National Hockey League President John Ziegler; and

• New York Yankees owner George Steinbrenner in his Yankee Stadium office, where I met "Mr. October" Reggie Jackson.

As a lifelong baseball nut, I fought hard inside to withhold excitement, and sought no autographs or mementoes. Only the NHL interaction surfaced a possibility. Zeigler was considering hiring a legislative representative to work both Washington and New York to improve the visa process for the many Canadian players on the American clubs. He thought I'd be perfect, and I said I'd consider it. Weeks later, after several exchanges, he said their board decided not to establish this position.

George Steinbrenner: New York Yankees.

John Ziegler: National Hockey League.

Interviews in person and by phone with academic administrators soon convinced me that without a Ph.D., any attempts to find mutual solutions was not worth pursuing. That's when Wilmington entered the picture.

TIME TO DEPART THE CIRCUS

My New Hanover High School and Carolina classmate Jim Fountain, a successful Wilmington Realtor and great guy, offered an enterprising opportunity. He and Doky Saffo, father of future Mayor Bill Saffo, had formed a real estate franchise company called Select One Real Estate Corporation of America, modeled a bit after the surging Century 21 concept. Believing my titles with President Ford and the Department of Housing and Urban Development, and promotion to Navy Reserve captain promised box-office appeal, they asked me to become president. I accepted and moved alone to Wilmington in 1977. Meant to be a trial case for the company, its money people, and myself, the idea was to develop a plan, push it, and see where it went.

The goal and plan made good business sense. They paid me enough to live on, expenses, and rented me a condo at Station One in Wrightsville Beach. Carroll continued working in Virginia and took care of the kids, and I often either drove or flew home for weekends, including Navy Reserve duties. After nearly a year of limited progress, the Select One principals and I agreed the idea wasn't catching on, and we parted company. Nice try, but we were way too small to dent the market, and they lacked the finances and fortitude. So, back to Alexandria, and back to job-hunting.

Working my political sources, I landed potentially a key position with the United States Chamber of Commerce in their stately building across from the Old Executive Office Building. They called it public affairs director, also perfunctorily overseeing the Chamber's political action committee (which had a director), but it was loosey-goosey. From month two, this wasn't going to work out. Dammit. I never knew what my real job was. Navigating the country's leading business organization hierarchy was as tough as Washington

The US Chamber of Commerce in Washington. My time at work in that grand headquarters was short.

politics. Their own game of politics, that is. We mutually decided to go our ways. Unemployment line for the fourth—and final—time.

My best efforts went into these opportunities, but the matches just didn't fit.

My paid "political staff career" thus ended. That pay, by the way, at each step was barely enough to maintain my family's expenses. Carroll wasn't employed until 1976 after Ford lost when she became a residential realtor. After a couple of months of digging, in 1979 an old Navy friend rescued me from looming poverty, as seen below.

A CRAZY, WIDE-RANGING POLITICAL STAFF CAREER LOOKING AFTER SOMEONE ELSE

Before leaving my political career, here's its chronology, which continues to a different degree:

• Volunteer, Barry Goldwater for President headquarters, San Diego, CA, 1964

• Precinct chairman, Los Angeles County, CA, Republican Party, and candidate for LA Central Committee, 1965

• Professional staff, Republican Associates of Los Angeles County, in Los Angeles, 1965-67

• Chief field representative for Congressman Ed Reinecke (R-CA), in Van Nuys, 1967-69

• Campaign assistant and personal advisor to congressional candidate Barry Goldwater, Jr., 1969

• Chief of staff for Congressman Barry Goldwater, Jr., (R-CA) in Washington, 1969

• Executive director, Committee for the Re-Election of the President in New Hampshire, 1972 (Nixon 72%, highest state percentage east of the Mississippi River)

• President Richard Nixon Inauguration Committee, coordinator for logistic support from US General Services Administration; and inaugural ball host, 1973

• Advance representative and assistant to President Gerald Ford in The White House, 1975-77

• United States Chamber of Commerce, Washington, director of public affairs, 1978-79

• President Ronald Reagan inaugural ball host, 1981

Also, these related positions:

• Confidential assistant (Schedule C, political) positions with the US Department of Housing and Urban Development (special assistant to the secretary), and US General Services Administration (special assistant to the commissioners of public buildings and federal supply service), in Washington, 1969-1970's.

• Non-political separate positions (on temporary loan duty) with two senior Department of Defense politically appointed officials, three years in 1989 and 1991, The Pentagon: special assistant and speechwriter to the under secretary of Defense (acquisition)

Since 1997 in Wilmington, North Carolina:

• Associate member, Lower Cape Fear Republican Womens Club, 2008-current

• Appointed by the Republican Governor of North Carolina, Pat McCrory, to the USS North Carolina Battleship Commission, 2013-17, including one year as chairman and one as vice chairman

• Donor to numerous Republican organizations, including New Hanover County Republican Party, in Wilmington; Republican Senatorial Campaign Committee; Republican National Committee; and North Carolina Republican Party, 1970's-current

• Donor to campaigns of North Carolina US Representatives Mike McIntyre (D, 7th District) and David Rouzer (R, 7th District); North Carolina US Senators Elizabeth Dole (R), Richard Burr (R), and Thom Tillis (R); and North Carolina state senators and representatives; New Hanover County commissioners and Wilmington City Council campaigns, Republican and Democrat—current.

TO THE PENTAGON 'PUZZLE PALACE'—HALLELUJAH!

The Pentagon!

Every red-blooded American ought to do penance in The Pentagon. Really. Armed Forces officers might say, a.k.a. "purgatory."

In 1977 I achieved the rank of captain in the Navy Reserve, twenty-one years after commissioning, and continued my Ready Reserve status at the training centers in Alexandria, VA, and Washington, where I commanded two separate units. My Navy connections proved highly beneficial after leaving the United States Chamber of Commerce. Exhausted from uncertain employment patterns, I contacted an old friend from long-ago active-duty days, Admiral James Hogg, to enquire about being recalled to active duty. He was close to the Chief of Naval Personnel who could decide.

THE PENTAGON
WASHINGTON D.C.

Fate and fortune collaborated, and in early 1980 I returned to active duty in the Pentagon's Office of the Chief of Naval Operations (OPNAV), Deputy CNO for Logistics (OP-04). This recall to active duty for a line officer (ship driver) four-striper captain was the first in anyone's memory in the Bureau of Personnel, so I heard. Heady stuff, but never mind, I wasn't out to set records. Through mutual agreement, the OPNAV folks had a need, and mine's was a good job. And, my stellar Navy Reserve accomplishments sealed the deal. Also, a captain's pay—the most money I'd ever made—finally elevated me from potential food stamps, and my children returned to three meals a day.

THE PENTAGON SPRINGBOARD

Hallelujah! It certainly was. Never mind all the cracks I'd heard about duty in the cavernous "Puzzle Palace of the Potomac." It promised stability. Never stepped foot in the Pentagon, but neither had the other 23,000 workers at one time. Duty in the Pentagon became a springboard for everything in my working life that followed.

For the next four-and-a-half years, I served as director of the OP-401 Branch, supervising two to three civilians and occasional officers, and became the naval weapons systems acquisition integrated logistics specialist in Navy headquarters. Right, a specialist in something I knew zero about previously. This necessitated an extremely quick learning curve, an immediate head-first dive to learn the defense acquisition process and its ten-million technical aspects. So, I confidently walked the building's five rings incubating contacts, asked questions, followed orders, performed my job rather flawlessly, and made myself indispensable to filling the requirements our warfighters demanded. It felt good being a tiny fraction contributing to our nation's defense.

To highlight my 28-year Navy career, I commanded an amphibious assault support unit which operated with Marines at the Virginia Naval Amphibious Base.

My job was to evaluate nearly all Navy weapons acquisition programs for inclusion of integrated logistic support (ILS) principles and plans at various stages of development through their life cycle. That cycle began with a concept, then research, building prototypes, test and evaluation, into full construction, and deployment. Excluded were the huge-ticket system platforms themselves, such as new aircraft, guided missile destroyers, carriers, and nuclear submarines. Many of their subsystems, however, had to pass an OP-401 review.

Each weapon system program had to show how it would support and sustain from birth to eventual retirement years hence. We used common checklists, but each system was diverse. This was a heavy mandate necessitating both available information, projected near term, and even off-the-wall projections. The chain of OP-401, then my boss, a two-star admiral as OP-40, and then the three-star OP-04, if necessary, had to sign off ("chop") for the program to progress. If we found discrepancies, back the submission would go for a rework. Rear Adm. Frank Collins, OP-40, just arrived from duty as US military attache to the deposed Shah of Iran, and was in Tehran when the Islamic clergy took over the government in 1979.

This regimen sound baffling? Okay, so could the Pentagon itself. I'm writing nitty-gritty stuff here. If you've never been in this industry, and squeamishly feel you're being pressured to do that heretofore mentioned penance duty, just hold on tight while we whiz you through. Won't be long and it will inform. Is it the same milieu today?

PENTAGON REGIMEN: HOW TO POSTPONE A DECISION UNTIL THE NEXT MEETING

In reviewing ILS data in weapon systems proposals, we used a cut-and-dry, boiler plate checkoff list according to command directives and decisions, plus "J factors" (Jesus or judgment) cranked in. Our chain did not second guess the operational need or basic requirements for the weapon system. That we left to the warfighters in the surface, submarine, and aviation communities within "the building." Our mandatory OP-04 review and advice, including mine as the first leg on the chop chain, was readily sought by individual program officers championing their systems through the wickets. Not boasting, just reality because that's why I got paid, and, we in the bowels were assured the weapons systems consequently were better managed.

Passing OP-401's eyeballs was essential to program progression. Consequently, planning and review meetings in all warfighting communities frequently included my presence. Staff officers constantly rotating through the Pentagon billets to punch their ladder tickets, often more concerned with returning to their aviation squadrons or sea duty, unabashedly needed my input.

The Pentagon loved meetings. Sometimes these sessions, including office individual meetings, two or three a day, could be humbling. Around a table with ten or twelve senior officers, most would be admirals or maybe a Marine Corps general and all were Regulars wearing rows of decoration ribbons and previous command insignia. My measly two rows and presumed Reserve identity "self-restrained" me from considering dominating the meeting. However, I was treated properly, just sort of left on the end of the table, so to speak, until it my my turn to influence decisions. It worked, and they liked it for four-and-a-half years.

Earning a living in the Pentagon is unlike any other in Washington. First it's the gigantic building itself, opened in 1942 in World War II, the world's largest office structure, with some 23,000 workers and its five concentric octagon rings of six floors, and a who-knows-how-large secret basement area. One feels consumed, small, as if you could go missing for a week without being noticed. Seemed like 10,000 other people outranked me.

The big brass, military and civilian and their staffs, occupied the outside E-ring. That's the best view particularly if you're on the east side looking at the District of Columbia. An office lying within the rings views only the other guy's office twenty-five feet away looking at yours. Discerning the weather and day or night were possible. I didn't quibble over rings, but with OPNAV I was on the D ring. Later in 1990 when dispatched as a civilian to work on loan for the under secretary of Defense, I advanced to the E-ring, but on the opposite side of the corridor. Moving on up.

Security in the Pentagon then, before constant terrorist threats, was fairly simple: ID check and x-ray scanner pass-through. I haven't been back there since retiring in 1996, and can only imagine today's conditions. From my days as a Navy ensign through retirement from the DOD, I always had a top secret security clearance. That's saying something prideful.

A City Itself, and the Defining Mid-Day Workout

Located on floors beneath the Pentagon offices was a concourse—a sort of momentary respite away from the grind—with drug store, mens and womens stores, post office, medical clinic, and restaurant (among many quick-eating establishments throughout), and access to the bus dock and the DC Metro subway system. One had to walk everywhere. Great exercise, no kidding, including where you parked.

But for real exercise, we hit the POAC (Poh-Ack, or Pentagon Officers Athletic Center) next door. Converted from a large WWII-constructed air raid shelter, it charged member dues and contained workout equipment, lockers, showers, and a snack bar. Hundreds jammed the place daily. My routine was to go in late morning daily if otherwise I had no commitments. Pentagon duty was tough going. So, signing out to the POAC cut one long, sh—y day in the Pentagon into two, shorter sh—y days in the Pentagon. Oh well. Thank goodness.

My duties as a captain in the Ready Reserve included field exercises here at Marine Corps Base Camp Lejeune, North Carolina, in 1975.

One awful, unforgettable event occurred on January 13, 1982, the Air Florida Flight 90 that crashed into the 14th Street bridge next to the Pentagon. In a heavy snowfall, freezing temperatures, and with ice-laden wings, the aircraft took off from nearby National Airport and never got airborne. Pilot error was blamed. Seventy-eight people died, including four on the bridge. We heard about it immediately. For days traffic was diverted and snarled. Just awful.

Although I commanded two Ready Reserve units in Virginia and DC, as a reservist on active duty without major command experience, I competed with much more experienced and qualified Regular Navy captains for promotion to flag rank. Thereby, I was passed over when my year group entered the selection zone twice, and was not allowed to remain on active duty short of intervention by Zeus, the god of war. Thoroughly understood the system. Moving on again. But this time, it was completely different and wonderful. I retired! And, when hitting sixty, would start drawing a Navy pension and Tricare for Life (DOD health insurance.)

In today's ongoing national defense combat operations against global Islamic terrorism, deservedly the culture has rewarded military participants with a multitude of decorations. See any flag officer tunic today as an example. Operational requirements appear to have no conclusions. In my Pentagon days in the Reagan administration, however, with an entirely different landscape, the culture eschewed awards for achievements above and beyond the call of duty, particularly to "desk jockeys" like me. Therefore, despite my immediate-admiral superior's proposal up the chain of command, OPNAV denied any award such as the Defense Meritorious Service Medal. Just wasn't being done, I was told. My OP-04 colleagues did present me upon retirement with a lovely shadow box with flag and insignia, which has mounted my office bookshelf since.

My twenty-eight years of active and inactive duty fell within the classic Cold War era. I never saw combat or had a shot fired at me. During the Vietnam War the Navy chose not to activate my Los Angeles Reserve unit as well as other Reserve units.

I retired as a captain in the US Navy Reserve. Here, Carroll and I on our way to a formal Navy function.

However, long term official recognition mattered little. My reputation and visibility in acquisition logistics reached officials of the Defense Systems Management College located on Fort Belvoir, VA, a half hour south of Washington and fifteen minutes from my Fort Hunt home. Before retiring in May 1984 I accepted their offer to join the faculty immediately in the acquisitions plans department as the equivalent of a GS-14, whose pay was close to a captain's.

Oh yes, I actually Did Enjoy those four-and-a-half years of penance believing I positively contributed to our nation's defense. Little did I know I'd be able to contribute again.

TWELVE YEARS AT FORT BELVOIR IN ARMED FORCES
ACADEMIA: THE LONGEST STAY ANYWHERE

In June 1984 at Fort Belvoir I ended a spider-web career pattern of interrupted, occasionally incomplete, but accomplished work experiences and settled down. An ideal, rewarding, twelve-year stay at the Defense Systems Management College (DSMC) allowed breathing room and a broadened horizon with new mountains to climb. Each of us knew what the other offered, forming a solid professional relationship.

DSMC, which soon significantly expanded into the broader Defense Acquisition University (DAU), educated students in national defense weapons systems acquisition plans, methods, policies, and procedures. Students were from the active duty armed forces, DOD civilian workforce, and weapons industries. The college also performed acquisition research, held seminars, and published books and journals to our community, and was the DOD's core acquisition educational center. Students included mid-grade military officers and DOD civilians, and defense contractor personnel. Ergo, it taught how to create, buy, field, and maintain weapons systems of all types.

Our DSMC faculty primarily consisted of active duty or retired armed forces acquisition officers and civilians with DOD specialist disciplines. The commandant, a flag officer from rotating military services, was backed by a Ph.D. civilian as provost and experienced officials of the government's civilian senior executive service. Our commandant reported to the under secretary of Defense (acquisition), with direct ties to the assistant secretaries for acquisition in the Air Force, Army, and Navy. Staff also consisted of enlisted armed forces and junior civilian personnel.

My title as professor of defense acquisition management allowed me to (a), develop and teach myriad courses in defense acquisition (at least 2,000 hours); (b) perform research into the defense acquisition process and develop a reputation in that field; (c) write articles and books; (d) manage projects; (e) interact and mentor promising students in the disciplines; and (f) be available for loan to senior Defense Pentagon officials. I enjoyed the routine, the challenges, being able to produce, and work closely with students from the defense systems universe. DAU had a makeshift but adequate fitness facility where I spent many a lunch hour, then returned from the campus cafeteria to eat desk food. Great jogging around Fort Belvoir.

When I retired from the DAU in July 1996, this would be the longest time served in one job or place in my working life—for somebody else—which included nearly forty-one years of service to the DOD as a naval officer or civilian.

Through experience, longevity, initiative, and performance, I earned another title as a member of the Defense Acquisition Corps. In my assignments in both the acquisition policy department and the research and information department, I was elevated to associate dean. This responsibility included managing our large, respected, and utilized publications operations. I established the DOD acquisition management library and archives and the juried journal *Acquisition Review Quarterly*, and oversaw the monthly publication of the popular magazine *Program Manager*.

WELCOME TO ARMED FORCES ACADEMIA

Doctorates and other advanced degrees permeated the faculty. It seemed we spent as much time aspiring to be the Belvoir equivalent of the Massachusetts Institute of Technology as we did a nuts-and-bolts school churning out educated program managers within our charter. Certainly we delivered on the latter. No question. But, some borderline snobbishness like reminding those without extra degrees, could—if not prudent—fester a bureaucratic and cumbersome environment. As I inched toward retirement in 1995, management told professors like me that a doctorate would be required for continued employment. They forced me into pursuing one in public administration from the University of Southern California's Washington extension. So it went for about a year of weekend classes and papers, struggling through statistics, until DAU's doctorate money pot evaporated. Our combined pursuits ended, thank goodness.

Folks got along; that's not it. But, we were hierarchal one week, informal the next, probably overstaffed, and not without inter-department egos, rivalries, office politics, and expectations, and unusually social. What would be new? Ah, social. Almost every other week there was a hail-or-farewell luncheon, party, awards ceremony, for some arriving or departing officer or civilian. Lots of officers at the lieutenant colonel or commander grades used DAU as their last stop before retiring. Evening socials meant Carroll could enjoy them with me.

We always tried to stay even with or a step ahead of Pentagon doctrines, directives, and forward thinking. They utilized our expertise and campus like a laboratory and a retreat from the "Puzzle Palace." Didn't blame them. If we faculty were smart, we established and maintained strong connections to our Pentagon sponsors.

Senior officials encouraged and exploited my writing interests and abilities, allowing me to write numerous DOD-published articles and books on national defense issues and acquisition. In affect this opportunity launched my decades-long profession and passion of writing for public publication. My favorite books included *Congressional Involvement and Relations: A Guide for Department of Defense Acquisition Managers*; . . . . *Glossary of Defense Acquisition Acronyms and Terms*; . . . . *From Packard to Perry: A Quarter Century of Service to the Defense Acquisition Community*; . . . .and the one I finished in 1999 under contract after retiring, *Arming the Eagle: A History of US Weapons Acquisition Since 1775*, a 500-plus page, immensely researched masterpiece with many photos and illustrations, which unfortunately went out of print by the Government Printing Office within a couple of years. The DOD acquisition professionals used and praised the book, including scholars in Hong Kong and Australia.

One of my favorite memories of DAU was with my granddaughter Carrie, Patricia's child. Carroll and I assumed legal custody of Carrie in 1986 at age two after essentially providing for her since birth. She was our godsend in many ways, and the responsibility for raising her positively changed our lives together. We loved her so much and welcomed her into our home. Today she is in her fifteenth year teaching third grade in Wake County, North Carolina, married to a loving man, Matt, who runs his own public relations firm, and has two lovely children, Brooks (seven) and Charlie (four, a girl!), my only great-grandchildren. Readers briefly met them in the Prologue.

Anyway, frequently I brought Carrie to work. Carroll loved making her clothes, or buying her quality classy outfits, and she'd show up looking little-girl spiffy and acting big-girl behaved, eliciting compliments and making me proud. She'd help out with xeroxing, running errands and messages, assembling study guides, anything to help the staff. Her early work exposure ultimately benefitted her in school and in summer jobs.

THE CHALLENGE OF TEACHING ADULTS, AND THE INTRODUCTORY COMPUTERS

Would you rather try teaching children or adults? The difference: school children know little or nothing. Adults know something or everything already. Preening adults challenge by supposedly correcting the instructor or interjecting their experiences which either proves or disproves what is being presented to the class. That adults faced examinations on classroom information and project results, and their end-of-course performance evaluations, impacted just how far they took it. Thus, most often they restrained from complaining too much or taking on the instructor's information. Air Force and Army majors rising in the acquisition corps were the most annoying. But, we faculty members pushed and mentored students through our long and short courses, and they became productive program managers and acquisition specialists after graduation. Mutually shared pride.

Besides writing and associate dean responsibilities, my workload included platform-teaching approximately 2,000 man hours to adults. Duties included teaching weapons acquisition; creating the basic acquisition policy course curriculum; traveling nationwide to educational sites; working on the team that established the DAU from its DSMC foundation; serving as assistant and speechwriter to the commandant; and—let the trumpets blare—being loaned on temporary detached duty to the under secretary of Defense in the Pentagon.

One commandant, Air Force Brigadier General Claude Bolton, the proud

African-American son of a World War II Tuskegee Airman ground crewman, liked public speaking and had me write several speeches about the Airmen. I enjoyed learning more about their heroic exploits, which I would use often as a historian for years following. For a couple of years he had me perform "assistant" duties in addition to my faculty responsibilities.

By the late-1980's, electronic technology vaulted DSMC into a new era. Management wanted to impress with its own great leap forward. Each of us received either an Apple Macintosh or IBM desktop computer, email address, and the charge to learn it ourselves. MS-DOS replaced IBM Selectrics. Soon, age-old office-door or water-cooler chats between professionals morphed into terse computer messages usually leaving the recipient confused regarding the sender's mind and intent. Exchanges broke down. And the paper this all was supposed to replace? Oh yeah, you too, huh?

BACK TO THE PENTAGON, ON LOAN TO THE DOD NO. 3

On two separate occasions in 1989 and 1991, the commandant sent me to the Pentagon's E-ring during President George H. W. Bush's administration to work as a special assistant and speechwriter. First it was for Assistant Secretary of Defense (Acquisition and Logistics) Bob Costello, whose title was soon upgraded to under secretary (acquisition), for a year, and later Under Secretary John Betti for a year and a half, just as the 1991 Gulf War began. Both were well respected in their industrial business careers. We developed a mutually satisfying professional relationship.

John Betti, under secretary of defense.

I was proud my experience and abilities could help the DOD's third-ranking civilian official do his job. I'm certain my Navy captain rank, previous Pentagon duty, and writing ability influenced them. Certainly all factors gave me a maturity and professional edge in dealing with the bureaucratic military and career swamp. Required long hours and some weekend work, but not daunting. My office was right down the hall from Secretary of Defense Dick Cheney, the second time I served under him.

This was a stimulating opportunity for continued service to country. It didn't include politics, but when completed, I could note seven-and-a-half cumulative years in "the building." Enough of penance, some would say "Pre-Purgatory," but service to country above self. I wouldn't trade anything for that satisfying, hide-toughening, battle-veteran experience. I got nice thank-you's, rode it out, and won.

Overall I liked working at DSMC/DAU, a mutually rewarding redirection. Management, with the occasional exception of policy department manager Don Freedman, whose self-instituted importance was as gross as his belly and loudness, was amenable. At what DOD was paying me (my highest paid job reporting to someone else), management had a right to demand. Okay, I produced. Management allowed me to continue my professional career umpiring baseball and officiating basketball games. As long as my work was completed and eight hours punched, or taking annual leave, I was able to schedule afternoon games. More about that in Chapter 12.

My favorite DSMC/DAU colleague was Dr. Franz Frisch, an Austrian national who became a US citizen is the 1950's and landed at the school with vast enegineering experience. He earned professor emeritus. During the war he was a German Panzer artilleryman in the campaigns in Poland, France, the Soviet Union, Sicily, and Italy. He captivated me the day I watched him stare into the falling snow outside our offices. Why? I asked gently. Russia, Russia, he softly muttered. My gosh, he fought at Moscow. From there on, we established a close relationship resulting in the book *Condemned to Live: A Panzer Artilleryman's Five-Front War*, which contained a hundred Brownie camera snapshots taken on this battlefields. See Chapter 13.

Franz Frisch, author and ex-Panzer gunner.

In July 1996 I retired after nearly forty-one years of working in the DOD. Carroll also retired then from the prestigious firm of Long & Foster after a twenty-year residential real estate career. Reality notwithstanding, we fantasized for years about taking the Safari-To-East-Africa-Trip. Oh yeah, what to do with Carrie, and with what money? Seriously, we did, and I mentioned it at my ceremony when receiving the Department of Defense Superior Civilian Service Award for my twelve years, whose nice certificate is still posted in my house. Accompanying it was a simple medal decoration that's not authorized to be worn anywhere on any jacket, and if worn, would not even attract casual glances. Okay, I finally got my Defense medal.

Before visiting my sister and husband in Seattle in August, and Carroll's kin around Boston, taking Carrie, we decided on our Next Life. We wanted to leave Northern Virginia, and posed three options: Remain there, return to the Los Angeles area from where we moved in 1969, or relocate to Wilmington, a familiar place visited numerous times for years. She loved Wilmington—it's your home town, she said lovingly—and heavily influenced our decision.

So, while I continued writing non-fiction books, we put our Alexandria townhouse on the market in early 1997, and it sold in August. In September we moved into 4700 Chamberlain Lane in the Lansdowne South area off South College Road, almost an acre, and prepared for something entirely new. St. Mary Catholic School accepted Carrie into the eighth grade. Our boy poodle Sailor quickly adjusted to our vast back yard, so we were set. Except that . . . well, now you're ready for Chapter 11. Welcome to Wilmington, NC, a whole new land.

CHAPTER 11

WILMINGTON FOREVER: REMEMBERING MY PARENTS—AND PRESERVE OUR WORLD WAR II HISTORY, OR IT DISAPPEARS

Lordy-lordy, the hackneyed expression of "culture shock" hit us squarely in the face. Carroll and I survived five years in revved-up, high octane Los Angeles, then twenty-eight even more hectic years in the Washington area's straight-laced formality. We knew right away: got to shift gears quickly. We were heading to Wilmington, North Carolina.

Although we were predisposed to Wilmington's informal and laid back lifestyle from annual visits for years, and tried conditioning ourselves, Carroll took nearly twelve months to acclimate herself. Me, almost that, a consistent gear down-shifting. Getting something done was always "*manana, domani mattino*," whether using home repairmen, handymen, plumbers, installers, store owners, landscapers, hairdressers, doctors, or anybody who promises anything—like deliveries. The better the weather, the chances were those folks went off fishing, boating, golfing, or escaping even if it meant postponing appointments. Their obsession, our frustration. But, as Wilmington continued into the modern era, so did service responses.

And, the ultra-casual nature of dress for business after one of blue suits, ties, and overcoats was a cultural aberration I still refuse to bow to completely. Consequently, I often show up overdressed just for wearing a blazer. And, going to "the theater" (Thalian Hall, the queen) in the evening, after Washington's scene, means seeing unattractive wardrobe combos on people lacking self pride. If I'm ever king, my first order would be to abolish flip-flops worldwide, starting here. Then tank tops, and then making it criminal to possess more than one pair of jeans. From traveling abroad, I find that Americans show little self pride for the way they dress. And the uber-casual way some Presbyterians come to summer church: my parents would croak.

Celebrating retirement, 1996. From left, with son Andrew, granddaughter Carrie, Carroll, and daughter Patricia. Next stop: Wilmington, NC.

Got a bit off the subject. Anyway, adjusting to Wilmington in 1997 before half of Ohio, Connecticut, and New Jersey accelerated their migration in force took patience.

Once we began settling in, we gave it full bore and never looked back, becoming active and trying otherwise to assimilate. We weren't "joiners" *per se* but sought modest social connections. In 1998 lifelong good friend and classmate Bill Humphrey sponsored me in the Wilmington Rotary Club, established in 1915 and the largest civic club in Eastern North Carolina. Rotary quickly became a huge outlet for my community and international projects involvement, and social associations.

Had Wilmington not changed for the better from my memories of yesteryear, we would have gone somewhere else. Yes, it was "better."

Hah, but as years rolled by, Wilmington's cosmopolitan transformation reversed its culture shock to my high school classmates who stayed here. Outlanders arriving after I-40's completion here in early 1990's brought a preference for chardonnay, Chivas Regal, volunteerism, activism, and ideological liberalism. This stunned the old families. Their domain was being watered down. People came, so they've told us, for a small town, major university, theater and arts, beaches, golf, bike paths, lifelong learning, historic plaqued houses, green spaces, a commercial airport, travel base, relaxation in retirement, and that it was Hollywood East, a movie-making mecca..

They also brought successful businesses that employed people and attracted even more residents, contributing smartly to a vigorous economy. They picked Wilmington from the map, Google, and after spending a weekend. Carroll and I? We just came because it was going home.

LEADING THE NATION

Another item we were told: In 1997 Wilmington led the nation only in fast food eateries. Now it appears we've surged ahead in numerous categories to lead the world for a community this size:

Opioids abuse, craft beer breweries, corner drug stores, chiropractors, chic boutiques, banks which continuously change names, cupcake and bagel bakeries, two-man lawn companies, restaurants opening and closing weekly, mobile pet groomers, financial planners, nondenominational churches, unchecked apartment construction, disheveled-musicians rock bands, summer outdoor concerts, housecleaning services, community theater companies, slick local-color magazines, injury attorneys, residential realtors, and large competing medical practices. Reader, what did I miss?

One very positive note. Residents and businesses in Wilmington and New Hanover County are blessed with having outstanding local governments, elected officials, professional staff, and law enforcement. Responsive, efficient, helpful, worth the double taxes paid by those of us who reside in the city. Working with them has been a pleasure.

To Mother and Daddy, don't even think about coming back to visit. You would be astonished and justifiably terrified with how this place has "changed." Our old home at 102 Colonial Drive now sports a historic plaque with our names inscribed, and the physical neighborhood looks almost the same. But, fewer and fewer traces remain as increasing commercial development devours property and creates burgeoning traffic problems. At this rapid rate, I might live to see the last pine tree standing on the last vacant lot in town.

However, reader, don't be turned off, because we preordained what we were getting into and had grown over years of visiting to love the town regardless. Back home is back home. Coping with a new way of living after the hellfire and brimstone of the nation's capital was easier than portrayed. We made it, and we adjusted and loved it. My intention is to stay here and join my parents and Carroll on our Oakdale plot.

SAYING "WELCOME" BY TEARING DOWN OUR USO

Now, Wilmington abruptly said "hello" and "welcome" to us. On our first day here, September 23, 1997, we waited to meet with our closing attorney to take possession of 4700 Chamberlain Lane. Radio WMFD reported the city planned to demolish the city-owned Community Arts Center, the World War II USO building at Second & Orange Streets and the venue for many local activities, and sell the property to the art museum across the street for PARKING. Whaaat? I couldn't believe it. Tear down our "USO"?! Man the battle stations.

Over the many years of coming to Wilmington after being officially gone for forty-one years, I frequently visited the USO, as Hannah Block and I always called it. Just two years earlier, Carrie and I had a smashing good time there commemorating the 50th anniversary of the war's end. By then it was listed on the National Register of Historic Places.

My connection goes back to 1941. My father served on the New Hanover County Defense Committee which worked with both local and federal governments to construct and in December 1941 to open that USO. A plaque to this establishment is located inside the main entrance including his name. My sister, a college graduate and shipyard clerk, in the summer of 1943 met her future husband of almost sixty years, a young Camp Davis Army officer, through a referral by staff at that USO. Hostesses sent him to our home for dinner. One glance, and the love affair was off and running. Daddy took me there often during the war to mingle with the soldiers and Marines. In high school, the building hosted our social events, sock hops, and basketball games. You can see the attachment.

With the late Hannah Block, in lobby of our WWII USO building that's now named for her, in 2008.

Meanwhile, opposition to the building's destruction mounted. The Thalian Association, which managed the building, and the Community Arts Center Accord already began saving it, and I partnered with them. The legendary Hannah, whom I would later nickname "Mrs. World War II Wilmington" because of her stellar programs entertaining the armed forces at that USO, led in spirit. Resident and Tony Award winner Linda Lavin pitched in. Hannah, who lived around the corner from me in Forest Hills, had known me all of my life. Her son Franklin, future attorney and state senator and lifelong friend, was a playmate. In 2006, at my request, the City Council renamed it the Hannah Block Historic USO/Community Arts Center. Naming sensitivity by the national USO organization forced us to add the "Historic," since it had ceased operating as a bonafide USO facility in 1946 when purchased by the city from the federal government. But I'm jumping ahead.

Our proactive team efforts paid off, and in 2000 the Council voted unanimously to save and preserve the USO, period. All along and to this day, the project received complete backing of the mayors, Council members, and city professional staff. The entire community—say, even Southeastern North Carolina—benefitted from this combined operation. The need to stay glued to the project persisted, however, and in 2005 constant attention, rationale, and persuasion resulted in a $2.2 million renovation and restoration decision and

I presided over the 2008 dedication ceremony for the restored USC and its mini-World War II museum.

a cohesive, cooperative public-private partnership project. By the way, our building is one of just a handful of WWII USOs left standing nationwide. She is my pride and joy, my refuge into boyhood and WWII. Some folks joke they'll bury me in the lobby.

REBIRTH IN 2008

In July 2008 we rededicated the building with a blockbuster "Star Spangled Weekend." The lobby area looks like it did in 1943. My World War II Wilmington Home Front Heritage Coalition, the building's de facto history preservationists, turned the space into a mini-museum of the Wilmington home front, and established a memorial to the 248 New Hanover County-related men who died in wartime service, and recognition of the two New Hanover High School WWII Medal of Honor recipients. Our USO is a magical blending of history and the arts, an exceptionally popular public venue for events, classes, theater, concerts, lectures, Bar Mitzvahs, meetings, wedding receptions, pottery groups, fundraisers, and more.

Of all my history preservation achievements since returning home in 1997, this is the one into which I poured the most time, energy, and sweat—and am the proudest. My service continues. I served as chairman of its City Council-appointed advisory board (first appointed to the board when the Council established it in 2008) which monitors its operations and maintenance, and works closely with the City Council and staff and building's management team in presenting WWII-related events and its preservation. As the hub of Southeastern North Carolina's expanded wartime activities and key to efforts to nationally designate Wilmington as the first "American WWII Heritage City," it remains our community crown jewel.

UNC Wilmington: Time, Effort, and Pride
in Hometown University

Once we settled, Carroll would not sit still. Not her nature. She let her realtor's license expire after twenty years and dived into docent-ing, the Daughters of the American Revolution, St. Mary Catholic Church, and local Republican women's activities. Unexpectedly, by pure happenstance, in 1998 the University of North Carolina Wilmington's librarian offered her a part-time job working in Randall Library's special collections as a research associate.

Wilmington's world was expanding to accommodate the newcomers, to the chagrin of the Old Line Residents. She became part of that expansion and relished the opportunity. Through tutoring, diligence, and self application she effectively organized personal papers collections, including mine, some of which are used in writing this screed. She endeared herself to local history researchers. Before retiring in 2009 after eleven years, also shutting down other activities because of her declining health, she organized and administered the university's oral history program.

Because my work as an author and historian immediately drew me to Randall Library, Carroll and I developed a rich and rewarding association with UNCW. Over the years I've donated mountains of items, including my career personal papers, those of both our parents, research material from books I've written; and military history books, magazines, and related items. Through my Will and agreement with the vice chancellor for development, I'm donating the remainder of my vast military history collection to Randall, with earmarked estate funds for the accession and maintenance. This includes books, magazines, art, artifacts, memorabilia, DVD's, photographs, and the like. With such a gift, I'm honored to be a member of the university's E. L. White Society of major donors.

Additionally, library officials and I estimate I've either brought in, or highly influenced, the accession of approximately twenty-five personal papers collections, many pertaining to military history. With material still in private hands, people frequently ask me, for example, "what should my family do with my grandfather's WWII records, photos, and memorabilia? If the subject is local, and the items noteworthy, I might recommend contacting Randall or alert the library. If the subject is from another state, or appears of limited value to Randall, I suggest other optional donation possibilities. Providing this unofficial and gratis counseling I consider as part of my pay-back.

This close association and contribution to the library is one of my most significant professional accomplishments. Two collections especially. The voluminous John Gunn Sports Collection, which I brought in, allowed UNCW to claim possession of the second largest university sports library behind Notre Dame. Its size required the chancellor's approval to accession. And, the US

Congressman Mike McIntyre Collection of his eighteen years of service to our Seventh District, which donation I highly influenced because of my working relationship with Mike. When my full donation is eventually accessioned, perhaps Randall can tout the size of its military history collection in my name.

WHY MY PERSONAL PAPERS TO RANDALL LIBRARY?

Thus my principal connection with UNCW is through Randall, then the development office because of my gift, and some relationships with individual history professors. Why did I gift to UNCW instead of my alma mater, Carolina, or the county library or historical society? First, UNC has enough collections and doesn't need mine. I'm small potatoes. The other local depositories aren't large enough. UNCW is my hometown's university. I remember when it started right after the war. As a Wilmingtonian, I share the pride of being home to this fine institution. My papers are more suited for Randall than anywhere else. They have the capacity, expertise, and visibility to provide my material to students, scholars, and historians, and make it available for my reference use.

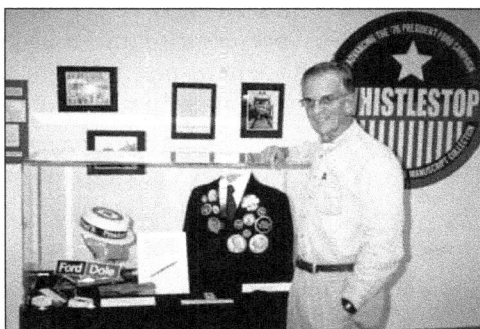

UNC-Wilmington's Randall Library put on an exhibition of my Ford administration materials in 2000.

But, the UNCW connection started off sourly in 1997 because of Chancellor Jim Leutze. Desiring to establish an adjunct teaching/ mentoring relationship with the political science and history departments, to provide some "street smarts," I made appointments with the chancellor to discuss if I could share my political and government experiences. For unknown reasons, Leutze cancelled our three separate appointments at the last minute. He lost my respect for this. Plus, the chancellor expressed no interest when told that my father-in-law, a highly decorated WWII naval officer who made admiral, commanded the destroyer USS *Leutze*—pronounced by the Navy "Loy-et-ze," vis a vis his "Loot-zee"—and was severely wounded at the Battle of Iwo Jima.

My meetings with those department chairs where I offered my services were polite but non-productive. I felt it was: don't bother our enclave with your Washington stuff. Soon realized the main problem, besides those individuals: I wanted to enter part-time academia without a doctorate? Since then I've lectured students once on campus. Didn't let that spoil my interactions with UNCW, or staff and faculty personally. Just wish the university would do more community outreach. Real shortcoming. So, my relationship with Randall Library has flourished.

COMMEMORATING THE CENTURY'S MOST PROFOUND EVENT IN WARTIME WILMINGTON

Remembering my Wilmington World War II roots, in 1998 I set out to do everything I could to preserve the area's WWII history, a journey of dedicated devotion I continue. With the grace and guidance of God, I will until my body and mind no longer let me. If it weren't for me, the story of wartime Wilmington likely would have been forgotten, then lost because no one else would assume the preservation responsibility. I got here at the right time. So said former mayor Dan Cameron, one of Wilmington's finest sons, among others like state Representative Ted Davis. Dumbfounded at how little or no attention had been given, I went right to work, uncovering its overlooked past while maneuvering amidst local politics to save it. We are so glad you came home, many said.

So, history preservation has ascribed my place in life for the past twenty-two years, a confident responsibility which reaped huge successes. But, I cannot find anyone who eventually will take my place.

'Wartime Wilmington' observance brought these African American Tuskeegee Airmen to town, 1999.

In 1998 the Lower Cape Fear Historical Society envisioned sponsoring an end-of-the century tribute to WWII and Wilmington's role, and asked me to lead the committee. Thus was formed an ambitious eighteen-month schedule of some 125 programs, exhibits, lectures and more under the banner of Wartime Wilmington Commemoration, 1999. As chairman, I worked with organizations of paid staff and volunteers in New Hanover, Brunswick, and Pender Counties to stage and publicize events.

It became almost a full-time job as I spoke all over Southeastern North Carolina, gave numerous media interviews, and simultaneously finished writing the book *Arming the Eagle* for the Defense Acquisition University. Also, I began researching what ultimately became the two popular, award-winning books on wartime Wilmington and Southeastern North Carolina.

Such a role was my sweetspot, intuitively my birthright. I came home expecting to write about WWII Wilmington, with fond and vivid memories, but where to start? The overwhelming community and media enthusiasm for the WWC 1999 project, and the amount of information the team uncovered, accelerated my determination.

Hard to realize how we did it, but we brought here the restored and flyable WWII B-17G bomber "Aluminum Overcast," operated by the Experimental

About to board the B-17 bomber 'Aluminum Overcast,' with a crewman, left, May 1999.

Aircraft Association of Oshkosh, Wisc., for show and flights. The first flight, for media and myself, was a lifetime's experience. Taking off from Wilmington's commercial airport, we circled the area and headed eastward across the beaches into the Atlantic. I'm sitting there thrilled as Holy Moses, heart beating like crazy, fantasizing out the window. We had just left an 8th Air Force airfield in East Anglia and were headed into the English Channel across the White Cliffs of Dover, on a bomb run over German Occupied Europe. I nudged my butt into the plexiglass nosecone bombardier's seat and looked straight down at the water. Gulp. That's not all. Returning to base, retracing our route, I broke out in "song," as loud as I could, *Coming in on a Wing and a Prayer!*

CONTINUING THE PRESERVATION MOMENTUM: FORMING 'THE COALITION'

What a team! At the beginning I never imagined we could accomplish so much. Momentum kept building. Helped elevate Wilmington's wartime contributions and our efforts to preserve that history, for which we received statewide and local history awards. When we shut down the Commemoration in 2000, the obvious need to keep rolling resulted in establishing its replacement, the World War II Wilmington Home Front Heritage Coalition. Historian Dr. Everard Smith joined with me in forming "The Coalition," and I became its only chairman since. In 2008 we got our 501(c)(3) designation and operate as a non-partisan, non-political, all-volunteer preservation organization. Our mission is to identify, preserve, and interpret the rich WWII legacy of Wilmington and SENC. We recruit and list our organization and individual supporters but ask for neither money nor meeting attendance. Purely supportive in name or for a favor when asked. The

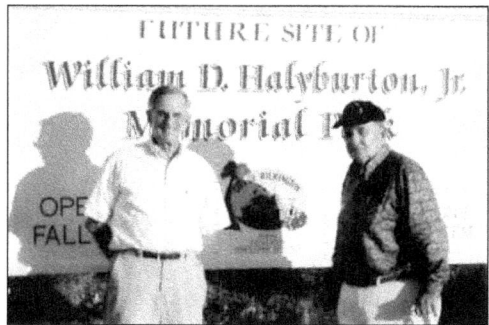

The late John J. Burney, Jr., a WWII veteran, helped with efforts to get Wilmington to name a new park for hometown Medal of Honor recipient William D. Halyburton, Jr. Here, we're at the park site in 2004.

In 2005 with WWII Medal of Honor recipients Frank Currey, left, and Charles Murray, namesake of New Hanover County's Murray Middle School.

Coalition's first major effort was continuing to save and preserve, then renovate and restore, the city's WWII USO building, the Community Arts Center.

Over the years I've raised directly or indirectly about $100,000 for the building's restoration, preservation, and mini-museum of the home front, along with other preservation projects, through grants, donation requests, fundraisers, special events, and gifts. History accomplishments since are way too numerous to list, but later on we see a sampling.

Two notes.

For years I dreamed about how best to serve the beloved battleship *North Carolina*. World War II's most highly decorated battleship, moored in Wilmington since 1961, is the state's memorial to some 10,000 Tar Heels who lost their lives. In 2013 Republican Governor Pat McCrory appointed me to the USS North Carolina Battleship Commission as vice chairman. For the 2014-15 year, he appointed me chairman, and I served on the Commission until rotating off in 2017. No honor or privilege has meant more to me. During the "McCrory Watch," we raised the funds—nearly $17 million—to begin construction of a long-term cofferdam as the first step

For more than two decades, our Coalition has held memorials every December 7, honoring our region's dwindling number of Pearl Harbor survivors.

to making required hull repairs to prolong its life another forty years. And we began building a 360-degree walkway around the ship, donated by the State Employees Credit Union.

The Department of Defense flirted with me for a year or so about writing another big book on defense acquisition. This led to my attendance in September 2001 at a national DOD history conference in Tysons Corner, Northern Virginia. The contract never happened, but 9-11 did while I was there. On the morning of the eleventh as I started my car to head for the conference, I got the first World

Trade Center crash news. On arrival, we glued to a communal TV as the other WTC building went down, and then—the crash into the Pentagon just two miles away.

The conference was about to adjourn, and since I'd checked out of my hotel, I got the hell out of Dodge. Smoke from the Pentagon was visible. Because I lived in the area for twenty-eight years, I knew the back roads and figured I-95 would be jammed. I was right, and wound my way through Fairfax County traffic to way south of Washington on to 95 and home, with only the radio for news. I phoned Carroll, heard what she heard, and sped to Wilmington.

WILMINGTON, THE FIRST 'AMERICAN WWII HERITAGE CITY' —WHEN? WE'RE ON THE GOAL LINE

And now to the most uphill, maximum-effort project—or goal—I've undertaken. Yet, the one with the greatest professional and personal rewards. The conclusion always seems on the horizon, within reach, but elusive. I've maintained optimism and confidence. Maybe tomorrow it will breakthrough. My role: Keep working it and don't let go, never giving up.

Okay, let's explain. The project is a twelve-year-plus effort to have Wilmington designated as the first "American World War II Heritage City," based on two criteria: our contributions to the war effort, and how we preserved that history. Ultimately, once realized, this project becomes a case study in how to navigate a noble civic idea through political wickets into a national history preservation success.

Great news emerged in early 2019 when Congress passed our bill (Section 9007 in S.47) in February and President Donald Trump signed it into law on March 12. The bill establishes the national history preservation program Wilmington initiated and assigns designation authority to the secretary of the Interior.

U.S. Senator Thom Tillis spearheaded bill in the Senate.

US Rep. David Rouzer helped push WWII Cities bill.

March 12, 2019

WASHINGTON, DC – Today, Congressman David Rouzer (R-NC-07) and Senator Thom Tillis (R-NC) applauded President Trump for signing the John D. Dingell, Jr. Conservation, Management, and Recreation Act [S. 47, "The Natural Resources Management Act"], which includes a provision [Sec. 9007] authored by Rouzer and Tillis to direct the Secretary of Interior to annually designate at least one city in the United States as an "American World War II Heritage City," into law. Wilmington, North Carolina is likely to be among the first cities to receive the honor.

The Senate and House of Representatives passed S. 47 in February. From the office of Congressman Rouzer:

Capt. Jones—I am happy to inform you that last night [Feb. 26th] the Natural Resources Management Act [S. 47], which included our bill text establishing WWII Heritage Cities, was passed by the House of Representatives. We are now the closest we've ever been to having this become a reality. A letter is being drafted to the Acting Secretary of the Interior to address Wilmington's selection as the first such city, to be sent as soon as this bill is signed into law by President Trump.

Congratulations, Capt. Jones, and thanks to everyone that has worked so hard on this initiative.

From the office of Senator Tillis:

Thank you CPT Jones for all of your work on this effort – Senator Tillis was very proud that it has passed Congress. You are an example of the best of democracy – constituents coming up with great ideas and working to accomplish them!

The Wilmington *StarNews* regional newspaper reported with a page A1 banner reading "Donald Trump puts Wilmington in line as World War City":

The World War II Wilmington Home Front Heritage Coalition, chaired by retired Navy captain Wilbur D. Jones Jr., had campaigned for the designation for more than a decade. Bills to authorize the designation had passed the House several times but had always stalled in the Senate until this year. Rouzer thanked Tillis and US Sen. Richard Burr (R-NC) for their strong support for the measure.

"It's marvelous," said Jones, a military historian whose books include *A Sentimental Journey* about wartime Wilmington. 'We're so close now, after all these years. We're on the goal line. All we need now is to get the secretary of Interior to sign a sheet of paper."

Gaining "Heritage City" designation would be a boost to destination tourism in Wilmington, Jones said. More important, he hopes the act will promote preservation of World War II heritage throughout the United States.

The Sec. 9007 measure lists examples of the two criteria we proposed at the outset: wartime contributions, and preservation accomplishments. All along it was non-political, non-partisan, and requested no funds. In July 2019 the entire North Carolina congressional delegation signed a Rouzer letter to the Interior

Retired US Rep. Mike McIntyre, here in 2012, was a key ally in efforts to create WWII Cities program.

Mr. Jones

In 2018, Rep. Rouzer and I testified on his bill before the House Natural Resources Committee.

secretary urging swift designation of Wilmington as *The First*. The secretary will also be guided by these fundamental facts about Wilmington:

Contributions to the war effort

• North Carolina Shipbuilding Co. constructed 243 cargo ships for Merchant Marine and Navy and state's largest employer

• All five armed forces stationed here, British Navy also

• P-47 fighter training base; anti-aircraft artillery advanced training base

• Official "Defense Capital of the State"

• Defense industries: shirts manufacturer, pulpwood, fertilzer producers, dairies, truck farming

• Principal state port along Cape Fear River

• Two Medal of Honor recipients from white high school

• Many servicemen decorated for valor including carrier pilot with 3 Navy Crosses

• $40 million raised for war bonds

• Three German prisoner of war camps

• Atlantic Coast Line Railroad headquarters and terminal

• U-boat fired on chemical plant

• County population triples to ca. 100,000

• 5,495 public housing units built for white and black war workers

• 14 USO facilities in county

• 248 county men in uniform lost their lives

Preservation accomplishments

• Shining star attraction since 1961 is Battleship North Carolina, state's memorial to its WWII dead.

• Formed World War II Wilmington Home Front Heritage Coalition. A 501(c)(3) non-political, all-volunteer preservation organization. Mission: identify, preserve, and interpret the WWII legacy of Wilmington and Southeastern NC

• Saved, preserved, renovated, and restored Hannah Block Historic USO/

Community Arts Center, the area's WWII activity hub
• Coalition raised nearly $100,000 for building's restoration, preservation, and other activities
• Staged WWII veterans meet-and-greet jamborees and USO-style dances;
• Added exhibits, artifacts, memorials to the 248 New Hanover County dead, its aviators, Medal of Honor recipients, and outstanding veterans; and National WWII Memorial giclee
• Celebrated the seventieth anniversary with students through music, drama, and dance: "Christmas 1944 at the Wilmington USO"
• Celebrated the seventy-fifth anniversary with the original musical play "Mrs. World War II Wilmington: We Fell in Love at the USO"
• 2017 annual Pearl Harbor ceremony with survivors (99, 97, 95) plus 25 other veterans
• *New York Times*, WarHistoryOnline, and *Our State* magazine: as potential tourism destination
• Named a school and city park for two WWII Medal of Honor recipients, erected memorials at New Hanover High School and the HBHUSO/CAC
• Formed WWII Remembered Group of veterans, home front workers, and enthusiasts
• Erected markers, including for two German prisoner of war camps
• Published and distributed three editions (100,000 copies) of the "World War II Heritage Guide Map of Wilmington and Southeastern North Carolina"
• About the subject, Coalition chairman has given nearly 800 presentations and media interviews, written two books, and wrote or been principal source for some 300 print articles

—o—

Wilmington's initiative has thus established a new nationwide WWII history

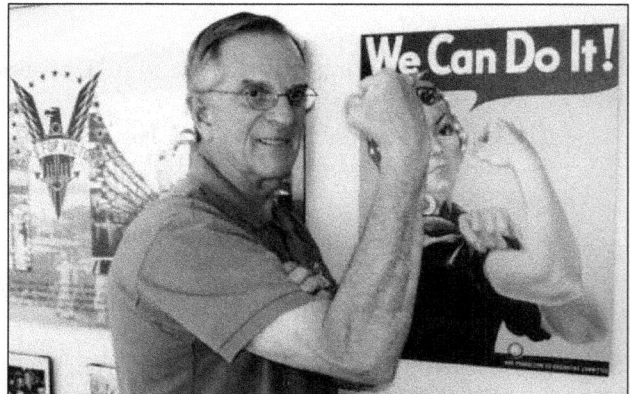

Flyer for 2017 performance and poster in USO building betray my fondness for 'Rosie,' icon for World War II home front war effort.

preservation program which will entice any city to seek such recognition.

It started with a blank piece of paper, subsequently generating pathways of encouragement, minor successes, steps both forward and backwards, road blocks and frustrations—plus skilled intervention and staff work by Senators Richard Burr (R-NC) and Tillis, Congressmen Mike McIntyre (D-NC) and Rouzer, and their capable professional staffs.

And, I proudly add, plus my detailed research, undying attention, polite encouragement, unrelenting insistence, and obvious dedication.

In early 2008 I began a project seeking national recognition for Wilmington as "America's World War II City," based on our area's contributions to the war effort, and what we had done since to preserve that history. With the war concluded sixty-three years before, I checked and found no city claimed such a title. Then, why not Wilmington? We moved to fill that vacuum. Starting with resolutions proclaiming it from the County Commissioners and City Council, and encouragement from the convention and visitors bureau, the *StarNews* Media, business and organizations supporters, and myriad back-slappers, the attempts to obtain that designation became my full-time volunteer job.

Realizing that some entity had to make it official, I enlisted the support of Wilmington's Congressman McIntyre. He liked the idea and agreed to work together to ask everybody and his brother who might have interest, responsibility, and authority to say "Yes."

To my parents Wilbur and Viola Jones who contributed diligently to the Wilmington war effort.

Wilbur D. Jones, a member of the Second and Orange Dedication Committee, Exchange Club, and American Legion Post 10

Viola Murrell Jones, a Volunteer Red Cross Nurses Aide and Post 10 Auxiliary Historian

To my sister Elizabeth Jones Garniss

She worked as a shipyard clerk and met her husband of nearly 60 years, Camp Davis Capt. George H. Garniss, through this USO.

Capt. Wilbur D. Jones, Jr. USNR (Ret.)

July 2008

I sponsored this plaque in the USO in honor of my parents' and sister's contributions to the war effort.

I prepared a mountain of background reference information to support our claim, listing wartime contributions and preservation accomplishments. This data is free and available to anyone requesting it, and includes:

• Facts on wartime contributions to the war effort, including the shipyard, armed forces bases, defense industries, home front efforts, Medal of Honor recipients, exploits of men in uniform, etc.;

• Listing all WWII sites, memorial, facilities, exhibits, etc., in Southeastern North Carolina;

• Timeline of actions on the WWII City project since 2008;

• Testimony before the House of Representatives Veterans Affairs Committee in 2012, and the House Natural Resources Committee in 2018; and
   • Accomplishments to preserve the WWII legacy of Southeastern North Carolina.

LET'S GO FOR THE PRESIDENT:
WAR II CITY BY ACT OF CONGRESS

Together in 2012, McIntyre and I both testified before one of the VA Committee's subcommittees. He garnered sixty-five House co-sponsors including men, women, blacks, whites, liberals, conservatives, Democrats and Republicans, and every member of the state's delegation but one.

Here follows excerpts from my update op-ed piece published in the *StarNews* on July 29, 2018, "Battle for Recognition: Optimism, momentum build in Wilmington's effort to become first 'WWII Heritage City.'"

> Buoyed by recent strong official and community endorsements, and constructive Capitol Hill conferences, optimism increases for Wilmington's ten-year project seeking national designation as the first "American World War II Heritage City" by act of Congress.

> In June 2018 the North Carolina House of Representatives unanimously passed HB 970, a resolution supporting Wilmington's claim and urging Congress to pass designation legislation. Wilmington Representative Ted Davis introduced and steered the bill. Congressman David Rouzer broached the idea to me eleven months ago.

THE HISTORY BEHIND THE HISTORY

> That stated, it's time to update the 'WWII City' project noting how we got here.

> First, the 'official' effort seeking national recognition began in early 2008. Second, understanding the proposed legislation's language is essential. Since 2010, our congressional delegation introduced similar one-page bills which would: (a) authorize a cabinet secretary to designate annually an "American WWII City"; (b) specify two such qualifications criteria; and (c) designate Wilmington as the first. Ah. There's the rub.

> The delegation and media, however, concentrated on only one criterion in (b): A city's war effort contribution. Like building atomic bombs, planes, tanks. Underplayed is the equally important second criterion: How has a city preserved its wartime legacy? Like restoring WWII facilities, preservation organizations, recognizing

veterans.

Wilmington, in this context including Southeastern North Carolina, overwhelmingly exceeds both criteria.

THE PRESERVATION CRITERION

Astounding aptly describes our area accomplishments which actually started earnestly twenty years ago, continually spearheaded by volunteers working with governments and organizations. Perhaps Wilmington trails cities posting larger wartime production numbers, or utilizing paid staff and fund-raising resources. But we challenge cities to match our combined criteria qualifications. Who else possesses our driving "X-factors": vision, passion, hard work, public support, and results?

This isn't just about preserving local history. It's North Carolina history. We are proud Tar Heels. What would Wilmington gain? Vast community pride, exposure to a huge national WWII audience, and WWII tourism destination promotion.

Of course, add the crown: Since 1961, our beloved Battleship North Carolina.

Wilmington encourages nationwide WWII history preservation, and welcomes other cities. Let them meet the criteria, organize, and justify as we have. Our coattails are long. Yet, Wilmington deserves to be The First "by act of Congress."

Understand this. Wilmington alone conceived the idea and has led all the groundwork. By 2008, sixty-three years following the war, no one claimed to be "America's WWII City." Wilmington occupied the vacuum and mobilized.

Although Wilmington City Council and New Hanover County Commission proclamations started the designation project, our quest traces to 1998 after I returned home. Preservation-friendly Wilmington had championed its Civil War history, historic district, and museum homes. Meanwhile, officials mostly ignored WWII history and risked losing it. No community leadership emerged.

SUDDENLY WILMINGTON SHIFTED GEARS

Realizing this, in 1998 the Lower Cape Fear Historical Society sponsored an end-of-century tribute to Wilmington's WWII role called Wartime Wilmington Commemoration, 1999. Throughout SENC our team executed an eighteen-month schedule of 125 lectures, exhibits, and related events. Following enthusiastic community and media responses, and material uncovered, obviously we needed a permanent education and preservation organization.

Parlaying this success, in 2000 historian Everard Smith and I formed the World War II Wilmington Home Front Heritage Coalition. Operating as a 501(c)(3) non-political, all-volunteer preservation organization, its mission is to identify, preserve, and interpret the rich WWII history of Wilmington and SENC. Our first accomplishment was helping to save, renovate, and restore the Hannah Block Historic USO/Community Arts Center, our WWII history hub and ultimate blending of history and the arts.

Astounding aptly describes our area accomplishments which actually started earnestly twenty years ago, continually spearheaded by volunteers working with governments and organizations. Perhaps Wilmington trails cities posting larger wartime production numbers, or utilizing paid staff and fund-raising resources. But we challenge cities to match our combined criteria qualifications. Who else possesses our driving "X-factors": vision, passion, hard work, public support, and results?

This isn't just about preserving local history. It's North Carolina history. We are proud Tar Heels. What would Wilmington gain? Vast community pride, exposure to a huge national WWII audience, and WWII tourism destination promotion.

Of course, add the crown: Since 1961, our beloved Battleship North Carolina.

Wilmington encourages nationwide WWII history preservation, and welcomes other cities. Let them meet the criteria, organize, and justify as we have. Our coattails are long. Yet, Wilmington deserves to be the first "by act of Congress."

Understand this. Wilmington alone conceived the idea and has led all the groundwork.

By 2008, sixty-three years following the war, no one claimed to be "America's WWII City." Wilmington occupied the vacuum and mobilized.

Although Wilmington City Council and New Hanover County Commission proclamations started the designation project, our quest traces to 1998 after I returned home. Preservation-friendly Wilmington had championed its Civil War history, historic district, and museum homes. Meanwhile, officials mostly ignored WWII history and risked losing it. No community leadership emerged.

SOLUTION: CONGRESSIONAL LEGISLATION

Wilmington realized that national recognition required more than self-proclamations and sought our congressional delegation's assistance.

The relationship began with a 2008 request to Senator Elizabeth Dole which went nowhere. Her successor, Senator Kay Hagen, did little. But, our Congressman McIntyre wholeheartedly participated. In 2010-11, McIntyre and I contacted national organizations including the National Trust for Historic Preservation; National USO; National Battle Monuments Commission; Smithsonian Institution; and National WWII Memorial organizers Senator Bob Dole and Tom Hanks. Several responded with: Swell idea, you probably deserve it, but we lack responsibility or authority.

McIntyre and I concurred: The president has the authority. So, we worked the legislative process with, and testified before, the House Veterans Affairs Committee on the original bill. McIntyre's 2013 bill passed the House. An identical one from Rouzer, his successor, passed in 2016. Both lapsed in the Senate. McIntyre's dedication and leadership infused our effort. Rouzer enthusiastically continued in that role.

Senators Richard Burr and Thom Tillis also introduced bills since 2010, trying to attach them to veterans affairs and related bills, but received no traction. Envious states opposed: "Why Wilmington and not us?" and thwarted any legislation. Regarding Burr's bill, the VA committee chairman wrote me stating, good record, nice going, maybe you guys earned it. He pursued no action.

Ideally, our bills are neither political nor partisan, nor request funds. But, our senators did not foresee Majority Leader Harry Reid's minutiae or colleagues' bipartisan pettiness, namely: Hawaii, Louisiana, Washington State, and the thorn Utah senator. Nonsensical. Without the legislation, there's no designation program. No law, no cities will participate.

Daily I advocate for this project. All along, Wilmington mayors, City Council and staff; County Commissioners; community organizations; and two governors and state officials have provided support. Still, you'd think that introducing a benign measure like history preservation, which nevertheless must navigate archaic wickets managed by more strategic-issues oriented individuals, would be easier.

Burr, Tillis, and Rouzer are committed to the project. No doubting that. I won't give up. Working together we are finding a solution. There's no alternative, or American WWII history could return to that vacuum.

When Congress passes the legislation, the president should sign it into law on the battleship. Friends, now wouldn't that be Something.

—o—

By early 2019, because of petty two-year opposition by Utah's Senator Mike Lee, who held up action, Tillis and Rouzer were obligated to remove "Wilmington as the first" from their measure to get it through. (He likened it to an "earmark," outlawed by the Senate years ago.) The negotiated consequence gave designation authority to the Interior secretary after the president signed it

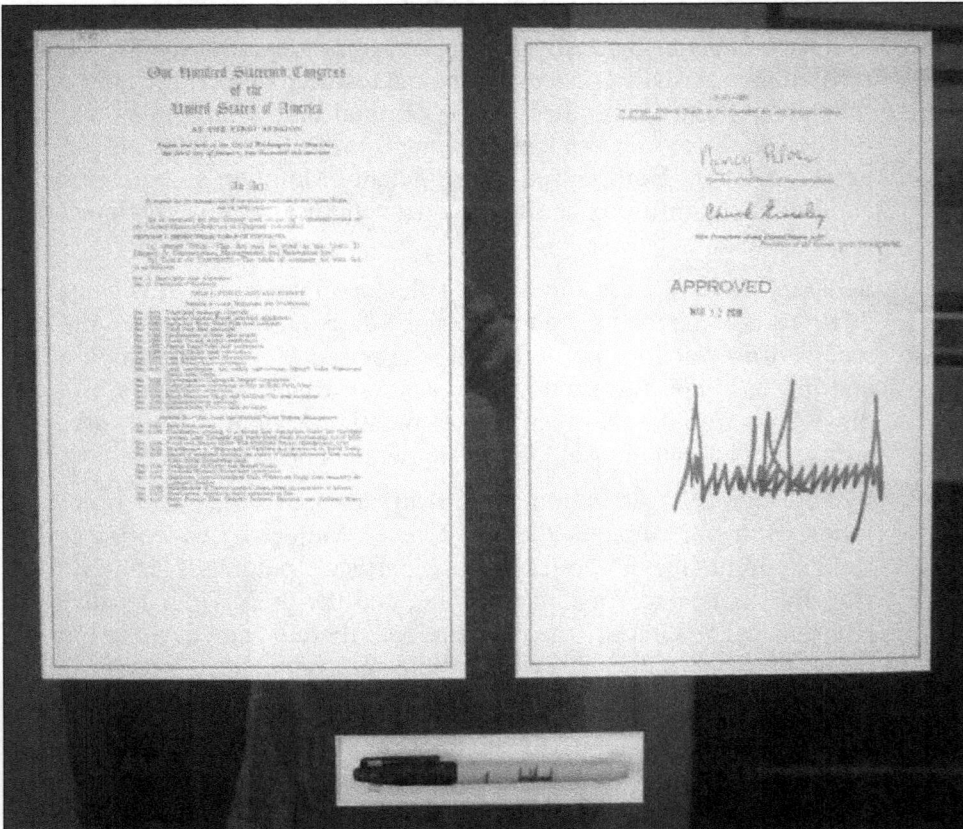

This is a 'red line' replica of the first and last pages of Senate Bill 47, signed by President Donald Trump.

Impact of Being the First "American WWII Heritage City"

Destination Tourism: People Will Come Here to See WWII Connection

State and City Pride

Increased Battleship Visitation

Boost Local Economy

Enhanced Cultural Appeal and Reputation

Exposure to Global WWII History Community

Preservation of North Carolina History

Our No. 1 WWII Heritage Attraction

Info on How We Exceed Law's Criteria: *www.wilburjones.com*

This slide, about preservation of the Battleship North Carolina and its impact on the city and state, was part of my presentation about why Wilmington should be the first World War II City.

into law. Thus our original goal of the president as the authority we sought was not achieved. However, we made it to the goal line with a first down.

Obtaining designation is not just for Wilbur. What do I get out of it? Only the love and dedication I have for recognition of my hometown, our accomplishments, and tribute to our WWII veterans and home front workers. Disregarding all the actions and obstacles to date, I'm confident North Carolina will get this distinction.

The history of our state, county, and city deserves this recognition. Readers and friends, I will never give up. But I'm still searching for someone to take over from me as the years speed by.

AN UPDATE, JANUARY 15, 2020

The National Park Service, charged by the secretary of the Interior with handling the Section 9007 WWII Heritage Cities program, informed Congressman Rouzer of the following: The NPS is preparing procedures to comply with the law; establishing the two selection criteria; an application process for interested cities; and a timeline of early Fall 2020 for the designations.

Wilmington must apply. We patiently await. By the time this memoir is published, our WWII Heritage City project will be in its thirteenth year.

Check my website (www.wilburjones.com) for updates on this and other preservation news.

Chapter 12

Moonlighting as a Professional Umpire and Referee, and Leading Global World War II Battlefield Tours

Hey Blue, you're a one-eyed cyclops! That was brutal! You need a wheelchair. Call 'em both ways!" (Blue, the jargon noting an umpire's shirt.) Was this loudly shouted by a local pastor, or was it a county commissioner whose son I just called out on strikes? Soft and sweet compared to . . . can't tell you. My publisher's obscenity rules. I heard much, much worse over the years. At least this guy credited me for being able to see.

Officiating baseball and basketball is an extremely tough profession. Few are those who venture forth into it, especially professionally, and as their only income source. While contemplating and exploring what it was all about, no one said to me at the outset: Hey, come on in, you'll enjoy the fresh air and exercise and meeting lots of new people who come to see you perform. Sure, fame and fortune. You make a little money, and it'll be fun away from wife and kids.

Then, why do guys like me get mixed up in this? What's the appeal? Daredevil challenges and proving toughness and decisiveness answers the first. Give me something that ninety-nine percent of everybody else can't or won't do. Somebody has to bring law and order to the game and set and maintain its high standards or else it won't be played. Another form of local leadership.

All my life I've lived by law and order and doctrine and discipline and one's self assuredness. I've never shied away from making decisions, and that's what officiating is all about. Thus for me it appeared natural. Perhaps that's why those sports attracted lots of armed forces officers who were my associates in the National Capital region.

But, was I still crazy to do it? Every long march takes its first step. Mine germinated in 1973, son David's first Little League season, Hollin Hall Elementary ball field. Umpires didn't show up for the game. Of course, I was pressed from the sidelines kicking and screaming out to stand behind the pitcher's mound. The coaches said, call 'em from here, just as you see 'em. Use your fingers for balls, strikes, outs, innings, and of course, you must remember the score. And, no favoring David's team.

My part-time career as an athletic official began with my involvement in youth teams at Fort Hunt, Virginia. Here, in 1975, I'm with son David's team.

How careers are born. I can say it went uphill from there, and soon our Fort Hunt Youth Athletic Association (FHYAA) was blessed with my volunteer Blue and Grey and Striped Shirt baseball and basketball uniform talents for many seasons. I'd say I succeeded. What a way to moonlight for recreation and a few extra beer bucks, a pleasurable and satisfying experience, and it kept me in shape.

Getting back to the opening paragraph, once inside the club, programming one's mind to tune out what is directed at the official during a game—from coach, player, or fan, and resist the urge to respond, is necessary for success. "Rabbit ears"—listening—creates ridicule and failure. Which is why it takes a Whole Lot to insult me to my face. Burn, maybe, but brush it off and keep moving. No doubt many years in the occasional ugliness of staff politics helped lay the foundation.

In early 1980's, while stationed at the Pentagon, I began pursuing a moonlight career as a professional baseball umpire and basketball referee. I joined the Northern Virginia Baseball Umpires Association, (Virginia) Commonwealth Basketball Officials Association, went through their training, achieved certification, and started calling high school baseball and basketball games.

For ten years around Washington I umpired baseball games at the NCAA (National Collegiate Athletic Association) Division I, high school varsity (one state championship game), men's semi-pro leagues, American Legion, and Little League programs. Games included two Little League fifteen-year old

Senior Division World Series. I accepted pay, such as it was, for all the above except Little League.

I retired without serious injuries but broke and dislocated several fingers working the plate because I positioned myself over the catcher's shoulder. Once a high school pitcher's fastball to a right handed batter was so inside it found its way into the bend between my forearm and biceps. Thud, stayed there. Yes, I called it a dead ball, removed it from a stinging arm, and threw it back. You don't want to read about the batted balls that hit the plate and conveniently bounced back at my plastic athletic cup. Bells rang. I liked getting close to the play.

WORKING UP THE LADDER IN NEIGHBORHOOD LITTLE LEAGUE

I learned early that officiating any sport can be "hazardous duty." If it's in one's own community, double the likelihood. *Ours was the Fort Hunt section of South Alexandria, next door to historic Mount Vernon, an upper-upper middle class consisting of many government officials, armed forces officers, and professionals.

In games of children, conscientious parents and coaches often reacted too seriously to a decision made counter to their interests. If I'm outside of the neighborhood, maybe a different story. These reactions could engender immature anti-social behavior levied against the official—me or one of my crew—while supermarket shopping, or by an angry phone call. For a father who's endured a bad office day his kid's baseball and basketball participation that evening provides open fora for taking it out on the official. If that guy is a neighbor, so what; I'm supposed to handle it.

My principal job was as the thankless chief umpire and chief basketball official. This full-time volunteer job meant recruiting, training, motivating, educating, stroking, interceding in their game problems, and continuous game assignments. That's what Sunday nights seemed to be for, the house phone constantly humming.

Decisive umpiring at an American Legion baseball game in Alexandria, Virginia in the early 1990s.

Nevertheless, experience as a professional let me develop another "leather ass" and block it. Usually, anyway. Not fun if these neighbors pressed the issue with threats about my service to the community. This essay doesn't chronicle my experiences alone, but also the other volunteer officials whose "misgivings" I'd hear about because I ran the program. If you're asking, no, the complainers wouldn't volunteer to help umpire or officiate. Having written this, before I paint a picture of sub-development mayhem and civil unrest, these are the extremes. Games were won and lost because of the teams, not the officials. In the end, neighbors still spoke, barbequed and drank wine together, and kept up with each other's careers, the times one remembered.

In the FHYAA Little League, I earned my advance through Virginia State and Southeastern US Regionals to two Senior League (fifteen-year-olds division) World Series in Gary, IN. I worked two championship games at first base and at the plate won by Curacao, formerly of the Netherlands Antilles. After a few years, and many games, the kids, coaches, and parents grew up and came to appreciate and value my experience, judgment, and dedicated organizational work. Neighbors on the whole appreciated the work of those who planned and supervised the youth activities and by and large thanked us. Carroll made it easier by spending so much volunteer

I umpired in the Little League World Series, Senior Division, held in Gary, Indiana, in 1983 and 1985.

time as a team mother, snack bar honcho, sponsor, and jackie-of-all-trades. So, the potential "horror stories" painted herein are illustrative only and do not represent the long-term productive community youth sports engendered.

Sons David and Andrew don't let a week go by without referring to those days, their friends, their teams, their coaches, or many calls I made. This is very healthy. I remember fondly so many kids whose games I officiated, especially those who were friends, teammates, and classmates of my sons David and Andrew, who played all three youth sports. David played Fort Hunt High freshman baseball and jayvee basketball, and Andrew played all three sports then concentrated on football as an offensive lineman on the Bishop Ireton Catholic High School and Fort Hunt varsities. Carroll and I saw at least ten-thousand of their games over those years, it seemed. She was the proud, quintessential Team Mother, and bless her heart, she never got on the officials (that I knew of).

In sum, the principal benefit I gained from youth sports was the positive impact I had on the kids and their development. What could matter more?

THE SERIOUS COLLEGE GAME

My college baseball games were concentrated in the Northern Virginia and District of Columbia areas, sometimes to Baltimore, at Georgetown, Howard, George Mason, Catholic, and American Universities. I memorized the locations of every 7-Eleven store and invariably stopped for a Coke Slurpee to refresh en route home. My colleagues elected me president of the professional Northern Virginia Baseball Umpires Association, a true honor in this "foxhole-brotherhood society." Seems like leadership roles drew me to these men, a duke's mixture of truck drivers, government bureaucrats, store owners, retirees, and officers. I retired after the 1991 season, realized I left too early, and returned to umpire my final season in 1993.

At the Pentagon (1980-84) and Defense Systems Management College/Defense Acquisition University (1984-96), I often took annual leave to depart work early for afternoon baseball games, sometimes changing into my umpire uniform in my office. Otherwise, umpires had no locker room accommodations requiring changing in the front seat of my car. I got used to it but it was a squeeze. Also, because the ball fields lacked toilet facilities available to umpires, I soon developed a procedure of (1) restricting my liquids prior to a game, (2) ate carbohydrates/stomach fillers to absorb any liquid, and (3) peed into a cup from the front seat.

We umps learned to stick together. Here, youth baseball, Virginia, 1990.

Umpires and basketball officials worked as a pair, with obligation to phone prior to a game to ensure the other would be there. Also, we decided who would work the plate since that requires the umpire to don chest protector, shin guards, protective cup, and steel-toe shoes. I stayed in shape to officiate. Most of my colleagues reversed this doctrine.

To ameliorate summer sweltering and steamy baseball games, I took a large thermos of water and placed it by the fence so I wouldn't have to use a team's water supply. Summer doubleheaders found me one game on the bases

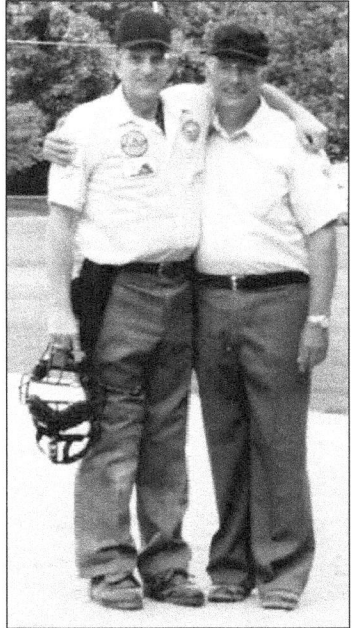

and the other at the plate. I preferred the plate, my better position. There I called a number of high school and American Legion no-hitters behind the plate, including two by Pete Schourek, the National League Cy Young runnerup in 1995 with Cincinnati, and an eleven year veteran, and one by Bill Pulsifer, who later pitched for the Mets. Get the ball around the plate, son, and I'll work with you.

Behind the plate, my preferred umpiring position, at a Virginia American Legion state tournament game, 1992.

Hah. I found this checking on Pete—veiled recognition of us umpires in his early years, as reported in Northern Virginia's *Connection Newspapers* on August 7, 2012. "Things were different on the mound in the big leagues, but as much as things changed for Schourek, the concepts and rules of pitching—though at a higher level—remained the same. Back in high school, obviously, throwing as well as I did I was able to get away with a lot more pitches in the middle of strike zone," said Schourek. "As you get older and the opposition gets better and better, it's almost like you have to throw slower to make sure you are out of the middle of the plate. That was harder for me because I always wanted to throw as hard as I could, as long as I could.

"And that's exactly what Schourek did in his high school days, leading Marshall to back-to-back Northern Region championships and to two state finals appearances before graduating in 1987." I worked one of his state championship games. Ah, Pete, you were the smoothest lefthander I ever called. Where are you now? You owe me at least a six-pack.

A number of my players played major league ball, my favorite being Jim McNamara who caught for the Giants for two years. We joshed back and forth when I worked his games. My favorite game for years was the July 4th Legion all-star festival game. Learning how to deal with head coaches was a constant challenge. Their personalities and attitudes generally ran from amiable to downright agitating. Deflecting their amateurish attempts to intimidate or harass were the result of professional maturing, and resistance to sucking up to them. Once around the circuit, it got easier.

RISING THROUGH VARSITY AND COLLEGE BASKETBALL

In basketball, I rose through girls high school varsity, then boys varsity, sometimes working back-to-back jayvee and varsity games as needed. Mia

Hamm, later all-world-everything American soccer star, of Lake Braddock High, was my favorite basketball player. For recreational mens league games, referees (always two at each level—we learned the NCAA three-man scheme as I was retiring) usually worked multiple games, two on a week night and perhaps three back-to-back on Sundays. To train for the profession, I twice attended summer officiating camps working with college-rated officials and some of the nation's top high school players.

Working my way up from neighborhood youth leagues, I was soon officiating basketball at the high school level, as here in the 1990s, and college.

My most memorable Sunday was working three games at Lee High School on the day of President Reagan's second inauguration in January 1985, bitter cold, icy, with snow. For youth and mens league games, we dressed at home. For college or high school games, the schools provided a changing area. I often worked girls high school games with females, with the changing room areas providing minimum privacy—but we ignored whatever it was we were supposed to ignore.

For two seasons in the mid-1980s, in addition to my Northern Virginia work, I also officiated in a Maryland college officials organization, working games in Washington, Baltimore, Eastern Shore, and those areas primarily at the Division II/III level, although I did work a couple of George Mason and American Division I games. Women's basketball was catching fire, and I witnessed it. However, the travel, lousy pay, quality of team play, and inconvenience with my job caused me to quit the women's organization.

Refereeing college basketball, 1990s, at Division III Frostburg State University in western Maryland.

Umpiring and officiating pay was minimal, almost scarcely worth it, considering that the officials assumed all expenses: mileage, uniforms, equipment, organization dues, etc. The best one could do was breaking even, but time spent couldn't be recovered. Pay for a high school game was about $30, recreation games about $15, and FHYAA games for free. Some colleagues over-worked trying to make money. Good for them.

FAMILY PLAYS THE NEIGHBORHOOD SPORTS

My association with the FHYAA besides with my sons was deep and intense. Youth sports thrived—some would say dominated—in the Fort Hunt area near Mount Vernon. Parents, managers, coaches, the board members all took it seriously, maybe way too seriously because it could interfere with personal, family, and community relationships. For years I served on the FHYAA board and endured amateurish neighborhood politics. Yet still, we maintained a model Little League field and ran a first-class youth organization which endures today.

If that wasn't enough, I tried being the head coach of two baseball teams and two basketball teams. Definitely not my strong suit. None had decent won-lost records. My fault. I knew each sport front-wards and backwards, but . . . couldn't teach the hit-and-run, or man-to-man defense I suppose. Also, some of my players who I had to "draft" just weren't worth a darn. My sons endured frequent hitting, fielding, and rebounding practices and skull sessions, but we aimed to bond as dads did in those days. Gave us hours together in addition to my officiating in a sports-crazy household, as Carroll always politely complained. In sum, all those hours and days, my countless attention to sons and neighborhood kids, were my contribution to preventing juvenile delinquency. Yep.

The year I head-coached Andrew's Yankees Little League team, 1976, found me totally occupied with President Gerald Ford. Should never have taken the coaching position, but the challenge to head a team was extremely competitive and political among neighborhood fathers that I took the team because it was "my

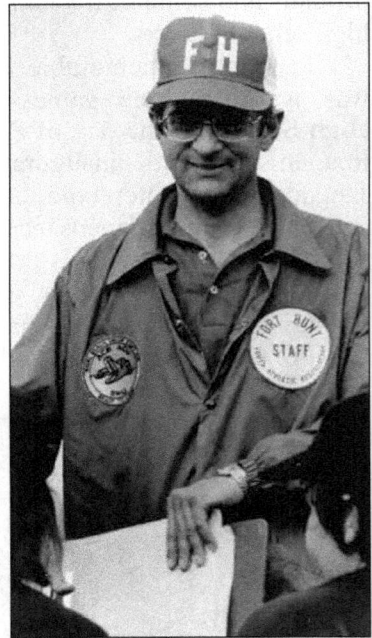

A big wheel in Fort Hunt youth athletics, focused on my sons' teams at first.

turn," a prize. But, I had to back off and turn the team over to another person who was even worse as a coach than I.

Where was wife and mother Carroll during all of this? She totally supported my involvement in youth sports, partly because it was a family affair. She drove to games all over the county, bringing me a sandwich and water for between recreational games. I suppose she was often bored as heck but came anyway, bringing granddaughter Carrie, whom we were raising. Couple of funny instances. Carrie, ages between three to eight, would stand behind the home plate backstop and speak to me: "Pop Pop hello, Pop Pop, hello." Pretty soon the loudmouth fans near her on the losing end, mocked her and shouted out to "Pop Pop. Get in the game, Pop Pop!" Man alive. Carroll would then corral her with, *hush, sweetheart, shhhh.*

Thus the Joneses were a family of dedicated jocks (a.k.a., nuts), she always said, while heading out for another (10,000th?) game. We pushed the boys, shipping them to summer basketball camps in the Poconos and Chapel Hill for Coach Dean Smith's. When Carrie began playing basketball and softball at Queen of Apostles Catholic School in Alexandria, and continued in Wilmington at Hoggard High School, my job was just parent-fan-scorekeeper-timer. She appreciated that, but we worked together on shooting and hitting and I sent her to Carolina Coach Sylvia Hatchell's summer camp, among others. She played jayvee basketball and varsity softball at Hoggard, the latter as a starter her senior year in 2002 following membership on the 2001 state championship runner-up team.

HERE COMES 'WILL-BURR'

Nevertheless, serving my community from 1978-93 in helping to build our youth for life was a pleasure. A number of them, particularly Andrew's friends, occasionally stay in touch, and might remember my birthday on Facebook. We share memory laughs. They remember games when I called them out on strikes, or a charging foul that nullified a basket, but we all agree on this one. Dressed to umpire the plate for a Little League game, I walked on to the Darsey Field to start the game. Heard giggles and rumbles from one dugout or another from a bunch of eleven- and twelve-year old hotshots. "Here comes WILL-BURR," a future prison lifer would say. Walking over to the dugout, my stare froze their faces and sat them upright. "Okay, gentlemen, I'm not gonna ask who said that. But I tell you. You can call me by my first name." Whewww, they sighed. Wait. "It's Mister Umpire," I said . . . (Pause) . . . Now let's play ball."

Another fond memory. Between umpiring morning and evening Little League games, I was resting at home when "some kid on a bike" rushed to the front door to tell me that son David had just hit a home run for the White Sox— over the fence, no less—and it won their game. And I wasn't there.

These kids knew I was good, and I'm doggone proud of the positive impact I had on their lives. Law and order on the field and court, but with understanding and empathy. By 1993 I retired from both sports respectively. Mostly pleasant memories. Enjoyed it immensely.

FROM PARIS TO KIRIBATI, AMSTERDAM TO IWO JIMA:
WALKING WHERE WORLD WAR II HISTORY WAS MADE

The opportunity to lead or participate in World War II battlefield tours to Europe, the Mediterranean, and Pacific since 1995 has been another of life's true blessings. Exciting, enriching professionally, mostly enjoyable but at times harrowing. What a privilege to see historical places I might otherwise have missed. To walk on our American battlefields is an honor as I help preserve the history they made.

Before exploring the globe's romantic, alluring, cultural and Third World spots, let's start with the Southeastern North Carolina tours in and around Wilmington. Individuals and groups enlist my services, and off we go by car or bus.

Area sites including the North Carolina Shipbuilding Company; Camp Davis Army anti-aircraft artillery base, and Fort Fisher, its advanced training base; the Hannah Block Historic USO building and mini-museum of the home front; German prisoner of war camps; historic downtown, post office, and stores; New Hanover High School memorial to its two WWII Medal of Honor recipients; wartime housing projects and neighborhoods; and the Battleship North Carolina. Organizing and conducting these tours has been another way for me to preserve area WWII history.

On a logistically challenging 1999 tour of remote Pelilieu I met local islanders and the daughter of wartime Japanese Prime Minister Hideki Tojo, right.

Foreign tour-leading days are over, but memories hold fast. I've worked for three tour companies, primarily for Valor Tours in California, but also two ship voyages on the RMS *Queen Mary 2* and SS *Clipper Adventurer*. I was paid to lead some, a pittance for the pre-trip and on-site work required, but expenses were always covered. The opportunity mattered.

Tour group sizes ranged from five (Invasion of Southern France) to thirty-five (Peleliu). The latter created a huge logistics problem moving them from the West Coast on the same flights to terribly remote Koror, and then keeping track of them in the Palau Islands. In Europe, once onsite, we traveled by over-the-road coach or van. In Europe we engaged a Dutch travel company's Gerrit Jansen, the Continent's Best Driver by far. He never met a Medieval French village's narrow streets he couldn't navigate. Whew, some close calls, especially when backing downhill, but we made it without a scratch. Dear Gerrit, what would I have done without you on those ten tours?

TO MY PASSENGERS (GOD BLESS THEM): PLEASE HEAR ME

Except for the Iwo Jima tours with many WWII veterans, groups usually had one or two veterans and escorts. We tried meeting preferences such as finding their foxhole in the Ardennes Forest. No kidding. We'd go out of the scheduled way to search just to see that a barn went up there forty-five years ago. Most passengers were veterans' family members and dedicated WWII history buffs.

Generally passengers followed instructions for their own good as well as the group's. Always I asked them: please hear what I'm saying about where we are. Often the Tour Butthole(s) came forth right away, demanding, blaming— unhappy, usually unsatisfied, and making their point: "I'm going to report this to the tour company when I get home." Go ahead, but the thing is, your trip fee doesn't include all attractions, and this one at General Eisenhower's Reims headquarters costs just two euros. No use. Trouble was, the weak-kneed owner might side with the complainer before hearing the full story. Plus, she needed repeat passengers and tour leaders were dispensable.

Met some very nice people along the way, foremost George and Judy Cressman of Georgia, who toured with me at least five times in Europe. George, a world-class amateur WWII historian, and I have become friends and colleagues. He now leads tours for Valor. Wilmington couples Smitty and Emma Jewell, and Bill and Golden Humphrey, the boys my lifelong friends, traveled with me frequently in Europe sharing grand experiences, but not beer and wine. They wouldn't touch it.

Want to hear the bane of my existence? The people who, after the bus stopped, would quickly wander off without telling anybody, not knowing the lay of the land (didn't

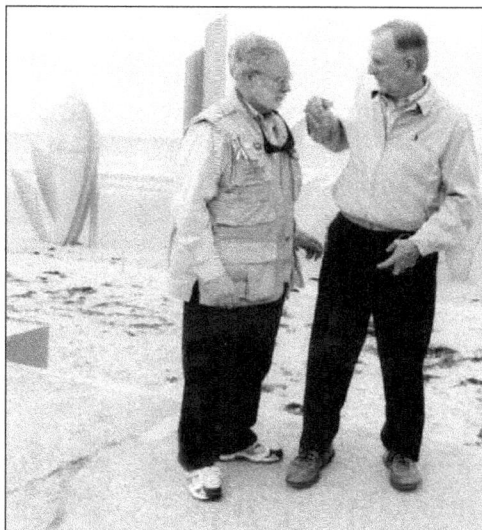

George Cressman was a favorite, knowledgeable tour client. Here, we are standing on Omaha Beach during a D-Day tour of Normandy in 2011.

hear me); and the photographer who had to shoot everything and got in the way of others shooting the same subject. Or, the woman who waited and waited in the gift shop line forever, or in the toilet, delaying our departure. Oooh. Polite admonishments might work. Restraint tested. Some trips had the guy who never changed clothes during the eight or ten days. No kidding. Just awful. At least the odor misery inflicted all equally, and passengers avoided him at mealtimes.

Buddy System, Counting Heads, and Erroneous Guides

Sometimes we instituted the buddy system, but couples traveling together figured it didn't apply and went out of sight. Before leaving a site, I always counted heads to ensure everybody was back. This worked except for once, exiting the parking lot at the Dachau, Germany, concentration camp. Running late, I glanced down the aisle and told Gerrit to shove off. My mistake. Once outside the lot, the "buddy" of our young, adventuresome ESPN writer, John Lukacs, said, wait! John's not here. Errrkk!!! went the brakes and we turned around. I walked the quarter mile back to the "*Arbeit Macht Frei*" gate to find him sauntering forth. Without a watch, he left his cell phone in the bus. So, he lost track of the departure time.

Infamous 'Work Makes You Free' sign at Nazis' Dachau concentration camp near Munich, 2011

Incidents like this subtracted months from my life, but he apologized and bought me a Loewenbrau that evening.

Local guides hired for half-day tours, or, like the Battle of the Bulge three-day outing in Belgium, generally were knowledgeable, spoke decent English, and were personable. On one Bulge trip, however, the guide, a Scotsman totally full of himself promoting a book he had just written, was giving out bum dope, as the Navy called it. Erroneous info. Our people were hearing the wrong stuff, and so on several occasions I politely corrected him publicly. After all, it was My Tour Group and they paid for the facts. For instance, when he said the 101st Airborne Division did not occupy the southern defense line of Bastogne, when I knew its combat engineer battalion damned well did. Oh boy. At our next stop he angrily told me never to do that again and actually threatened me physically. I set him straight and eventually he calmed down, and we drank Belgian beer together, but he festered anyway. I wanted our people to get their money's worth. Yes, it did considerably lighten the tip I customarily gave each guide at the end. Later I heard he complained "officially" about the tip, and posted a nasty note online about me, daring me not to return to Belgium. You see, tour leading is a contact sport.

The best guide I ever had escorted my group on a Tour of Nazi Munich. We visited many of the places where the movement began, flourished, and touched, including the Munich University where Hans and Sophie Scholl led the 1943 White Rose Movement against the Nazis, and Hitler's office where in 1938 he coerced the French and British into the Munich Pact—"peace in our time."

Airline flights have lost or delayed your baggage, right? En route to your holiday destination perhaps? Here's my Tour Horror Story. May 2007. I signed on as a historian/ lecturer and shore tour leader for the WWII Italian Campaign tour conducted from the small cruise ship, SS *Clipper Adventurer*. About 85 passengers, great group, most associated with the National WWII Museum. The 10-day tour began in Malta with stops in Sicily, Sorrento, Gaeta, and Civitavecchia. Malta then was reachable only by a couple of daily Air Malta flights direct from the two London airports. Malta has an airline? Gonna be some ride.

My very tight schedule showed departing from Heathrow; so that's from where my baggage was tagged. I did keep my attache case with notes, speeches, PowerPoints, etc. Flight postponed. I simply had to get to the ship before it sailed. Air Malta booked me on the next flight from Gatwick which, of course, meant hauling butt over there. Just made the flight, last seat available, landed at midnight in Malta. No baggage. Inquiry after an hour found it in Frankfurt, Germany. OmG—please dispatch it to Malta ASAP/Emergency, c/o of SS *Clipper Adventurer* at Pier xxx.

After a short night's sleep,

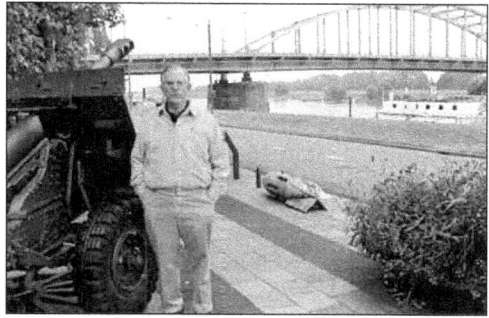

2010 at Arnhem, Netherlands, the Rhine 'bridge too far' of Operation Market Garden, the failed 1944 Allied airborne attempt to leapfrog into Germany.

Site of 'The Eagle's Nest' Adolf Hitler's demolished Alpine retreat at Obersalzburg, Germany, 2011.

Burgundy, memorial to the French Resistance, 2009.

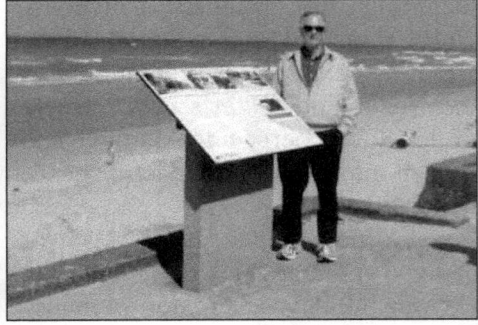

A preserved Sherman tank in Luxembourg during a 2011 tour of sites from 1944-45 Battle of the Bulge.

On Dog Green Beach, part of Omaha Beach, Normandy, remembered in 'Saving Private Ryan.'

without essentials or change of clothes, I found a slew of small shops nearby. Purchased a large shirt, shorts, and socks plus underwear. Man, they were Mediterranean-style chokers, form-fitting, but clean. I had to board by 4:00 p.m. Our ship was to depart Valletta that day at 7:00. Took a 10-mile bus ride to Valletta, did a little sightseeing, and boarded. No baggage yet. The tour director, aware of my predicament, said the crew could loan me clothes until.... Near panicking, I sweated, then sweated more as 7:00 drew closer. Damned Air Malta. Then fifteen minutes before we shoved off, the baggage arrived. Everyone cheered. I think they raised their glasses. I was a mess, for I was on the after-dinner program. First thing was to change clothes and brush my teeth. Yep. After the tour I visited Naples for three days to re-live where Carroll and I met—it had been 47 years since we left.

In Nettuno, Italy American cemetery I found the grave of Wilmington's Captain Henry Bragaw, killed in 1944 Cassino campaign.

HOLDING THEIR HANDS, FINDING THEIR TOILETS

My pre-trip routine differed from other tour leaders. Thinking it would enhance bonding, I telephoned each passenger to discuss the itinerary, answer questions, and ask for their preferences. This mutually advantaged both of us until they had something to complain about: hate hotel room douvet, no breakfast omelets, the driver smokes too much, and on. On every stop the first person off the coach was me, looking for direction signposts, coach parking, and toilets. Ah, toilets. After a while I knew pretty much where they were all over Normandy and other familiar stops. Then I'd announce their location. Arriving at the hotel, I'd head for the desk to check-in everyone, handing out room keys. Generally, the passengers easily fit into this routine.

At day's end, we descended upon the closest bar. Over the years French Kronenbourg's 1664 beer grew as my European favorite. I can drink it here by special order. The most popular, of course, Heineken's, was universal. Europe teems with great

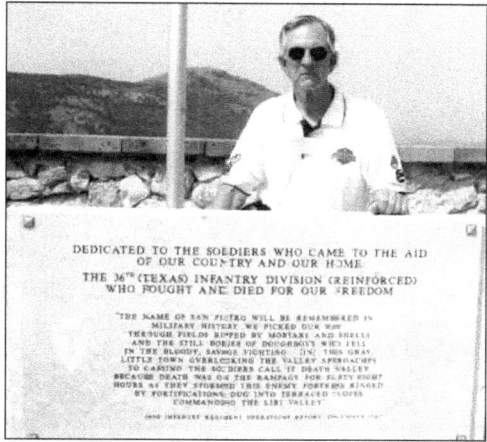

2017 tour of Italy included San Pietro, site of battle immortalized in 1945 John Huston documentary.

beers, Belgium in particular, but not always available throughout Europe. Local white or red wines rounded out dinner. For lunch while we were on the move, rather than sit down and order at a restaurant, costing sightseeing time, they

agreed to hitting a small supermarket, boulangerie, or pastisserie, for a baguette sandwich, cheese, water and wine to consume on board. Away we went. Love baguettes! Baguettes! The European staff of life.

As the group's Mother Hen, I was supposed to know everything, including what American infantry company occupied that farm house over there sixty-five years ago. Men comprised virtually all of the history buffs. Conversations with them over drinks or dinner ended up pleasurable even after random attempts to upstage the leader or tour's historian. A passenger had come to go where their relative had fought. We might have time to stroll, sightsee, take photos, enjoy the evening in an outdoor café. European life at its finest.

2010: at a cafe in Bénouville, France, site of Pegasus Bridge, taken by British airborne troops on D-Day.

Over Iwo Jima's bleak volcanic landscape, just as forbidding today as when US Marines landed in 1945, looms Mount Surbachi, site of famous flag raising. This picture is from a 1998 Pacific tour.

THE PACIFIC BATTLEFIELDS—NO PARIS, NO ROME

Trips to Marine Corps Pacific island battlefields obviously were more arduous than to European battlefields, without the accompanied Western sightseeing and cultural attractions. For example, to get to Iwo Jima, which the Japanese reclaimed in the 1970's, we based out of Saipan in the Northern Marianas for the 1995 fiftieth anniversary visit, and Okinawa for the 1998 one. Lots of long flights.

Iwo, without lodging or messing accommodations, was administered by the Japanese Self Defense Force. They allowed one annual February tour visit on the anniversary month. Indispensable US Marines from Okinawa pre-positioned vehicles and logistics. We flew in early in the morning, had organized or individual outings, gathered for a ceremony, trucked up to the summit of Mount Suribachi, ate box lunches, got back on our commercial aircraft, and departed. Spent about seven hours on the island, but long enough to get familiar. I also conducted informal research for the book *Gyrene: The World War II United States Marine*, that the Marine Corps had given me a grant to begin writing.

So much to experience. Crunching through the black volcanic ash invasion beaches, sweating through the command and hospital caves, climbing over pulverized concrete pillboxes, carefully stepping over steaming sulphuric rocks, and meeting the widow of Japanese island commander, General Tadamichi Kuribayashi, who committed suicide.

I brought home bags of volcanic black sand, shell casings, and bits of Japanese uniforms. I'm certain I found the pillbox on Iwo's Red Beach whose round exploded on the after bridge of my father-in-law's destroyer, the USS *Leutze* he commanded, two days before the landing, while covering underwater demolition units. He was severely wounded in the blast and taken out of action. He recovered three years later but remained partially paralyzed.

The reunion group of veterans of Company F, 2nd Battalion, 25th Marines (F/2/25), 4th Marine Division, had made me an honorary member. I walked on three of their invasion beaches, Saipan, Tinian, and Iwo with pride and respect. We developed a close relationship over three reunions, and I was so sad when they could no longer continue in the mid-2000's. I dedicated *Gyrene* to them.

Seeing Tinian, too, was special. The airfield from which the B-29 bombers "Enola Gay" and "Bock's Car," each loaded with an atomic weapon, made their round trip to Hiroshima and Nagasaki in August 1945. The islands all had a constant: entrenched Japanese defenders against Marines and soldiers landing with rifles and no body armor. One felt the horror, the noise, the sheer courage and determination of our boys, envisioned the blood. Didn't have to close the eyes. Near Tinian's Ju;ly 1944 White Beach we came upon a rusted but recognizable LVT

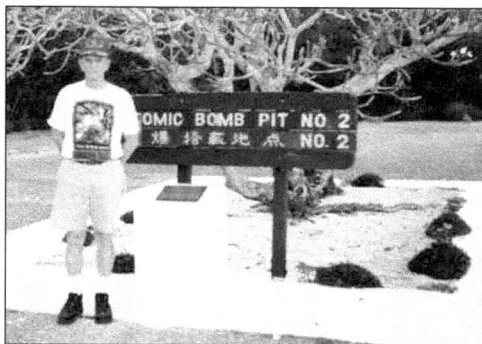

At a former US bomber base on Tinian are the sites where atomic bombs were loaded for final attacks on Japan that ended World War II. I visited in 1995.

amphibious assault tractor in the jungle, recently uncovered by natives. We found names of the operator and gunner stenciled inside and reported it to military authorities who told us not to say anything yet: the Marine Corps was trying to locate their descendants.

PELELIU AND TARAWA, ALONG THE EQUATOR
AND WAY OFF THE BEATEN PATH

These are isolated locations the average traveler would never visit. It's so easy for me to write more stories about Luxembourg, The Netherlands, Provence, and Italy. Readers have been there, especially Normandy. So, I'm concentrating on places like Iwo, Peleliu, and Tarawa which are barely visited. Here's an intro.

In 1999 Koror, capital of the Palau Islands in the Carolines, opened up for scuba diving tourists, but nothing else. Lovely, but so are hundreds of other Pacific islands and also extremely hot and sticky. But, the exceedingly remote Palau island of Peleliu in September 1944 saw some of the Marines' bloodiest Pacific action. To get there, just north of the Equator, we took boats from our Koror hotel across gorgeous shallow lagoons through some of the world's finest diving areas and submerged Japanese aircraft to get to this Less-

Than-Third-World (LTTW) island, which just began constructing power poles and had minimum running water. Battlefield relics dotted Peleliu and its caves and impassible mangrove swamps: human bones, unexploded shells, helmets, weapons, crashed aircraft, amphibious tractors, everywhere.

But the trip home turned out to be the most memorable portion. Six flights from Koror via Guam and Honolulu to Los Angeles, Houston, Atlanta, then Washington Dulles to my car. Ninety-two hours to get home, from LA eastward and then driving down I-95's frequent detours, everything was knocked crazy because of the massive Hurricane Floyd and its flooding rains. On Koror we saw it coming via CNN, and I telephoned Carroll from there to discuss her plans for leaving or not leaving Wilmington. She stayed. Ninety-two hours until I saw the damage at home.

THE BATTLE OF TARAWA, AND ONE OF
THE MOST REMARKABLE PERSONS I'VE MET

Visiting Tarawa atoll in 2008 and 2009 I met the sisters of the Sacred Heart convent, including local-history archivist Sister Margaret Sullivan, below.

One of my most challenging travels was leading tours to the Battle of Tarawa anniversaries in November 2008 and 2009 in the Republic of Kiribati, formerly the Gilbert Islands. Its surprise reward allowed me to associate with one of the most remarkable persons I ever met: dear Sister Margaret Sullivan, of the Catholic Order of Our Lady of the Sacred Heart. At least 90-plus now, this marvelous lady served as the spartan convent's (ergo, the island nation's) archivist and historian. An Australian, she devoted her life to the Tarawa Atoll population since her early twenties. We immediately struck a chord. She was exceptionally accommodating and hospitable to our tour group and research. The nuns made us comfortable among the natives, who, while congenial, live in another LTTW with miserable housing and infrastructure and limited functioning water and power. They lacked resources except copra and fishing, and generally appeared non-productive. In 2008 Kiribati's president, Anote Tong, hosted our group at a festive outdoor traditional dinner. We enjoyed a pleasant conversation while his stud-like bodyguard almost hung on his sleeve.

Seeing Tarawa's many technical and library needs, on return home in 2008 I launched a Wilmington Rotary Club project to collect and ship her numerous items: new laptop and software; archival materials; books on WWII Pacific history; DVD's; and administrative items. We raised the money to purchase and ship them to her, the final leg on a US Navy ship making a periodic good-neighbor visit to Tarawa and other depressed Pacific islands. On my 2009 visit, I saw how much difference those items made to the joyful sisters. Two years later by email she made another request for a laptop and associated items. We raised the money and shipped the boxes via DHS, the only international carrier going to Kiribati.

The only way to fly to Tarawa was on two weekly flights from Fiji and return. On one trip we were delayed overnight there because of no flight. If you hear about Kiribati, which straddles both the International Dateline and Equator, it's because the new year starts there annually, and—regarding sea levels rising, that soon it will drown. Many Japanese guns and emplacements and pillboxes remain on Tarawa's Betio Island, where the main battle raged and whose highest land point is about six feet above sea level, some near the water's edge in the same location as 1943. I couldn't reconcile how alarmists could predict the overwhelming waters when nothing near such occurred in sixty-five years. By the way, the stops in Fiji marked my only times ever in the Southern Hemisphere.

BUARIKI, END OF TARAWA, PERHAPS CIVILIZATION

As the Marines drove the Japanese from Betio in November 1943, the retreat headed about fifty miles to the northernmost island in the atoll, Buariki, the remotest of the remote. Conflict ceased there. Twice my groups took a boat across the famous Betio lagoon (you can see Marines wading ashore from landing craft) up to Buariki, where we too waded ashore to meet the local chieftain. I came supplied with gifts of cigarettes, which I was told would be exchanged for his gift. What a fascinating virtually uninhabited spot, barely a structure, no power or water. We took our box lunches and water. The heat and humidity as we traversed the island looking for the final battle site, and Marines' original graves, had to be 100/90 easily. Our boys with packs and weapons handled it. So would we. The chief, barefoot in sarong, accepted our gift and offered their prized pandanus plant leaves used for a variety of reasons from food to weaving and minimal fabrication. To us, a token gesture; to them, a valuable commodity.

There's more here in paradise. Next, a hair-raising but two ultimately fearless twin engine light passenger aircraft lifts to Butaritari Island in Kiribati's

Makin Atoll, an hour northeast of Tarawa, where Marine Raiders attacked the Japanese in 1942, and the US Army invaded victorious in 1943. Views of the glorious azure blue coral atolls passed beneath us. Crowded, scrunched is better, our only ventilation came from a few three-inch diameter forced air vents on the fuselage. Hot as hades. Are we carrying enough bottled water?

Greeted by village elders and school children on 2009 visit to Kiribati's Makin atoll, with Tarawa the sites of hard-won American victories in 1943.

The island's air strip is an irregular graveled, asphalt-like remnant from the war, almost overgrown. A few villagers with nothing else going on welcomed us. The lone truck took us to the main village of stilted tropical huts to a warm waiting reception of villagers who performed dances and smartly paraded to show their appreciation for our visit, and acknowledge America's liberation role.

After exchanging greetings and gifts with the island elders, my group sat down for a Kiribati lunch of coconut milk and pulp, mangoes, bananas, and other fruits before driving to WWII sites. A large Japanese seaplane still rested at the shore line of the Army's invasion beaches, another plane lay in the bush. We visited the crude gravesites where recently the US had removed the bodies of thirteen Marine Raiders killed and buried there in 1942. Very moving. The elders pressed me, as the leader, for financial help from America for their school. I listened but could make no promises. This happened on both trips and was a bit disarming and difficult to handle as guests on their territory.

One more highlight. While in Honolulu for the 2011 seventieth anniversary of Pearl Harbor, a local resident friend of Japanese descent took me to the weekly Saturday brunch of her late father's WWII unit, the all-Nisei 100th Infantry Battalion (the "One-Puka-Puka") at their Waikiki-area clubhouse. What a thrill and privilege to be among these men whose exploits in Italy and France fighting separately or with the famed 445th Regimental Combat Team are legendary. They warmly welcomed

In Honolulu, 2011, I dined in their clubhouse with Japanese-American veterans of WWII's legendary 100th Battalion/445th Regimental Combat Team.

me, and because I had walked on their battlefields, such as the Vosges Mountains site where they helped rescue the 36th Infantry Division's "Lost Battalion," we shared stories. But mostly I made notes silently in awe. Once home, I wrote a piece for the *StarNews* about my rich encounter headlined, "A Legacy Worth Preserving." Appropriately, that's been my life's purpose since long before.

There's not enough paper or ink for me to spend the next few months telling you all sorts of interesting tales about my WWII tour trips. If you want more, just dial 1-800-WILBUR and ask for the tour leader.

WITH LAREAU, TO WONDERFUL EUROPE
FOUR TIMES IN THREE YEARS

But note that within three years beginning in 2014, my sweetheart lady friend Ann LaReau and I made four extensive WWII and cultural business trips to Europe. Twice after visiting France and Italy I've written *StarNews* articles on their wine, cuisine, and culture, geared for novice travelers wishing to learn and experiment. I had a ball researching and writing them and appreciated the flattering reviews. I'm a well-informed, dedicated, and much appreciative enthusiast of French and Italian wines. This adds an important cultural dimension to my small-town Wilmington boy's backdrop.

A highlight visit was being in London for the seventieth anniversary of V-E Day, the end of the war in Europe. This was a big deal over there. For months I worked with the British government to cover the events for the *StarNews*. On May 8, 2015, they put me in the cat-bird seat at the Cenotaph War Memorial press area in Whitehall. My photograph of wreath laying by Prime Minister David Cameron; Prince Andrew, the Duke of York; and Labour Leader Ed Milliband made the newspaper's front page. Cameron's Conservative Party the day before had wiped out Labour at the polls. One of the finest shots I've taken, it emphatically embraces my living room wall.

In June 2017 we sailed on the *Queen Mary 2* transatlantic westbound voyage from Southampton to New York, via Halifax, Nova Scotia. My assignment was to write about why its passengers booked the *QM2*, the world's most famous and glamorous ship. This was my third sailing on her, including the maiden eastbound transatlantic voyage in 2004. An international story emerged: our mid-North Atlantic rescue of a lone stranded yachtsman in his boat disabled by a fierce gale through which we had sailed. Later I told Captain Chris Wells the way he maneuvered the *QM2* for the pickup was the finest piece of seamanship I'd ever seen.

What a wonderful part-time part of my life these trips have been. I could go on and on and on. How much time do you have? Let's get together for a bottle of wine.

Here's my WWII history global travel experiences since 1995:

•Business trip to WWII Italian Campaign and cultural sites in Naples-

Salerno, San Pietro, Anzio-Nettuno/Sicily-Rome American Cemetery and gravesite of Capt. Henry Churchill Bragaw, 36th Infantry Division, killed in action in 1944, Wilmington resident; Cassino-Rapido River; and Rome, Italy; and Portsmouth, Southwick, England. Returned home on RMS *Queen Mary 2*—May-June 2017.

On return, wrote three articles for the Wilmington *StarNews* Media.

• Business trip to WWII and cultural sites in Bordeaux, Acquitane, Dordogne, Rhone, and Provence—May 2016.

On return, wrote articles for *StarNews*.

• Business trip to WWII sites in London, for seventieth anniversary of V-E Day; Normandy and Paris—May 2015.

Filed *StarNews* article from London.

• Business trip to WWII and cultural sites in Amsterdam and western Netherlands; a Rhine River cruise; Germany; and Alsace, Burgundy, and the Rhone River, France—April 2014.

• Tour leader for Pittsburgh, PA, private group to Normandy, France—September 2013

• Historian for Pearl Harbor, Hawaii, tour for the seventieth anniversary of the Japanese attack that launched the United States into World War II. December 2011.

Filed *StarNews* article from Pearl Harbor on December 7; wrote two articles prior and one upon return.

• Tour leader for "Battle of the Bulge to Hitler's Eagle's Nest" tour to WWII and cultural sites in France, Belgium, Luxembourg, and Germany: Paris to Munich -- June 2011.

• Tour leader for WWII and cultural sites and D-Day sixty-seventh anniversary tour to Normandy and Paris—June 2011.

• Tour leader for "Crossing the Rhine: Market Garden to Remagen Bridge"tour to WWII and cultural sites for 1944-45 Rhineland Campaign and sixty-sixth anniversary of airborne Operation Market Garden. Frankfurt to Amsterdam: Germany, Belgium, Netherlands—September 2010.

• Tour leader for "Operation Dragoon: Riviera to the Rhine" tour to WWII and cultural sites in Provence, Rhone River Valley, Alsace, and Vosges Mountains, France and Germany. Invasion of Southern France. Nice to Frankfurt—September 2010

• Tour leader for D-Day sixty-sixth anniversary tour of WWII and cultural sites to Normandy and Paris—June 2010.

• Tour leader for "Battle of the Bulge to Hitler's Eagle's Nest" tour of WWII and cultural sites in France, Belgium, Luxembourg, and Germany. Paris to Munich—June 2010

• Tour leader for tour of WWII sites on Tarawa and Makin Atolls in the Republic of Kiribati (formerly Gilbert Islands) for sixty-sixth anniversary of

Battle of Tarawa, via Fiji. Central Pacific—November 2009.

• Tour leader for "Operation Dragoon: Riviera to the Rhine" tour to WWII and cultural sites in Provence, Rhone River Valley, Alsace, and Vosges Mountains, France and Germany. Sixty-sixth anniversary of invasion of Southern France. Nice to Frankfurt—August 2009

• Tour leader for tour of WWII sites on Tarawa and Makin Atolls in the Republic of Kiribati for sixty-fifth anniversary of Battle of Tarawa, via Fiji. Central Pacific—November 2008

• Tour leader for "Battle of the Bulge to Hitler's Eagle's Nest" tour of WWII and cultural sites in France, Belgium, Luxembourg, and Germany. Paris to Munich—June 2008.

• Historian, on-board lecturer, and shore-group tour leader of the WWII Italian Campaign and cultural sites on board the small cruise ship SS *Clipper Adventurer* to Malta; Sicily; and Italy—May-June 2007.

On return, wrote article for the *StarNews*.

• Historian and lecturer on board the RMS *Queen Mary* 2 eastbound maiden voyage from New York, NY, to Southampton, England – May 2004.

• Tour leader to WWII and cultural sites in London area and Normandy for the 60th Anniversary of D-Day.

Remained in Normandy for 10 days on assignment from the *StarNews* covering Anniversary events. May-June 2004

Filed three articles for the *StarNews* from France.

• Tour leader to Peleliu, Palaus, for fifty-fifth anniversary of Marine Corps Battle of Peleliu. September 1999.

• Assistant tour leader for Battles of Iwo Jima, Bonin Islands, and Okinawa, Ryuku Islands. February 1998.

• Historian, Battle of Iwo Jima for fiftieth anniversary, Bonin Islands; and Saipan and Tinian, Commonwealth of the Northern Marianas. February 1995.

COUNTRIES AND MAJOR ISLANDS VISITED, 1956-2017

North America
    Canada (British Columbia,
      Ontario, Quebec, Nova Scotia)
    Mexico (Baja California)
Africa
    Morocco
Europe
    Austria
    France
    Germany
    Great Britain/United Kingdom
      (England, Wales)

Greece (Crete, Rhodes)
Italy (Sardinia, Sicily)
Luxembourg
Malta
Monaco
The Netherlands
San Marino
Switzerland
Spain (Mallorca)
Middle East
    Lebanon
    Jordan

Syria

Turkey

Far East

China (Hong Kong)

Japan (Honshu, Iwo Jima,
   Kyushu, Okinawa)

Philippines (Leyte, Luzon)

South Korea

Taiwan

Pacific

Commonwealth of the Northern
   Marianas (Saipan, Tinian)

Fiji

Guam

Kiribati (Makin, Tarawa)

Marshall Islands (Kwajalein)

Midway Island

Palaus (Peleliu, Koror)

Wake Island

PLUS, SOME GREAT CITIES OF THE WORLD VISITED

Amsterdam, Athens, Barcelona, Beirut, Bordeaux, Cannes, Cologne, Damascus, Florence, Frankfurt, Genoa, Hiroshima, Hong Kong, Istanbul, Jerusalem, Kyoto, London, Lyon, Manila, Milan, Montreal, Munich, Nagasaki, Naples, Nice, Paris, Quebec, Rabat, Reims, Rome, The Hague, Tokyo, Toronto, Toulon, Vancouver, Venice, Vienna, Yokohama, Zurich.

Chapter 13

Why I Write, Shoot Photographs, and Speak

Writing, shooting photographs, and public speaking are principal vehicles through which I have dedicated my life to preserving World War II history. They are the products emanating from an exceptional ability to plan, organize, think through, and execute ideas and projects.

Over the years, each of the three evolved from a beginning interest into an accelerated avocation, then into an flaming profession. All three are primary avenues for accomplishing my preservation goals and paying back. I seek neither awards nor monetary gains, only to codify and protect where Americans have already been. As I concluded in Chapter 11, if not me, then who will?

I incorporated Wilbur Jones Compositions, LLC, in 2003, after starting the business in 1988. Through this company I write, consult, speak, and lead WWII tours, although most of my time is spent as a volunteer. As the 2000 co-founder and only chairman of the WWII Wilmington Home Front Heritage Coalition, I receive no compensation and essentially have bankrolled the organization.

The Genesis of my absorption with these avenues, get this, started in 1946 as a Forest Hills School twelve-year old, eighth grade "editor-in-chief" of the school "newspaper" following my absorption with WWII. In 1950 during my senior year I became editor-in-chief of my New Hanover High School newspaper, *The Wildcat*. Later I wrote for a while for Carolina's *Daily Tar*

Heel. An ability to write emerged long before realizing I possessed an ability to communicate effectively on my feet, or interact as a source with electronic and print media, or employ fine Japanese cameras.

I thoroughly love to write, was born to write, am forever willing to write. My theory: inexhaustible natural desire and hard work produces a multitude of useful and noteworthy books, papers, and articles. Couple this with a stimulating pace which sees no letup and the result also is hundreds of speaking engagements and interviews to national and local media. From the beginning, give me a blank sheet of paper, a typewriter, and a subject and watch what happens. Humbly speaking, I pride on being a self-starter. No one has ever had to push me.

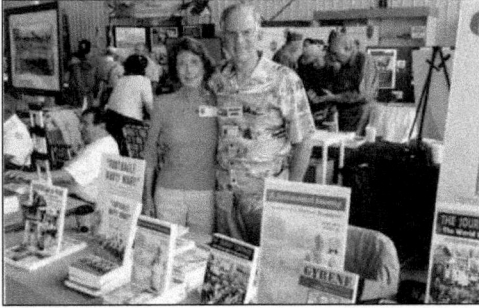

With Carroll at a World War II event in Reading, Pennsylvania, 2012. My titles are displayed on table.

Writing may be my lone God-given talent. If so, it's been willingly exploited to further the study of national defense and to preserve our history. See, that blank sheet is filling already.

NINETEENTH BOOK

The one you are reading now is my nineteenth authored book. Most subjects are military history and national defense. One can find reviews, endorsements, awards, and recognition noted on my website, www.wilburjones.com, under Book Titles. From 2016 to 1997, the books are:

• *"She Shot Her Way to Success": How China's Empress Dowager Ci Xi Launched a Photographer's Trail-Blazing Career*, with Carroll Robbins Jones
• *Football! Navy! War!: How Military "Lend-Lease" Players Saved the College Game and Helped Win World War II*
• *The Journey Continues: The World War II Home Front**, the natural sequel to
• *A Sentimental Journey: Memoirs of a Wartime Boomtown**
• *Forget That You Have Been Hitler Soldiers: A Youth's Service to the Reich*, with Hermann O. Pfrengle
• *Hawaii Goes to War: The Aftermath of Pearl Harbor*, with Carroll Robbins Jones
• *Condemned to Live: A Panzer Artilleryman's Five-Front War*, with Franz A. P. Frisch
• *Arming the Eagle: A History of US Weapons Acquisition Since 1775*
• *Gyrene: The World War II United States Marine***

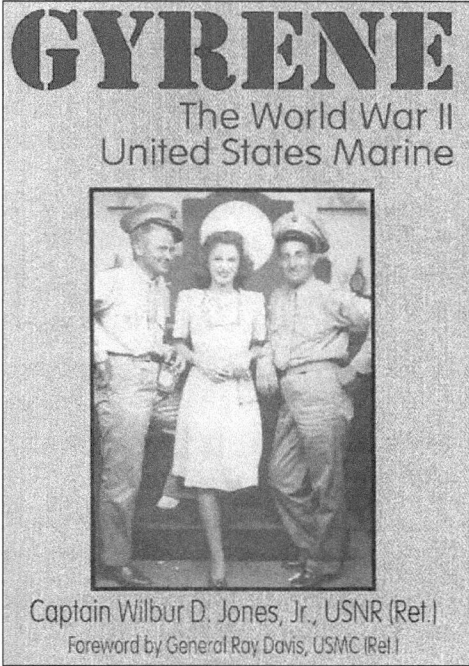

'Gyrene' was used as a reference for the Steven Spielberg-Tom Hanks miniseries 'The Pacific.'

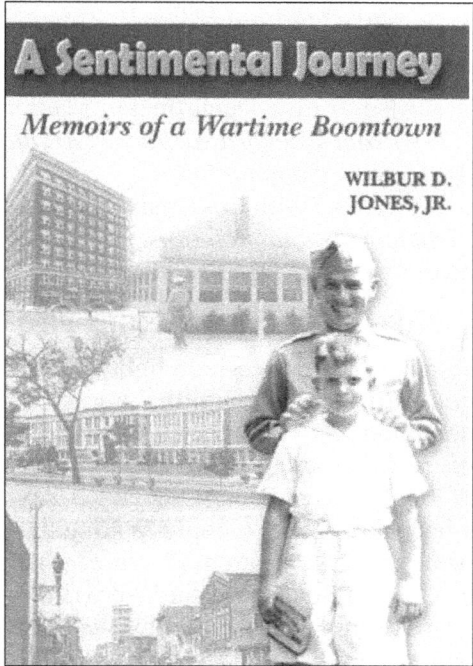

Along with its sequel, this was my most personal work. That's nine-year-old me on the cover.

Researching 'Gyrene' I had the honor to interview the novelist Leon Uris, a World War II Marine and author of 'Battle Cry,' in New York City, 1995.

A tale of two Wilburs: with my fellow professor from the Defense Acquisition University, Wilbur V. 'Bill' Arnold, each of us plugging our own books.

• *Giants in the Cornfield: The 27th Indiana Infantry*

And the monograph *A Brief History of St. Andrews-Covenant Presbyterian Church, Wilmington, NC, 1858-2008.*

Also, for the Department of Defense and/or Government Printing Office:

• *From Packard to Perry: A Quarter Century of Service to the Defense Acquisition Community*

• Titles with extensive revision reissues, including *Congressional Involvement and Relations: A Guide for Department of Defense Acquisition Managers*; and *Defense Acquisition Acronyms and Terms.*

NOTABLE EXPERIENCES FROM RESEARCHING AND WRITING

Performing research lights my fire. Never know what you'll discover when you start inquiring and kicking over rocks, or gently turning yellowed, musty documents. For certain, without researching there's no end product of books or articles. Oh, you'll say what about the Google-Wikipedia-web universe searches? Sure, that too, but so much of what I've written stems from jewels found by walking battlefields and cemeteries, oral interviews, and countless hours—say millions—in public depositories. It all adds up, and it's thrilling. While looking for one item, you might also see something out of the blue that startles, fills in a blank, or prompts a new direction for the project.

Most of my historical work concerns World War II, but in the 1980s I did field research for one Civil War book, 'Giants in the Cornfield,' as here in Virginia.

Here's three instances showing what unexpected research can uncover.

LEE'S LOST ORDER

That's what happened when I began researching my first commercial book, *Giants in the Cornfield: The 27th Indiana Infantry*, about the Union Army's tallest regiment that gained honors at Antietam's Cornfield, Chancellorsville, Gettysburg's Third Day, New Hope Church, and other battles. I learned that the 27th's soldiers found Confederate General Robert E. Lee's "Lost Order" No. 191 in a clover field south of Frederick, MD, wrapped around three cigars. That discovery initiated the 1862 Battle of Antietam whose results redirected the course of the Civil War. One of history's intriguing and most significant intelligence coups. My digging led me into the National Archives and Library of Congress, where I held the actual Special Orders No. 191. Exhilarating history.

Historians knew about the 27th's involvement, but none ever determined

Historical marker remembers the Indiana soldier who found Robert E. Lee's marching orders before battle of Antietam—but the year is wrong.

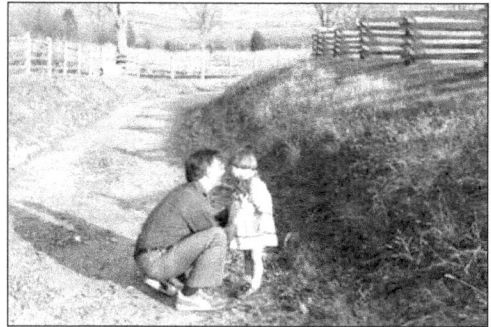

While researching 'Giants' in 1987, visited the Antietam battlefield along with my granddaughter Carrie, here at the notorious 'Bloody Lane.'

who lost it. Lots of wrong finger pointing at Confederate General D. H. Hill and unidentified carelessness. I knew, by discerning fascinating, credible circumstantial evidence. I had written extensively about the "finders" in *Giants in the Cornfield*, and concentrated on the "loser" afterwards. Consequently, I wrote two journal articles explaining the story. (Too bad, my Southern friends, it was an officer extremely close to the sanctified Stonewall Jackson.)

Yes, I walked the battlefield numerous times and every square yard of the clover field, then little changed from 1862. My findings generated little interest, unfortunately, because the Civil War scholarly genre, to which I didn't belong, overwhelmingly sympathized with the Confederate cause. Heavens, we can't let this get out! I lectured a few times on the subject and will at any time. Still have three repro cigars and a dried ear of corn. Call me.

CONDEMNED TO LIVE

Everyone on the Defense Acquisition University faculty and staff loved Dr. Franz Frisch as pleasant, charming, and witty, besides being an expert in his field, engineering for weapons systems. A soft German accent hinted only that this Austrian native immigrated to America in the 1950's after achieving his doctorate. Associates assumed his slow, shuffled stride with cane indicated only his age, maybe to something during World War II. This short, modest man, with whom I had known few lingering moments, was actually holding back, sharing nothing with colleagues.

My points here trace to one season's first snowfall on campus, when both Frisch and I poured a cup of coffee in the office mess. I saw him, a short man, a distinct professorial mustached figure replete in customary tweed jacket and bow tie, leaning on the cane staring pensively out the window at the falling snow, locked on to some distant spot. He didn't notice me. "Franz, my friend," I said, "*Guten morgen*." No response. I continued, "Ah, the snow, you are looking at the snow. This must remind you of your home in Austria—the winter sports—did you like the winter sports when you were young?" "No," he replied, never moving. Feeling drawn to his cogitation and not offended by this usually personable old man, I asked: "Well then, what does this remind you of?" Seconds later, still motionless and transfixed, he softly answered: "Russia, Russia."

From then on for weeks we discussed his service in *Wehrmacht* panzer artillery units in five European campaigns: Poland, France, Russia, Sicily, and Italy. Oh yes, he would let me write his story. For the first time in forty-plus years he felt comfortable in remembering. Information poured from his memory. I bought books on the German Army and artillery and read all I could find on their side of those campaigns.

Vanity license plate shows how being a World War II historian is central to my duty.

One morning he entered my office and tossed on the desk a large, shopworn manila envelope tied with string. "Here, see what's in there. Use whatever you want to. I just found them." Out came hundreds of small, aging photographs in varying arrays marked by country, taken with a Kodak Brownie box camera he carried in service, and documents and small mementoes. A researcher's mother lode. His comrades, their weapons and camps, dead enemy soldiers, French refugees, burning tanks, peasant Poles and Russians, frozen German trucks outside Moscow, hanged partisans, outdoor cafes in Paris. None had been published. Soon they became the foundation of our book, *Condemned to Live: A Panzer Artilleryman's Five-Front War*.

'FOOTBALL! NAVY! WAR!'

On October 17, 2003, a North Carolina sports legend, Charlie "Choo Choo" Justice, died. Number 22. I'd say he'll forever be the state's most famous football player. Kids today know the name and fame, tutored by grandads who saw him play, and dads who heard their fathers' stories about how Justice earned grandiose honors for the University of North Carolina Tar Heels and Washington Redskins. I never saw him, arriving at Chapel Hill a year after he graduated.

Our regional newspaper, the Wilmington *StarNews*, assigned me to write the obituary. Had to be quick. Following phone interviews with his widow Sarah and several Carolina teammates, and checking online, I beat the deadline. But my attention focused simultaneously on the name Bainbridge which kept surfacing. Bainbridge, the old Navy training station in Maryland? Certainly. Justice trained there and starred on their 1943-44 base football teams. He was a teenage phenom with the football, leading Bainbridge to lofty heights and poll rankings. The team, which played major colleges and other powerful armed forces squads, consisted of All-Americas and National Football League players. These teams kept football alive during the war and are credited with preparing future officers for combat to help win the war.

In 2000, I returned to the Defense Acquisition University for a book signing. I wrote three specialized works for the DAU.

I continued researching and got a contract after writing the book manuscript for *"Football! Navy! War!": How Military "Lend-Lease" Players Saved the College Game and Helped Win World War II.* The book broke fresh ground on a subject heretofore not covered, and attracted endorsements from numerous football luminaries, including the foreword by Beano Cook, considered ESPN's most prominent college football analyst. Research included NCAA rule books, commercial pre-season publications, game programs, player interviews, newspapers, a visit to the abandoned Bainbridge station, and more. I learned a lot and enjoyed the work. Quite naturally I named the Bainbridge Commodores the nation's top wartime military team.

FAVORITES FOR THE WILMINGTON STARNEWS

The *StarNews* is a daily (and Sunday) regional newspaper serving primarily Southeastern North Carolina. It's the state's oldest continually operating daily. I've enjoyed numerous writing assignments from the *StarNews* to preserve our history since returning to Wilmington. We began doing business in 1950 (see below). They gratify me with confidence in and appreciation of my work to preserve history. Here are a few of my favorites.

2003—As the paper's military authority, I wrote thirteen page A1 articles on the Iraq War, from the planning and run-up, through the invasion and advance through to the capture of Baghdad. The pieces contained art and maps I constructed with technical staff.

2004—The sixtieth anniversary of D-Day Normandy invasion, June 6. Stories about Wilmington's involvements before departing, and filed story on June 6 from France.

2007—The Sicily-Rome American Cemetery in Nettuno, Italy. Visited the gravesites of six, yes six, Wilmington boys who died in that campaign, and wrote their stories. With photos.

2009—Tracking the WWII exploits of Wilmingtonians Lt. Charles Murray, Medal of Honor recipient, and Sgt. John Burney in Alsace, France, 1944. With photos.

2011—The seventieth anniversary of the Japanese attack on Pearl Harbor, Hawaii, stories before departing for Honolulu, and one filed from there on December 7, 2011 about the three Wilmington boys who died there that day. Sent photos.

2011—Visit for brunch with survivors of the all-Nisei 100th Infantry Battalion in the Waikiki, Honolulu, clubhouse. Shared stories of walking on their Italy and France battlefields.

2015—The V-E Day seventieth anniversary story filed from London mentioned in Chapter 12. Sent photos.

2016—Intimate interviews with two Wilmington Pearl Harbor Survivors on the seventy-fifth anniversary, along with stories of Wilmington on December 7, 1941. With photos.

2016 and 2017—From visits to France and Italy. Lighthearted but legitimate stories on French and Italian wine, cuisines, and culture. With photos.

2017—See the following "Newspaper Memories from the 1950s."

2018—At the conclusion of the World War I Centennial, wrote story of how local 120th Infantry Regiment and the NC National Guard 30th Division broke the Hindenburg Line which crushed German resistance leading to Armistice.

SMALL-FRY PHOTOGRAPHER

Nagasaki to Normandy
Seven Global Decades of Images:
War and Peace, Peoples and Cultures

Photography by Wilbur D. Jones, Jr.
Captain, US Navy Reserve (retired) / author / historian
www.WilburJones.com

February 25-March 26, 2015

Hannah Block Historic USO /
Community Arts Center
120 South Second Street   Wilmington, North Carolina

Free Admission

This poster promoted a 2015 exhibition of my photos from around the world, starting in the 1950s.

My serious connection with photography began in 1956 shooting black-and-white 35-mm roll film with a Japanese Nikon F when I first landed the Far East. Since then, I've loaded tons of albums with family shots, foreign travels, and travels within the US, all properly captioned. Those compiled from my many foreign trips, a mix of WWII and military subjects and cultural sites, are worthy of donation to UNC Wilmington for posterity.

Never studied the art, but taught myself through trial and error in a day when the shooter had to mail in rolls of film to Kodak for processing and return, even when deployed to the Far East or Europe. Seems like decades ago before digital photography and SD/memory cards. Today's photographers can't comprehend what the trailblazers went through, such as my mother-in-law Pat Robbins in the book I wrote about her in *"She Shot Her Way to Success."*

Fortunately, I developed a knack for the art and look for angle, perspective, depth, lighting and of course subject. Not a snapshot freak, more serious than that. In fact, I'm a small-fry, exhibited, semi-professional who sold a few. In 2015 I opened a large exhibit of my collective lifetime work in the Hannah Block Historic USO/Community Arts Center titled, "Nagasaki to Normandy: Seven Global Decades of Images: War and Peace, Peoples and Cultures." Folks liked it.

One photo years ago hung in the Smithsonian Air & Space Museum; another in an Indiana museum. My residence walls look like a gallery. Two favorites especially: Hitler's Eagles Nest retreat near Obersalzburg, Germany, in the Alps (what a grand view!); and the seventieth anniversary of V-E Day wreath laying in Whitehall, London, by Prime Minister David Cameron and Prince Andrew. Many images illustrated my books and *StarNews* pieces.

Once I carried two camera bags with lenses, accessories, and tripods and all that. Too burdensome. So in recent years have carried only the packable, pocket-handy Canon digitals. So convenient when traveling. Even tried videoing for a short while, but not for me. What did it? The physical burden of hauling a weighted shoulder bag with all that stuff and film while edging through the thick undergrowth on my 1998 visit to Iwo Jima. Sweating, missteps into holes, sinking, sharp cutting plants, never again.

SPEAKING TO THE PUBLIC AND THE MEDIA

I've experienced that the ability to speak, or lecture, before the public can be a demonstrative form of leadership and a distinct professional advantage.

Veterans' Day 2015, Wilmington National Cemetery.

Developing and honing aptitude and delivery methods are the results of continuous process improvements, particularly since moving to Wilmington in 1997. Essential was the earlier experience of lecturing for 2,000 or-so hours before astute adult students at the Defense Acquisition University. See Chapter 9.

Speaking platforms, or audience organizations, have included a potpourri of groups including:

Civic clubs, libraries, church groups, historical societies, museums, military organizations, preservation and anniversary ceremonies, cultural and ethnic groups, book signings, social organizations, school students, and

In 2015, for the 'StarNews,' I covered the seventieth anniversary of V-E Day at the Cenotaph in London's Whitehall district. My photo of the wreath laying showed, from left, then-Labour Party leader Ed Milliband; Prince Andrew, the Duke of York; and Prime Minister David Cameron.

women's and men's clubs.

As examples: the RMS *Queen Mary 2* maiden eastbound transatlantic voyage, C-SPAN Book-TV; small-ship Mediterranean tour; National Archives; US Navy Museum; Wilmington Rotary Club; US House of Representatives committees; 100 Black Men of North Carolina, Inc.; National Conference on the Battle of Iwo Jima, and others.

I speak to educate, inform, and influence potential support. PowerPoint slide shows which I produced often accompany the presentations. Since 1997, I've given close to 800 speaking engagements and media interviews, and held more than 200 book signings. Virtually every one of the foregoing have been to preserve history. I encourage being "in demand," and rarely turn down a request. Usually I am not offered an honorarium. You have to love the job.

Besides interacting with Southeastern North Carolina media, I've interviewed with so many including *The New York Times*, *Sports Illustrated*, Smithsonian.com, *Our State* Magazine, the Federal Reserve Bank of Richmond magazine *Region Focus*, Raleigh *News & Observer*, *University of Iowa Alumni Magazine*, and others.

THE WILMINGTON STARNEWS MEDIA RELATIONSHIP

Boy, this association goes way-way back and still flourishes. For the *StarNews* newspapers, since 1998: almost 300 columns, op-ed pieces, features, letters, as either the writer or a principal source for another writer.

Ah hah. As the paper celebrated its 150th anniversary in 2017, the executive editor asked me to write my memories of working there as a high school and college student in 1950-52. They flowed easily.

'NEWSPAPER MEMORIES FROM THE 1950s'

October 11, 2017

a.k.a, Memories from the *Star-News* Stone Age

Fortunately, Althea Gibson proved me dead wrong. My July 27, 1952 *Morning Star* report on her sport locally unwittingly reflected historical estrangements between Wilmington's white and black communities, not factual tennis.

Years later, re-reading the opening paragraph plainly indicated how little we knew about each other's backyards. My naivete? Inexperience? No. Culture. Inquiring never occurred.

"Tennis in Wilmington isn't at such a tremor that this Coastal city will probably ever send a native son or daughter to the famous Wimbledon matches in England, but with a little more aid, the net game has possibilities of rooting itself more firmly into the local athletic scene.'"

Sheer irony. Just blocks from where I gathered material at Robert Strange Park's courts, Ms. Gibson, already a rising star, was perfecting her future Wimbledon championships game under Dr. Hubert Eaton.

By now publicly acknowledging this predictive imperfection, its 65-year professional embarrassment is assuaged, even if no one ever noticed or cared.

INTO THE WRITING PROFESSION

From 1950, as a 15-year old New Hanover High School junior, through the 1952 summer while at Carolina, I worked part-time as a sports writer and copy editor in "the paper's" Murchison Building headquarters at Front and Chestnut. Duty began right after school adjourned and on weekend and summer mornings. Legendary newspapermen R. J. Powell and Paul Jennewein mentored me.

The *Morning Star* hit the streets about 6:00 a.m. Its companion edition, the *Wilmington News* (informed people read both), printed mid-afternoon. Separate staffs used the same facilities. Desk and equipment sharing likened to wartime shipyard workers hot-bunking. A combination staff published the *Sunday Star-News*.

Offices and production facilities occupied at least two floors. A woman manually operated the elevator. Managing editor Al Dickson, who reported to publisher Rye Page, both friends of my father, hired me. What they paid me still registers as a teenager's pittance. Nevertheless, prestigious work.

Until I drove, my one-car parents usually transported me to and from my job. His Carolina Building & Loan office being nearby facilitated this. Sometimes I took the bus, a hairy nighttime prospect.

THE NEWSROOM SETUP

Except for the women's section editor, newsroom staff and reporters were all white males.

The city editor two desks over from sports managed news flow, page allocations and production schedules. Usually two persons manned sports until we "put the paper to bed" around 10:00 p.m. After a desk-copy cleanup and unless awaiting scores, with permission we departed. The editors trusted me to close alone.

Probably the only technological instrument still in use is a telephone. Sports had three desks and two rotary dial phones including a direct line, although a central operator serviced the office. Holding the receiver between ear and shoulder while taking items, especially box scores, quickly fatigued the neck.

Desks contained:

• In/out baskets for placing paper copy, the out-basket ready for linotype-setting.

• An eight-inch metal pin-spike for ramming copy awaiting action.

• A manual typewriter, whose fabric ribbon spool required frequent replacement. I've never learned to typewrite, just fine-tuned "hunting-and-pecking." Pound the letters. Un-jam the keys. Rub mistake erasers on original and carbon copies. Somehow, the index fingers survived ten trillion keystrokes since.

Teletype machines for incoming Associated Press and United Press paper traffic were called the "wires." You tore off items or reams looking for hot news, retaining newsworthy items, trashing the residue. Qualified operators dispatched outgoing items on the wires.

What We Published, and How

Sports used little copy from syndicate features or other publications which mostly consisted of women's news, health and gardening, information and comics.

The women's "Society Page" carried fashion and kitchen tips and associated features, engagements and weddings, club and social news, fewer stories with fancier headlines than regular news.

Segregation guided news policies, with limited—if any—photographs or stories of black citizens, organizations and activities.

We used AP Wirephotos of scanned images processed on a cylinder and transmitted over telephone lines, a principal source for international, national and sports images. We also used pre-packaged images impressed on a paper mold into which hot lead was poured, cooled, then set on the typesetter's matrix.

Sports pages layout by inches, all manual, began at the desk. We typed the copy from the wires or notes, pasted copy and photos or illustrations on a matrix, and wrote headlines. Typesetters already placed advertisements. We fit copy around them, or designated locations, and walked the completed layout or copy to the typesetters.

Operators with keyboards "automatically" assembled matrices/molds of hot lead letters, including some 18 fonts, which became the printing form. Lead was recycled. Linotype machines, the industry's high-tech, processed and formatted pages for printing, which we did in-house. From frequent visits to the linotype room, I recall the noisy, clicking, whirring machines and lead's crisp metallic odor, shards spotting the floor. Like inside a 1950 factory.

1950s By-Line Production

During 1950-51, the paper let me cover the Post 10 American Legion Junior baseball teams, serving also as scorekeeper-"manager." Sonny Jurgensen, future NFL Hall of Famer, played third base. His authoritarian father drove the bus.

Because I covered everything imaginable, it warranted countless bylines, starting with the city's first Little League-forerunner game in 1950. Pepsi-Cola beat E. W. Godwin's Sons, 12-0, at the 21st and

Wolcott field. Future NFL star Roman Gabriel pitched a no-hitter. Also: city recreation activities; professional wrestling; college football; elementary school basketball; semi-pro baseball; and my editors' "cats-and-dogs."

Note: The *Star-News* employed other family members: uncle David Murrell, a writer (1930s); son Andrew, sports "ACC Insider" (1998-2008); and grandson-in-law Matt Vaughan (mid-2000s).

In 1998 we re-established a continuing working relationship in which I've written or been a principal source for more than 300 byline or referenced news items.

Sixty-seven years since the Stone Age. Man, how the paper has grown up.

—30—

The *StarNews*. For sixty-nine years, a mutual highly-respected relationship, and always will. It's where I got "my start." Each has succeeded.

EPILOGUE

Okay, my children, you have what you asked for, and I am free to state, Mission Accomplished. Whew.

Once published, I'm certain I'll remember events, people, and photos that should have been included. But remember, this is about my life only, and perhaps someday you should write your own. If you want, I promise to write a postscript in five years, and an update chapter in ten years, because I'll still be working.

That said, so where am I?

I feel fine and have no health issues. . .

Enjoy freedom of physical movement and mental sharpness . . .

Am crisis-free . . .

Run my small Wilbur Jones Compositions LLC as an author and military historian . . .

Buy Belks clothes on sale . . .

Sustain comfortably on three Federal Government pensions, and some LLC income . . .

Able to pay my bills . . .

Have a small nest egg; careful about how I spend . . .

Got one more satisfying Carolina NCAA basketball championship (our sixth) in 2017-- but gotta have at least one more. . .

Crave my work, won't stop . . .

Enjoy and support the arts . . .

Look at all sides of most issues . . .

Am proud to be an American: my country first and always . . .

Am proud of "Service Above Self" as a Rotarian . . .

Prefer being with people who understand what's going on in the world, and use their brains and common sense . . .

Turn off to boorish people . . .

Watch the clock and prefer routines . . .

Abhor wasting time . . . .

Try to avoid confrontations . . .

Detest loud anything especially restaurant music/noise and locker room jabbermouths. . .

Keep feet moving and brain cells percolating . . .

Am a totally immersed foreign traveler . . .

Work out at O2 Fitness five-six days a week . . .

Thoroughly enjoy some of God's greatest gifts: wine, beer, popcorn, and ice cream . . .

Oh yes, wine! Devoted connoisseur of French and Italian wines, considered "well informed."

Light wines, low tannins. Favorites: Provence rose and reds; Rhone, Burgundy, and Chianti reds; Chardonnay and sauvignon blanc whites.

Learn something new every day (and remember it) . . .

Read a lot . . .

On TV, watch PBS (UNC-TV), Smithsonian and History Channels, Nat Geo, documentaries, travel, TCM movies . . .

I tune into Fox News, Rush Limbaugh and Sirius/XM 40's music . . .

In the Olden Days would have been part of "the Washington Establishment," but not now, Thank Heaven . . .

Like to help others . . .

Enjoyed 54 married years with the love of my life, the late Carroll Robbins . . .

Raised four children who are succeeding . . .

Want to be remembered for my moral and ethical codes, decisiveness, leadership, and compatibility . . . and . . . '

Am the luckiest man alive. Ann LaReau and I have each other.

MY DEAR, STEADY LADY FRIEND

Ann and I no longer are an item around town. Everyone knows we're inseparable. Her husband of thirty-six years, Ron LaReau, a Notre Dame grad, well respected and accomplished businessman, University of North Carolina Wilmington adjunct faculty, and Rotary club president, died after a short illness in 2012. Ann later joined his/my Wilmington Rotary Club, but we never met

With Ann LaReau in Tuscany, savoring local wines, 2017. A Scotch drinker, she indulges my tastes in wine.

until after Carroll died in September 2013.

Ann is an experienced and reputable professional consultant rendering senior care giving and Alzheimer's/dementia services. Since I'm a senior, why not approach her? Seeking advice on the likelihood Carroll's dementia affected her slow, twelve-year demise with COPD, I traded a cup of Port City Java coffee for her opinions. Also, how did she dispose of Ron's vast belongings, downsize, and then sell their house? I turned to her for all sorts of guidance. In 2018 she established her own senior care business, Ann LaReau Alzheimer's Consulting, LLC

She politely and generously offered her professional opinions and how she handled life after Ron, helping me clear some unknowns. Right away, I liked the way she looked, talked, and walked. Several female fellow Rotarians, my "little sisters," urged us to go out. She wasn't certain about dating, I learned. But I couldn't resist and came on. Life is just too damned short. On our third date, we were completely struck. We are the best thing that could happen to each other.

Since late November 2013 we've been going steady, and enjoyed four extended business trips to Europe from 2014-17. We are great together. No. No plans for marriage—I can't do that to her (LOL)—and we both require "space" at our ages.

When I sold my Chamberlain Lane house in 2014 after seventeen years, she helped pick out the new downsized home, decorated it, and converted the backyard into LaReau's Wild Critterville Feeders Smorgasbord. This is her house, too, although she continues living in a charming apartment. She's most tolerant of my pleasures and obsessions, such as anything World War II and Carolina basketball and football. The latter gives her nearly fifty yearly evenings or weekend afternoons to hang out with her friends, or watch what she wants to watch on TV, or work. Not really a sports fan, she endures a game occasionally and sometimes dons a "Carolina NC" sweatshirt. Thanks, sweetheart, for being most tolerant. You are my life.

By the way, how do I say this other than extremely carefully? Ann and Carroll have So Many endearing, repeat endearing, common characteristics. Or, naively, maybe all women act the same? Let's start with:

(a) Stop. Stop. There's a parking space right here;

(b) You never want to dance with me;

(c) You just don't like Thai (Indian/Congolese/Eskimo/Taureg nomad, et al.) food. You said so once;

(d) I'm not interrupting you. I'm just interjecting conversation;

(e) I am not answering your question before you ask it;

(f) I know you don't like third-day leftovers. But shall I freeze these fish fry hushpuppies for another day when you eat alone?;

(g) Oh, you mean I've told you that story before (. . . 100 times . . .)?

And on, but we love 'em just as they are. Don't we, fellas?

THE REST OF ME

My children are settled and prospering. The oldest, Patricia (b. 1961), has been married thirty years to Willard Jacobson, a seasoned and successful airlines maintenance executive, and lives in South Florida. David (b. 1962) has made his mark as a solar power industry marketing executive in Connecticut. Andrew (b. 1966) is the senior or dean of North Carolina sports journalists covering the Atlantic Coast Conference for twenty-four years, and publishes TarHeelIllustrated.com. He has been married to Kimberly, a neo-natal nurse in Raleigh, since 2005. Their daughter Elizabeth (Ellie, b. 2009) is my other grandchild.

A favorite family photo, from Christmas 1986. From left, Carrie, Patricia, Andrew, Carroll, and David.

The Prologue introduced you to Patricia's daughter, Carroll Jones Vaughan (Carrie, thirty-three), married since 2008 to a terrific husband, Matt, who owns a successful public relations marketing firm in Wake County, North Carolina. They are doing so great together.

Daily I thank God for these many blessings of life and for allowing me to see the light of another day. Since relocating to Wilmington in 1997, I attend St. Andrews-Covenant Presbyterian Church, where I was born and raised, every Sunday I'm in town. Except for several one-time activities, and acting as historian when needed, I avoid church business, social life, and politics. Other outlets take my time. With my worldly background, I'm unsure if they've ever known how to accept me. I go to worship God in my own private manner.

Activities include: In 2007-08, member of the church's 150th anniversary celebration committee, which included establishing the church history corner, inventorying numerous church artifacts, and writing the church's history monograph. In 2017-18, member of

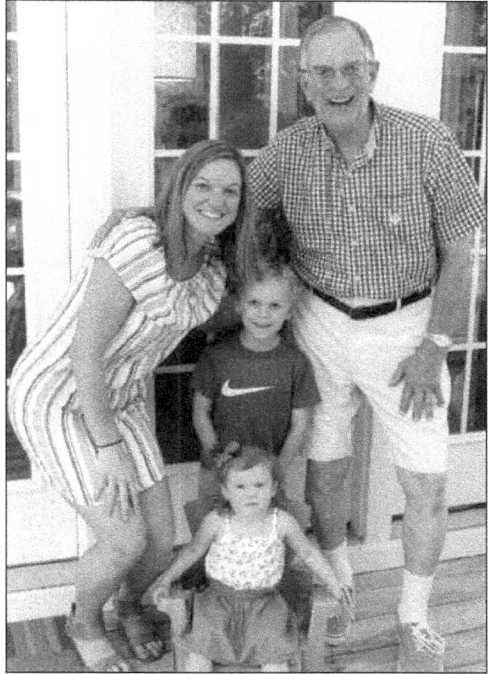

The next generation: with granddaughter Carrie Vaughn and her children, Brooks and Charlie, in Holly Springs, North Carolina, 2018.

the 100th anniversary celebration of Church of the Covenant, before its 1944 merger (I am the youngest merger Charter Member). In 2000, I conducted a complete inventory of old church records for discard, retention, or gifting to UNC Wilmington's Randall Library. Each of us pays homage to God, church, and community in his own way.

I intend to keep writing, shooting photos, and speaking to preserve North Carolina history until the old body and mind say No More. That's it. My two goals are to publish this book for anyone's pleasure, and to have Wilmington designated as the First American "WWII Heritage City."

Err, I mean, until the next major project comes along that requires my involvement. Carroll often asked, not always tongue-in-cheek, "Okay now, so what's your next project you're off to?"

Watch the news and stand by for my emails.

WWII
AMERICAN HERITAGE CITY

UPDATING CHAPTER 11
WILMINGTON, N. C., DESIGNATED FIRST AMERICAN
WORLD WAR II HERITAGE CITY
September 2, 2020

"...So you are just a tough cookie"

On September 2, 2020, in a ceremony at the Battleship North Carolina, President Donald Trump and Secretary of the Interior David Bernhardt designated the City of Wilmington as the first American World War II Heritage City.

President Trump remarked: "It is my tremendous honor to officially designate Wilmington, North Carolina, as our nation's very first World War II Heritage City."

On hearing him praise my work, I respectfully stood erect and snapped a sharp hand salute. I am a retired Navy officer and always will be. He is the Commander in Chief. The President returned my salute.

Acknowledging that other cities wanted this designation, and we got it and are now Number One, he beamed at me, "So you are just a tough cookie."

The day was my proudest honor.

The designation culminated an ambitious, vigorous 12-1/2 year project it was my professional privilege to start and lead through the auspices of the all-volunteer, 501(c)(3) World War II Wilmington Home Front Heritage Coalition. We sought such national recognition based on (1) the city's contributions to the war effort, and (2) how it has preserved that history.

The dedicated work of Senator Thom Tillis and Congressman David Rouzer resulted in the passage of S.47 in 2019, signed into law by the President in March 2019. It established a national WWII preservation program I originated with Congressman Mike McIntyre. Secretary Bernhardt signed the designation proclamation.

The president continued: "That's a big deal: our nation's very first, Wilmington. Congratulations to you all. (Amidst thunder) And God is saluting you up there.

"This mighty vessel in this magnificent town will forever tell that story [our heritage] with this designation. So I want to congratulate North Carolina and Wilmington. That's a fantastic thing.

"I want to thank Senator Tillis and Congressman Rouzer - stand up please - for their work to make this day possible. Thank you, Thom. Thank you, fellas. Great job.

"And let me also thank retired Navy Captain Wilbur Jones, who has championed the cause of World War II Heritage Cities. Wilbur, thank you. Thank you, Wilbur. Great job. Great job. So, Wilbur, you know a lot of people wanted this, right? So you are just a tough cookie. You got it. Number one. Number one in the nation. I want to thank Wilbur. That's great."

He concluded his remarks by pointing to me and saying, "Thank you for making it come true...Just a tough cookie." Thank you, Mr. President.

The United States of America.
Department of the Interior

DESIGNATION OF THE CITY OF WILMINGTON, NORTH CAROLINA,
AS AN AMERICAN WORLD WAR II HERITAGE CITY

By the Secretary of the Interior of the United States of America

A Proclamation

WHEREAS, the President of the United States signed into law on March 12, 2019, the John D. Dingell, Jr. Conservation, Management, and Recreation Act of 2019 establishing the American World War II Heritage Cities recognition program (Public Law 116-9, Section 9007), in order to "recognize and ensure the continued preservation and importance of the history of the United States involvement in World War II"; and

WHEREAS, under the authority of Public Law 116-9, Section 9007, each calendar year the Secretary of the Interior may designate one or more cities located in one of the several States or a territory of the United States as an "American World War II Heritage City"; and

WHEREAS, not more than one city in each State or territory may be designated by the Secretary of the Interior; and

WHEREAS, the "American World War II Heritage City" designation recognizes the historic contributions by a city and its environs to the World War II home-front war effort and achievements to preserve the heritage and the legacy of the city's contributions to the war effort and to preserve World War II history; and

WHEREAS, during World War II, the population of Wilmington, North Carolina doubled as numerous citizens contributed to rapidly expanding production in a variety of vital war industries, such that by war's end the city's shipyards had launched more than 240 cargo vessels; and

WHEREAS, the city and its surrounding area hosted training for all five military branches and thousands of its residents joined the fight as Navy frogmen, P-51 fighter aces, Tuskegee Airmen, submarine skippers, bomber pilots, Marine riflemen, Army artillerymen, physicians, nurses and volunteers; and

WHEREAS, since 1961, Wilmington has been home to the USS North Carolina, the most decorated American battleship of World War II and a memorial to those that served during the war; and

WHEREAS, in 1996, a group of veterans and historians established the Southeastern North Carolina's World War II Remembrance Group; and

WHEREAS, the World War II Wilmington Home Front Heritage Coalition, an all-volunteer nonprofit organization established in 2000 to identify, preserve, and interpret Southeastern North Carolina's rich World War II legacy, has been a catalyst for developing and leading efforts to preserve Wilmington's wartime history; and

WHEREAS, the City of Wilmington has memorialized the contributions of its two Medal of Honor recipients; has renovated and restored its National Register of Historic Places-listed USO building; and has erected multiple markers to commemorate a German U-boat attack on a local defense facility.

NOW, THEREFORE, in recognition of the unique significance of the City of Wilmington, North Carolina, in the history and commemoration of the World War II home-front, I, David L. Bernhardt, Secretary of the United States Department of the Interior, finding that the City of Wilmington meets the criteria set forth in Public Law 116-9, do designate the City of Wilmington as an American World War II Heritage City.

IN WITNESS WHEREOF, in recognition of this historic site, I have hereunto set my hand on this 2nd day of September, the two hundred and forty-fifth year o

Secretary of the Interior

GLOSSARY

AHEPA – American Hellenic Educational Progressive Association

AP – Associated Press

Blue – Slang name for baseball umpires who in my day wore light blue shirts

boatorcade – Long processional array of boats similar to motorcade

B–17G bomber "Aluminum Overcast" – Thrill of a lifetime to fly in WWII aircraft

bum dope – Navy for really bad info

Cal Berkeley – University of California

Carolina – University of North Carolina

Chevy – Chevrolet auto

"chop" – DOD word for signing off on a proposal

CNO – Chief of Naval Operations

COMPHIBPAC – Commander Amphibious Force, Pacific Fleet

COPD – Chronic obstructive pulmonary disease

CREEP – Committee for the Re-election of the President (1972)

C-SPAN – Cable Satellite Public Affairs Network

Cy Young runnerup – Top pitcher in Major League Baseball

DAU – Defense Acquisition University

DC – District of Columbia

D-Day – In this case, June 6, 1944 invasion of Normandy

"death watch" – Presss pool that always travels with the president to report on events

Division I/II/III – NCAA college sports levels

DOD – Department of Defense

drop-by – Presidential event where he doesn't stay long

DSMC – Defense Systems Management College

"earmark" – Including a specific funding provision in legislation

East Anglia – World War II air bases in England

E-ring, D-ring – Outer and next inner corridors of Pentagon building

ex-pat – expatriate, American now living abroad

"The football" – The nuclear weapons activation codes carried in a case

FRG – Federal Republic of German (West Germany)

"Gator Navy" – Navy amphibious forces

GOP – Republican Party

GSA – US General Services Administration

Hatch Act – Federal law prohibiting federal employees from engaging in political activity

HBHUSO/CAC – Hannah Bock Historic USO/Community Arts Center

Hitler's Eagle's Nest – Hitler's mountaintop retreat in Obersalzberg, Germany

ILS – Integrated logistic support designed into weapons systems programs in-towner – presidential event held in the Washington, DC, area

Japanese "Zero" – The flyover "attack" by restored WWII aircraft over the president's arrival at USS *Arizona* Memorial on December 7, 1975

LA – Los Angeles, CA.

latchkey – A child of working parents who spends much of his time unsupervised around the home

LOL – laugh out loud slang

"Lost Battalion" – 36th Infantry Division unit trapped in Vosges Mountains in 1944

Lt. Cdr. – Lieutenant commander (O-4), Navy

Lt. j. g. – Lieutenant junior grade (O-2), Navy

LTTW – Less-than-Third-World country

LVT – Amphibious tractor

"manana, domani mattino" – Tomorrow in Spanish and Italian

Market Garden- Allied parachute assault on German forces in the Netherlands, 1944

MBE – Minority Business Enterpriser program

Med – Mediterranean Sea

MS-DOS – Microsoft disc operating system

NatGeo – National Geographic Channel

NATO – North American Treaty Organization

NCAA – National Collegiate Athletic Association

New Deal – Progressive programs of President Franklin Roosevelt's administration

NFL – National Football League

NHHS – New Hanover High School

Nisei – First-generation Americans of Japanese descent

OCS/OC – Officer Candidate School/officer candidates

OMG – oh my gosh

"One-Puka-Puka" – nickname of all-Nisei 100th Infantry Battalion

Operation Dragoon – Allied invasion of Southern France, 1944

OPNAV/OP – Office of the Chief of Naval Operations/OPNAV program office designation

out-of-towner – Presidential event held outside of Washington, DC, area

"Pah-ree" – Paris, France

PBS – Public Broadcasting Service

"Puzzle Palace on the Potomac" – Slang for the Pentagon

Ready Reserve – Drilling, paid Navy Reserve component subject to being activated, USNR

Regular Navy – Non-Reserve Navy active duty component, USN

SACPC – St. Andrews-Covenant Presbyterian Church, Wilmington, NC

SALT – Strategic Arms Limitation Talks

SEAL – Member, sea-air-land Navy special operations force

Schedule C confidential assistant – Federal government political appointee not requiring senate confirmation

stop – A presidential event

SWAT – special weapons and tactical unit of law enforcement

TCM – Turner Classic Movies

topside – Outside on a ship's weather decks

UNC – University of North Carolina (Chapel Hill)

UNCW – University of North Carolina Wilmington

UPI – United Press International

USO – United Service Organizations

USSS – US Secret Service, a.k.a. "The Service"

V-E Day – Victory in Europe, May 8, 1945

VFW – Veterans of Foreign Wars

Watergate – Nixon administration scandal resulting from coverup of Watergate break-in

WHCA – White House Communications Agency

YMCA – Young Men's Christian Association

APPENDIX A

MOUNTAINTOPS CLIMBED: LARGE, SMALL, AND IN BETWEEN IN SERVICE TO COUNTRY

• President Gerald R. Ford, The White House—Advance Representative and Staff Assistant, Washington

• Congressman Ed Reineke (R-CA.)—Chief of staff, District

• Congressman Barry Goldwater, Jr. (R-CA.)—Chief of staff. Washington

• President Richard M. Nixon's 1972 New Hampshire re-election campaign—Executive Director, Concord, NH

- President Nixon's January 1973 Inaugural Committee—General Services Administration manager of logistics support

• Secretaries of Housing & Urban Development—Special Assistant to James Lynn and Carla Hills, Washington

• Commissioners of General Services Administration—Special Assistants to Public Buildings Service and Federal Supply Service, Washington

• US Navy, twenty-eight years of Regular Navy and Ready Reserve service—Earned promotion to captain

• Ready Reserve amphibious assault support unit, and ordnance support unit—Commanding Officer, Washington

• Commanded shipboard department of 150 men

• US Department of Defense—Nearly forty-one years of service

• Under Secretaries of Defense (Acquisition), The Pentagon—Special Assistant and Speechwriter to John Betti and Bob Costello, Washington

• Office of the Chief of Naval Operations, the Pentagon—Manager of integrated logistics support for naval weapons systems, Washington

• Defense Acquisition University, Fort Belvoir, VA—Associate Dean and Professor, Speechwriter to the Commandant, and Member, Defense Acquisition Corps—Twelve years, Washington

TO STATE AND COMMUNITY

• USS North Carolina Battleship Commission—chairman and vice chairman, four years as commissioner, Wilmington

• Friends of the Battleship North Carolina Memorial—chairman, Wilmington

• Northern Virginia [Professional] Baseball Umpires Association—president, Alexandria, VA

• Professional NCAA Division I, high school, and recreational baseball umpire—Washington, DC metro

• Commonwealth [Professional] Basketball Officials Association—Professional college, high school, and recreational basketball official—

Washington, DC metro
- Fort Hunt Youth Athletic Association—chief umpire and chief basketball official including Little League, and board member, Alexandria, VA
- World Series for Little League's Senior Division—umpire, Gary, IN
- Commonwealth of Virginia Equal Employment Opportunity Commission—member, Richmond, VA
- Wilmington Executives Club—president, vice president
- Wilmington Rotary Club—director
- Numerous community organizations—chairman, president, and board member, Wilmington
- Received numerous preservation, history, and community service awards and recognition, Wilmington

TO THE PRESERVATION OF HISTORY

- Wilmington *StarNews* Media Lifetime Achievement Award—recipient
- World War II Wilmington Home Front Heritage Coalition—co-founder and chairman, Wilmington
- Wartime Wilmington Commemoration 1999—chairman, Wilmington
- Hannah Block Historic USO/Community Arts Center Advisory Board—chairman and vice chairman
- Annual (twenty-one years) December 7th Pearl Harbor Commemoration ceremonies—organizer and emcee, Wilmington
- First anniversary commemoration of 9-11 attacks—chairman and organizer, Wilmington
- Author of nineteen books
- Author of or a principal source for some 300 newspaper and magazine articles
- Keynote speaker/presenter of some 800 history presentations, and print and electronic media interviews
- Global photographer for sixty-two years—an exhibited semi-professional: Washington, DC, Indiana, Wilmington
- Recognized by *New York Times*, SmithsonianMagazine.com, *Sports Illustrated* Magazine, Federal Reserve Board magazine *Region Focus*, *Our State* Magazine, WarHistory.online, and other national and state media for preservation efforts
- WWII battlefield tours in Pacific, Europe, and Mediterranean; and North Carolina—tour leader and organizer

TO EDUCATION

- Varsity lettermen's Monogram Club, University of North Carolina—president and vice president, Chapel Hill
- UNC varsity lacrosse and soccer teams—member

• New Hanover High School newspaper, *The Wildcat*—Editor in Chief, Wilmington

• Students at University of North Carolina Wilmington, East Carolina University, and high schools—Mentor and advisor, Wilmington

• E. L. White Society, UNCW, Office of Vice Chanellor for Development—Member, for major gifts donated and planned, Wilmington

AWARDS, RECOGNITION, AND PARTICIPATION (PARTIAL)

2017

Lower Cape Fear Historical Society—Society Cup for outstanding preservation of local history, Wilmington

2014

Chairman of the USS North Carolina Battleship Commission, appointed by North Carolina Governor Pat McCrory. First Wilmington chairman since Hugh Morton in 1961. The Commission monitors and oversees and monitors the operations, maintenance, and plans of North Carolina's state memorial to the 10,000 Tar Heels who died in uniform in World War II. Served until 2017.

2013

USS North Carolina Battleship Commission—Vice Chairman, appointed by Governor McCrory

2012

Wilmington *StarNews* Media—Lifetime Achievement Award

Congressional Record, US House of Representatives, "A Tribute to Captain Wilbur D. Jones," by Rep. Mike McIntyre (D-7th District, NC)

2011

E. L. White Society, University of North Carolina Wilmington—Along with late wife Carroll Robbins Jones, inducted into the organization which honors donors of $25,000 or more through planned giving

Earned Rotary International Paul Harris Fellow designation for donations supporting the Rotary Foundation

2010

United Daughters of the Confederacy—National Defense Medal

2009

Historical Society of the Lower Cape Fear—Society Cup awarded to the World War II Wilmington Home Front Heritage Coalition (chairman), for outstanding history preservation accomplishments

2008

Lower Cape Fear Chapter, The National Society of the Sons of the American Revolution—Bronze Good Citizenship Medal

2007

Production of the 2010 Steven Spielberg-Tom Hanks HBO mini-series *The Pacific* used the book *Gyrene: The World War II United States Marine*, as a "technical reference manual" to train actors. Spielberg wrote a thank-you letter for writing the book.

2006

American Association for State and Local History – National Award of Merit for Leadership in History, for books on World War II North Carolina and history preservation accomplishments

Lower Cape Fear Historical Society—Clarendon Award, for best regional history book, *The Journey Continues: The World War II Home Front*, Wilmington

Elderhaus—Senior Service Award Wilmington

2005

North Carolina Society of Historians—North Carolina Historian of the Year (East)

Three other NCSH awards for the book, *The Journey Continues: The World War II Home Front*; newspaper op-ed pieces and other articles in Wilmington *StarNews*; and to the World War II Wilmington Home Front Heritage Coalition statewide award, Federation of North Carolina Historical Societies – for history preservation

2003

NCSH Statewide book award for *A Sentimental Journey: Memoirs of a Wartime Boomtown*

2000

Lower Cape Fear Historical Society—Society Cup for Wartime Wilmington Commemoration

1999 (chairman)

NCSH—Two statewide awards to the WWC 1999, for history preservation

1966

Los Angeles (CA.) Junior Chamber of Commerce—Runner-up, Outstanding Member of the Year

OTHER CIVIC AND COMMUNITY LEADERSHIP ACTIVITIES

• Secretary and principal organizer of the Wilmington Kitty Hawk Concept Team which worked from 2006-09 to bring the retiring aircraft carrier USS *Kitty Hawk* to Wilmington as a museum ship. (The Navy stated the ship would remain in the reserve fleet for several more years.)

• Director, Museum of the Marine, Jacksonville, NC

• Member, Salvation Army Advisory Board, Wilmington

• Member, New Hanover County Public Library Advisory Board, Wilmington

• Member, 150th Anniversary (2008) Committee of St. Andrews-Covenant Presbyterian Church, Wilmington – wrote church history and established a mini-museum History Corner. Charter Member of the church (1944).

• Member, 100th Anniversary (2018) Committee of Church of the Covenant

Presbyterian Church, Wilmington
- Vice president and board member, Olde Camden Homeowners Association, Wilmington
- Member, Wilmington-New Hanover County Military Affairs Committee

APPENDIX B

A MILIEU OF PEOPLE WITH WHOM I'VE TRANSACTED BUSINESS (MODESTLY PARTIAL, OF COURSE)

Vice President Spiro Agnew, A highlight visitor for me during the Nixon 1972 New Hampshire campaign.

Ernie Banks, "Mr. Cub," baseball Hall of Fame—In his New York office.

John A. Betti, under secretary of Defense (acquisition)—Former Ford Motor Company executive vice president whom I served as Pentagon assistant.

Hannah Block, "Mrs. World War II Wilmington. For all she did to inspire the preservation of World War II history.

Brig. Gen. Claude M. Bolton, USAF—Son of WWII Tuskegee Airman. I researched and wrote his speeches about them, heightening my admiration.

James Brady and **Larry Speakes,** associates in Nixon-Ford politics, colleagues at the Department of Housing and Urban Development—Later President Ronald Reagan's press secretaries.

Vice Adm. Charles "Cat" Brown, USN, commander, US Sixth Fleet— Navy protocol stated I needed his permission to marry in Naples, Italy. Came to the wedding.

Bear Bryant, University of Alabama football coach—Got him to speak at President Ford 1976 rally in Mobile, AL. What a gentleman.

John Burney, WWII infantryman, two Purple Hearts, community leader, hall-of-fame lawyer, one of the dearest friends I ever had.

Sen. Richard Burr, North Carolina—Instrumental in the project to have Wilmington designated as the first "American WWII Heritage City."

Hon. Dan Cameron, former Wilmington mayor and WWII Army veteran—A true inspiration and supporter.

Red Cavaney, director of the White House Advance Office under President Ford—Outstanding advanceman, boss, and leader.

Dick Cheney, President Ford's chief of staff, and President George H. W. Bush's secretary of Defense—The advance office reported to him. Short of charm, his professional productivity and sound judgment were what mattered. Also served under him in the Pentagon.

Ann Compton (ABC), Sam Donaldson (ABC), Cokie Roberts (ABC), and **Lesley Stahl (CBS)**—Notable "young lions" among the national media and White House press pool with whom I indirectly associated. The women were pleasant, Donaldson maybe not so.

Gen. Ray Davis, USMC (Ret.), Medal of Honor recipient, Chosin Reservoir (Korea). World War II infantry veteran, and assistant commandant of the Marine Corps—Wrote the foreword for my book *Gyrene*, made me an Honorary Marine, and lectured on WWII in Wilmington.

Vince Dooley, national champion University of Georgia football coach.

Capt. Herbert Dowse, USN, commanding officer, USS *Nashville*—Exceptionally professional colleague working together on President Ford's visit to his ship on July 4, 1976 in New York harbor.

Lane Dwinell, former New Hampshire governor, and chairman, New Hampshire Committee for the Re-Election of the President—wonderful, delightful man who drew people to him and let me run with the ball.

David Eisenhower and **Julie Nixon Eisenhower,** grandson of President Eisenhower and daughter of President Nixon—Valuable visit to my New Hampshire Nixon re-election campaign. Reminisced with them many years later.

Bob Finch, Governor Ronald Reagan's California lieutenant governor and later President Nixon's secretary of Health, Education, and Welfare—Connected me to my first paid political position.

First Lady Betty Ford—Exceptionally nice to work with. A lovely person.

President Gerald R. Ford–The nicest boss I ever had. We worked our tails off mutually for each other.

Susan Ford, daughter of the president and Mrs. Ford—Enjoyed leading her to a New York parade holiday.

Franz A. P. Frisch, Ph.D, professor emeritus, Defense Acquisition University—WWII German army veteran and faculty colleague with whom I wrote: *Condemned to Live: A Panzer Artilleryman's Five-Front War.*

Rene Gagnon, World War II Marine and lone surviving Marine Iwo Jima flag raiser—At the Marine Corps's 200th anniversary ceremony.

Joe Garagiola, former major league baseball player, sports commentator and celebrity—A Ford supporter, enjoyed joshing about his playing days.

US Senator Barry Goldwater (R-AZ)—Inspired me as a conservative to get into politics. Later repaid him by getting his son elected to Congress.

US Representative Barry Goldwater, Jr. (R-27th District, CA)—Served as constant campaign assistant, instrumental in his election, and later his Washington chief of staff.

Mia Hamm, Lake Braddock High School, Fairfax, VA—Finest women's basketball player I ever officiated, and later world champion soccer star.

Norm Hatch, United States Marine combat cameraman—Shot epic motion picture film of Battle of Tarawa which became Academy Award-winning documentary, "With the Marines at Tarawa."

Hon. Carla Hills, secretary of Housing & Urban Development—She green-lighted me, as a special assistant, for Ford advance duties.

Adm. James Hogg, USN (Ret.)—Friend from early naval service who later got arranged my Pentagon duty.

Vice Adm. Ephraim Holmes, USN, commander, Amphibicus Force, US Pacific Fleet—Regular tennis partner who, since I was resigning, must have known I was breaking the Hatch Act.

Lady Bird Johnson, former first lady—Worked with this gracious, charming, personable woman and her staff on the Lyndon Baines Johnson Memorial Grove dedication in Washington.

Sonny Jurgensen, as his sandlot baseball teammate, I launched his Hall of Fame career.

Sir Ben Kingsley, Academy Award winner (*Ghandi*)—Along with executive director Captain Terry Bragg, gave private three-hour history tour of WWII Battleship North Carolina. Never said thank-you.

Dee Kinzel, Ingham County Republican chairperson, Lansing. Mich.—Most typical of the hard-working, productive, and appreciative volunteers in the hinterland (1976).

Hon. Henry Kissinger, secretary of State and national security advisor for President Ford—Difficult to deal with, but got his comeuppance from me in Newport, RI.

Bowie Kuhn, commissioner of Major League Baseball—Interviewed in his New York office.

Dawn Kuhn, my secretary at the General Services Administration and Department of Housing & Urban Development—Loyal, nice, terrific, and we stay in touch today.

Mrs. Lassiter and Mrs. Symmes, New Hanover High School veteran teachers—They encouraged, taught, and convinced me to write properly in English classes and as the newspaper editor.

Linda Lavin, Tony Award winning actress and Wilmington resident—Supported efforts to save, renovate, and restore Wilmington's WWII USO building, wrote endorsement for my book.

US Representative Alton Lennon (D-NC)—My neighbor and Daddy's friend, he lobbied the Navy in 1955 to accept me as an officer candidate.

US Representative Mike McIntyre (D-7th District, NC)—A model congressman, super person and strong colleague in preserving North Carolina World War II history.

Jim McNamara, James Madison High School, Vienna, VA—The best catcher I ever worked the plate with, loved to banter. Played for San Francisco Giants.

Gov. Pat McCrory of North Carolina—Appointed me to the USS North Carolina Battleship Commission in 2013, and as chairman, 2014.

Fred Malek, Nixon stalwart assistant in California and Washington—Recruited me as advanceman for President Nixon . Great guy, dodged Watergate, had brilliant industry career.

Helen Martin, my administrative assistant, New Hampshire Committee for the Re-Election of the President, 1972—Totally indispensable, the person I want in my foxhole.

Hon. William Middendorf, President Ford's secretary of the Navy—Worked with him on the Navy's 200th anniversary ceremony and the Bicentennial in New York harbor.

Alan Moore and Marvin Allen—My lacrosse and soccer coaches at Carolina who instilled toughness, teamwork, and leadership.

Hugh Morton—Wilmington native, WWII Army veteran, world class photographer, finest Tar Heel ever, wrote foreword for one of my WWII books.

Col. Charles P. Murray, Jr., USA (Ret.), Medal of Honor (Alsace, France, 1944)—Dear friend and colleague for whom I successfully sought Wilmington recognition and memorials.

President Richard Nixon—Served in his administration, ran his New Hampshire re-election, and coordinated 1973 inauguration logistics.

Tricia Nixon, daughter of the president and Mrs. Nixon—Arranged her date with Congressman Barry Goldwater for the 1969 Major League Baseball all-star game.

Lyn Nofziger, Republican political genius and media specialist—Nice gentleman and friend, later senior Reagan confidante, who ran Goldwater's opponent's losing campaign in the 1969 California 27th congressional district primary.

US Representative Devin Nunes (R-CA)–Hold him highest admiration for his efforts on behalf of the US Constitution and our laws. Autographed my book to him in Wilmington.

Terry O'Donnell, assistant to and body man for President Ford—The president's eyes and ears. If we needed to communicate with the president, we went via him.

Steve Owens, University of Oklahoma 1969 Heisman Trophy winner—The story of the "OU" football helmet at a Lawton rally that wouldn't fit the president is a classic about which I still shudder.

Maureen Reagan, daughter of Gov. Reagan, Republican activist—Nice lady, but vicious opponent during the 1969 California 27th congressional district primary (my side, Goldwater, won).

Gov. Ronald Reagan, of California—Met and bantered with multiple times prior to, during, and after his successful 1966 campaign, the last time at a Century City hotel's urinals. As a presidential candidate running against President Ford, I blocked him from upstaging First Lady Betty Ford in Iowa.

US Representative Ed Reinecke (R-27th District, CA)—Great boss for whom I ran his district office. Later California lieutenant governor.

Mary Rivenbark, assistant principal, Peachtree High School, Dekalb County, GA—Advancemen mortgage their houses for someone like her: one-stop contact and she got things done.

US Representative David Rouzer (R-7th District, NC)—Model constituent-related congressman. Super supporter of Wilmington's project to

228   WILBUR D. JONES, JR.

be designated the first "American WWII Heritage City" through congressional legislation and loyal friend.

Hon. Donald Rumsfeld, President Ford's chief of staff and later secretary of Defense—Served under him.

His Excellency Mohamed Anwar Al Sadat, president, Arab Republic of Egypt—For meetings with President Ford in Jacksonville, FL One of the most impressive, distinguished, and intriguing men I've met.

Mayor Bill Saffo, Wilmington, NC—Strong colleague in preserving Wilmington WWII history.

Hon. Helmut Schmidt, chancellor, Federal Republic of Germany—Worked with him and his staff on President Ford's visit to Bonn, FRG.

Pete Schourek, Marshall High School, Fairfax, VA—Umpired his no-hitters and state championship game, later runnerup for Cy Young Award with Cincinnati Reds.

George Steinbrenner, New York Yankees owner—Interviewed in his Yankee Stadium office for advice.

Sister Margaret Sullivan, Order of Our Lady of the Sacred Heart convent, Bairiki, Tarawa, Republic of Kiribati—One of the most remarkable people I've met. Led Rotary project to provide her country's archives with materials.

Leighton "Goro" Sumida, ringleader, WWII all-Nisei 100th Infantry Battalion, Honolulu—These heroes of Italy and France shared brunch with me in their clubhouse.

Rev. Kiyoshi Tanimoto, Hiroshima, Japan, organizer of the Hiroshima Maidens injured in the atomic blast who received care in America—Worked together on Christmas party for orphans on board my ship in Japan, 1960.

US Senator Thom Tillis (R-NC)— Stalwart man of action and supporter of Wilmington's project seeking designation as the first "American World War II City."

Hon. Anote Tong, president, Republic of Kiribati—Encountered him during two visits to Kiribati including when he hosted my tour group at dinner.

Leon Uris—Author (*Battle Cry, Exodus, Trinity, Mila 18* and others), WWII Marine in Pacific campaigns. Included my New York City interview with him in my book *Gyrene*.

Gov. George Wallace of Alabama—Personable, considerate, and accommodating in appearing with President Ford at Mobile, AL, 1976 airport rally.

John Warner, chairman of the nation's 1976 Bicentennial commemoration—Worked with him several times, including by arranging President Ford's appearance at his Virginia 1979 US Senate campaign rally.

Capt. Chris Wells, commanding Cunard's RMS *Queen Mary 2*—Interaction with him following the ship's 2017 rescue in the mid-North Atlantic of a stranded lone yachtsman.

Ted Williams, Hall of Fame baseball player and manager, Washington Senators—Worked with him in arranging Congressman Barry Goldwater, Jr., and Tricia Nixon's date to the 1969 All-Star game in Washington.

Bill Woolson, executive director, Republican Associates of Los Angeles County—Hired me as professional staff, my first paid political job, for four years.

John Zeigler, National Hockey League president—Interviewed in his New York office for position.

James Wortman, MD, my family physician since 1998—For Carroll and me, a trusted caretaker and advisor on our health.

SOME OTHERWISE FOLKS & CHARACTERS I'VE DEALT WITH

Toufik Asley, Beirut, Lebanon, taxi driver—Drove my party to Damascus in 1961. Still have his business card.

Danny Bean and **Chris Ryan,** Fort Hunt Youth Little Leaguers—Danny, my favorite catcher even though he chewed awful smelling grape gum when I worked the plate leaning over him, and Chris, my favorite Little Leaguer, later a Naval Academy graduate patrol aircraft pilot.

Jim Beatty, Carolina distance runner, first person to break the indoor four-minute mile (1962)—Swell guy, worked well together on Monogram Club activities.

Don Freedman, department head at the Defense Acquisition University—Loud, disorganized, chore to work with, professional magician: "Mister Mysto."

Cmdr. Smokey Gordon, USN, commanding officer of USS *Alameda County*—Was the idiot captain in "Mr. Roberts" personified. I requested and got a transfer.

H. R. (Bob) Haldeman and **John Erlichman**, extremely dedicated chief assistants to President Nixon—Knew them in California, shook hands in Washington, then no more direct contact. Watergate drowned them.

Reggie Jackson, "Mr. October" Hall-of-Fame baseball player—Twice, one-on-one conversations. Refused to give an autograph.

Christine Jorgensen, first person to become widely known for having trans-gender "sex reassignment surgery"—Delightful conversation seated by chance next to her on the Star Ferry from Kowloon to Hong Kong Island.

Sarge Keller, athletic equipment manager for Carolina varsity teams, Woollen Gym—Kept me supplied with clean jockstraps and socks for four years.

James Leutze, Ph.D, chancellor, University of North Carolina Wilmington—He gave me good reasons to lose respect.

Albert Long, Carolina's last four-sport varsity athlete—Classmate and good friend who melded well into Monogram Club activities.

Capt. Mead, USAF—White House aide who extremely carelessly left

"The Football" alone, requiring me to retrieve it before it fell into Jacksonville's St. John's River.

Mike, just Mike, Navy Seaman, my father-in-law's orderly on our flagship—Mr. Utility: wedding day driver, errand man, wisecracker, who shepherded my in-laws' nervous poodle when it rode the ship.

Old-timer gold miner, Mojave Desert, CA—Drank beer with him at the bar of a dusty saloon right out of a movie-set, his mule tied up outside, 27th Congressional District.

Blanche Parsley, my Sunday School teacher at an early age—Mother's tiny old-maid friend, a Confederate officer's daughter, who typically wore frilly, lacy clothing and feathery hats. In Carroll's face on meeting, she asked: "Are you from around here?" We kids loved her.

Tom Scott, University of Virginia lacrosse player—All-America in lacrosse and football, future National Football League player. We beat up on each other.

Katherine Von Glahn and **Emma Nauer,** my Forest Hills School principal and fourth-grade teacher—Old-fashioned disciplinarians who bent this growing tree in the right direction. Because of their German names, we boys just knew they were Nazi spies.

INDEX

B

E

Hotel Paradiso 55
Hotel Vesuvio 52
Neapolitan 55
Santa Lucia Harbor. 52
Narragansett Bay, RI 38
National Collegiate Athletic Association
(NCAA) 172, 201, 219
National Football League (NFL) 26, 30,
32, 201, 207, 208
Hall of Fame 26, 207, 226
National Hockey League 134, 229
Ziegler, John, president . .134, 229
National Society of the Sons of the
American Revolution Bronze Good
Citizenship Award 221
Navy, U.S., general . . 16, 63, 129, 138,
142, 161, 182, 222, 224, 226, 230 .
See also Bicentennial, Nation's; Pearl
Harbor, Hawaii - USS Arizona 34th
Anniversary; and U.S. Navy's 200th
Birthday
Navy, U.S. - Jones careerSee Jones Navy
career
Navy, U.S. - Office of the Chief of Naval
Operations (CNO, OPNAV) . . 137,
138-141, 219
Deputy CNO for Logistics (OP-04)
137, 139
OP-40. 138
Collins, Frank 138
Islamic revolution 138
Shah of Iran 138
Tehran, Iran. 138
OP-401 Branch
Navy, U.S., sites
Amphibious Base, Coronado, CA59,
61
Amphibious Base, Virginia . . 138
Balboa Naval Hospital, San Diego,
CA 64
Moffett Field Naval Air Station, CA
41
Naval Academy 229

Naval Hospital, Charleston, SC . 11
Navy Museum, Washington, DC 204
Navy Officers Candidate School 3 7,
38, 39, 42
Newport, RI . . . .
37. . . . .
Naval Station, Norfolk, VA 101
Pearl Harbor, Hawaii military bases
19
Barbers Point, HI. 41
Navy, U.S., ships
USS Alameda County . .47-49, 229
USS Constitution. 118
USS Essex 48, 49
USS Gerald R. Ford 102
USS Kitty Hawk 222
USS Lenawee 57, 58, 59, 64
USS Leutze. 155, 186
USS Mississinewa 49
USS Nashville . . . .
See Bicentennial, Nation's; and Jones
Advances for President Ford
USS Nimitz. 101
USS Paricutin 39, 40, 41, 42, 43-44,
45
USS Shaw 106
USS Yosemite 104
Navy, U.S., terms and units
Bureau of Naval Personnel. . 59, 61
Commander Amphibious Force, U.S.
Pacific Fleet (COMPHIBPAC). .5 9,
61, 64, 225
"Gator Navy". 57
Naval Beach Group Reserve . . 1 3 8,
140, 219
Navy Reserve (Ready)59, 64, 72, 92,
135, 137, 140, 141, 219
Regular Navy. 59, 61, 64, 139, 140,
219
SEAL(s), U. S. Navy. 16
U.S. Sixth Fleet . . 49, 53, 54, 224
. . . Commander Service Squadron
Six/Commander Service Force, Sixth

THE DAY I LOST PRESIDENT FORD

259

A MILIEU OF PEOPLE WITH WHOM JONES HAS TRANSACTED BUSINESS

SOME OTHERWISE FOLKS
JONES DEALT WITH

www.ingramcontent.com/pod-product-compliance
Lightning Source LLC
Chambersburg PA
CBHW060255100426
42742CB00011B/1759